ANNE
CARROLL
MOORE

BOOKS BY

Frances Clarke Sayers

ANNE CARROLL MOORE

A Biography by

FRANCES CLARKE SAYERS

Atheneum

NEW YORK

1972

For Storer

These pages betray her secret; which is that she was naturally exuberant. And her power came, as all power comes, from the control and direction of exuberance.

G. K. CHESTERTON   *Preface to* Love & Friendship *and* Other Early Works *by Jane Austen*

Is it not possible that the ultimate end is gaiety, music and a dance of joy—

JAMES STEPHENS

FOREWORD

> *Every reader for reading's own sake carries his own smoke screen, assumes his own protective coloring. If it were not so, then the children's rooms of public libraries would become mere laboratories or experiment stations instead of theaters in which books live and move and play their various parts in daily human experience.*
>
> ACM

$\mathcal{A}$T the turn of the century, to use a phrase cherished by Anne Carroll Moore, a new concept of reading in relation to children came into being. It followed fast on the growth of the Free Public Library in the United States. Destined to move beyond the walls of the public library and to become essential to formal education in its own country, its influence as a natural, spontaneous, and informal enhancement of the lives of children gave it such appeal to the traditional European mind as to make it widely copied and imitated in England, France, Belgium, Sweden, Russia; in India, Japan, and other countries of the East, as well as in Latin America.

That concept, taken for granted now some seventy years after the fact, was the radical idea that children be given free access to books in public libraries, without hindrance of age or capacity to read, and with minimal concern for cleanliness of hands.

One hundred years after the declaration of American Independence, the American Library Association was founded in Philadelphia, at the Philadelphia Centennial Exhibition. The librarians meeting there were, for the most part, administrators of college and university collections or librarians of private libraries supported by subscription. But all over the country, men and women were beginning to organize in churches, in trade unions, in sewing circles, and athletic clubs, in village and town meetings, for the purpose of making books available to everyone with the support of local tax monies. Andrew Carnegie gave impetus to the public-library movement with his gift of free public-library buildings. His largess, continuing from 1881 until 1917, resulted in a stereotype of library architecture, the greystone fronts rising like a national monument in towns and cities across the land.

Free books for everyone! That was the exhilarating idea, an ideal born of a young country whose founding fathers had recognized from the beginning that in a democracy education of the populace was a necessity for survival.

But the children were denied entry. They were considered to be unequal to the ideal. Straightway, they made their own persistent and unorganized demands, knocking upon doors that were not open to them. They literally climbed upon window sills to peer in at their elders, who sat at soap-yellow tables in high-ceilinged, mustard-colored rooms, or emerged from the building with armloads of books after a mysterious ceremonial ritual at the desk in the rotunda, involving rubber stamps and little boxes of pads purpled with ink.

With the rise of public libraries in the country, an awareness of an undefined responsibility began to trouble the minds of librarians, the responsibility of choice. Which books should be purchased for any given community? The responsibility vexes the professional thinking to this day. The question could be more easily defined and more readily answered in relation to children whose tastes were unformed and who were helpless in the face of authority. But whoever serves children in any capacity, no matter how tangentially, is haunted by an awareness of a commitment to the future. Dealing with adults, one works with the here and now. Each child, however, wraps about him the promise or the threat of all that is yet to happen. When, therefore, in 1882 Caroline Hewins, librarian of the Young Men's Institute of Hartford, Connecticut, presented to the American Library Association a report on the melodramatic, sensational quality of the reading of boys and girls, she found a receptive conscience in the profession at large and an awakened concern for the minds of the young.

By 1894, when the American Library Association met at Lake Placid, New York, eager but bewildered administrators took heed when Miss Lutie Stearns, of the Milwaukee Public Library, read a "Report on the Reading of the Young," which declared for a policy of abolishing age limitations, presented the necessity of providing special rooms for the young, staffed by attendants *"who liked children"* and were prepared to serve them with the same standards of excellence as obtained in libraries for adults.

The young women who found themselves assigned to those first rooms for children in their respective libraries soon discovered that nothing in their previous training or experience with books and people had prepared them for this new commitment to children and books. It was to involve them in heretofore undiscovered skills, attitudes, and subject matter. Their accustomed patterns of thought regarding librarianship were shaken with such violence as to force them to become innovators, improvisors, and pioneers in a whole new area of being. They worked before the days of child psychology and child study, with all the catch phrases ready to the tongue. They functioned without the benefit of professional library schools with their varied courses in library work with children, and floundered in a confusion of purpose and direction.

Out of this confusion was to emerge a new profession. It introduced a philosophy of education that functioned independently of pedagogy, created an undiscovered rapprochement between the world of the adult and the child, and brought into being a tradition, uniquely American, that was to excite the admiration of countries around the world. It reached outside the library walls to publishers' inner sanctums, bombarding them with certain knowledge of the demands of children and direct experience of their capabilities. The breed of librarians born of this profession acclaimed standards of taste and judgment with such consistency as to influence the production of books for children and to involve, on their behalf, writers and artists of significant magnitude.

One person more than any other gave shape and content to the new profession, to the greatest degree and in fullest measure: Anne Carroll Moore, of Brooklyn's Pratt Institute and the New York Public Library. To be sure, confluence of period and place set the stage for her achievement, but the color and character of her accomplishment derived from the quality of her imagination; her courage and stubborn determination; her shrewd,

New England practicality; her logical, analytical mind, which, like a pyrotechnical display, could turn and light up the sky with its rocketing commitment to joy.

From time to time, certain few artists transcend the magnitude of their unique inspiration to emerge not as artists in a given field but as profound prophets who reveal in a blaze of light some splendid affirmation at the heart of life: Isaac Stern at the violin, Artur Rubenstein at the piano, Picasso in all his manifold manifestations. Anne Carroll Moore was one of these. She lived and moved beyond the prescribed condition of her art: children, books, and the utmost reach of the public library.

ACKNOWLEDGMENTS

*M*y indebtedness for help in writing this book is great and includes many people. A large portion of gratitude is due the nieces of Anne Carroll Moore, Constance Moore Willey and Ruth Moore Owen, of Saco, Maine; and Rachel Moore Warren and Margaret Moore Bedell, of Northampton, Massachusetts. They provided family records and letters, offered New England hospitality as setting for interviews and reminiscences, and took me to haunts known and loved by Anne Moore.

I am grateful to two cousins, Dudley and Storer Lunt, whom Anne claimed as nephews by virtue of their devotion to her. Each read the manuscript with critical but sympathetic care. The book owes its origin to Storer Lunt, who suggested that it be written and then stood faithfully by through long years of waiting for its completion.

Anne Carroll Moore was prolific in her letter writing, and many recipients husbanded her letters through the years. To this circumstance I am indebted for floods of letters generously lent to me by the following: Bertha Mahony Miller, Siri Andrews, Katherine Carnes, Lillian Smith, Virginia Bowman King and her daughters, Ruth Sawyer Durand, Ruth Hill Viguers, Marcia Dalphin, Alexandra Sanford, and Margaret Warren Brown, Anne Carroll Moore's great-niece.

Certain of Miss Moore's friends wrote their impressions of her, and these gave me valuable syntheses of her effect upon a variety of people. Among these were Anne T. Eaton, Louise Seaman Bechtel, Martha Peterson, Florence Little, Julia Carter, Eulalie Steinmetz Ross, and Nancy Bedell Massey, Anne Carroll Moore's great-niece.

Special gratitude is due Flora Cutler Cohn, whose records of the early years were complete and substantiated by newspaper clippings of the time, and Alexandra Sanford, who went on many an errand in New York City to fasten upon some fact. I wish to thank Marjeanne Blinn, of Los Angeles, who checked and rechecked facts of place and time, and Louise Bruckner and Betty Izant, whose typing dignified the appearance of my scrawled pages. To the cat Flan I am grateful for the comfort of his frequent presence. Whatever courage, determination, and discipline I was able to muster in writing this book I owe to the support of my sister Marie V. Clarke, who sustained me also with food and drink and a daily bouquet of fresh flowers.

To E. B. White and the New York *Times* I am indebted for permission to reprint a part of an article appearing in the Book Review section of that paper. The Literary Trustees of Walter de la Mare and the British Society of Authors as their representative gave permission to reprint the poem of Walter de la Mare, "Not I," which appears as a chapter heading. A great measure of gratitude is due to *The Horn Book*, its editor, Paul Heins, and to Mary E. Manthorne, President of the Horn Book Company, for permission to quote without limit from its pages and publications.

CONTENTS

ILLUSTRATIONS

(between pages 144 and 145)

Anne Carroll Moore as an infant
Anne Carroll Moore at the age of seven
Luther Sanborn Moore
Sarah Hidden Barker Moore
Almira Boardman Barker
Alderwood
Anne Carroll Moore as a young lady
Anne Carroll Moore as a student, 1892
Anne Carroll Moore with Flora Cutler, Marit Blehr, and Alice Tyler
Anne Carroll Moore as the Supervisor of Children's Rooms, New York Public Library, 1906
Anne Carroll Moore as the Superintendent of Work with Children, in the thirties
Children applying for library books
The academic procession at Pratt Institute, 1955
Anne Carroll Moore with Anne Carroll Peterson, in the fifties

ANNE
CARROLL
MOORE

1

___

ANCESTRY

*Once upon a time, Creation, Eternity, a
hundred years ago, a century ago, my birthday—these are familiar phrases to children
who have lived at the crossroads of life and
literature.*

ACM

Anne Carroll Moore was born on July 12, 1871,
in Limerick, Maine, York County, southwesterly as the
state stands on the map, the youngest in a family of ten
children. Seven brothers had preceded her and two sisters who had died in the first years of their infancy.
When her mother felt that the birth of her tenth child
was near, she called to one of her sons and asked him to
fetch the doctor. "I'll not go," he replied, "unless you
promise it will be a girl."

She was christened *Annie* Carroll Moore, a name
adapted from that of one of the maiden aunts who lived
with the family in the wide, generous house, Aunt Ann
Eliza. The name was changed to Anne Carroll Moore
some fifty years later to avoid confusion with a teacher
at Columbia's Teachers College, Annie E. Moore, who

not only had a similar name but was in a related field of work. Both women were publishing books on the reading of children in the same period. At the suggestion of her editor, Eugene Saxton of George H. Doran Company, "Annie" became "Anne" when her second book appeared, *New Roads to Childhood* (George H. Doran Company, 1923). In certain untidy bibliographies, even today, a confusion exists between the two writers.

Carroll seems not to have been a family name but was chosen, apparently, because her mother liked the sound of it. It was an appropriate choice, with its connotation of Christmas and music, its foreshadowing of a lilting quality, characterizing her walk, the gestures of her hands, her voice and manner of speaking.

The landscape of Maine, the blue reaches of its sky, the hills that lift themselves to mountain heights, the thousand ponds and deeply wooded stretches, the boisterous coast and islanded shore, the rivers and valleys rich in Indian names, these constitute a national heritage threading through the literature of America to such an extent that even those who have never been there claim the state of Maine as a birthright of the American experience.

For Anne Moore it was inescapable. Maine was both root and refuge, especially its woods, fields, mountains, and country roads. These things she wrote of often with moving intensity.

> I had always loved the Cornish road for its woods and rushing brooks and, most of all, because it led straight on to the White Mountains. From its open stretches on a clear day, I could see Mount Washington white with snow.[1]

The roads to Cornish and Limington, linking small New England villages together, were the roads she knew as a

child, and she was to travel them many times in her lifetime. They were destined to take her well-nigh around
the world and bring her home again, where

> Spring still lingered with a gift of pink lady's-slipper in
> the Maine woods, and white lilacs and lilies-of-the-valley
> were blooming under the Christmas trees in the Old
> World garden of my childhood. Mount Washington rose
> white with snow in the distance and warm and clear and
> blue the June day held past, present, and future in its keep-
> ing.

Her lifelong reliance upon flowers was the result of
childhood freedom to roam woods and fields as she
pleased as well as of having had the good luck to be born
into a family of garden-loving people. It was a strong
and characteristic trait, not altogether typically American. She loved and employed flowers as do the Mexican
people, who depend upon them for fiesta, propitiation,
or merely for the humble comfort of holding them in
the hand; or in the manner of Northern people, the
Russians and the Scandinavians, for whom bouquets of
garden flowers, innocent of arrangements, are the natural
accompaniment of celebration and ceremony.

It was no affectation but a response to a need born of
instinct, like hunger or thirst, and it became a basic
premise in her philosophy of work with children. Time
and again she speaks of children and books "in natural
surroundings." She meant just that, asking of each Children's Room under her jurisdiction that, periodically in
the year's calendar of events, some gesture from the
earth, some small token of root and flower, be made the
focal point in the arranged environment where children
and books were brought together.

The wisdom of her insistence on flowers can scarcely
be realized unless one has watched with one's own eyes

the response of city-bred children to the actuality of
blossom and flowering branch. To see children standing
in line, waiting their turn to "smell the roses" (every
flower is a rose to many of the children in New York);
or to have a child ask, "Miss, the next time you go to the
country, will you bring me a little dirt? I've got a seed";
or to realize that for one boy the experience of seeing a
single spray of bleeding hearts in a small vase was literally
beyond his belief; "Miss," he asked the librarian, "did
you *make* that?"—incidents such as these reveal the enor-
mity of the gap between millions of children and an
elemental knowledge of nature.

In the early days at Pratt Institute, Anne Moore proved
her point:

> Very early in the work of satisfying children with
> books, I had discovered how many of the stories and
> poems known and loved by me as a child were meaning-
> less to children who had never seen the country in spring-
> time, and whose parents seemed to have forgotten their
> childhood. The "nature study" of the schools was as yet
> unfortified by botanical specimens, or by the expanding
> resources of the Children's Museum of Brooklyn.

The recognition of nature even crept into her criticism:

> I believe the secret of Mr. Altsheler's appeal lies in a
> deep love of nature, the ability to select from historical
> sources subjects of strong human interest, a natural gift
> for story-telling, and great modesty.

Anyone even remotely associated with Anne Moore
could scarcely escape the contagion of her involvement
with the flowering earth. A cataloguer in the library of
the University of Southern California recently recalled
a spring day in New York when she had been a member
of the staff of the New York Public Library, undergoing

one of those interminable "In-Service Training" sessions. Miss Moore had been scheduled to speak on the goals of library work with children. She had come into the room carrying a basket of spring flowers. The flowers and the weather had quite undone her, she announced, and though she was supposed to talk about the Children's Division, she had decided, instead, to make them a present of the spring by reading aloud the poetry of the season. "I've never forgotten it," said the California librarian, some forty years after the event.

This bright fixation had its beginning in the garden of her childhood, a large rectangular plot as wide as the depth of the house, bordered to the north by a stand of pine to break the wind. Anne spoke of the pines as Christmas trees. Good New England stone walls marked the separation from the open fields, orchards, and hills, and the road streamed beyond to the front entrance of the house, circled and branched off into a second road that led into the gaping mouth of the huge barn. A summer house—the fashionable gazebo of the period—added its open-work decor to the abundance of roses that grew there with all the other country flowers. "An Old World garden," Anne calls it, over and over again.

It was her mother who supervised the planting of the garden. "Born with a green thumb, she could bring the most reluctant plant to bud and blossom," Anne wrote of her. "She had the only greenhouse for miles around, and a gift of flowers from her hand was precious to many a visitor." But the allotted space for the garden had been part of the large design that originated in the mind of her father, Luther Sanborn Moore.

As a young man, Luther Moore walked three miles each way between the villages of Newfield and Limerick in order to attend Limerick Academy. He passed a stretch of woodland on that walk, bordered by an alderswamp, "not outside the village but skirting the heart of it." This was the place he determined to make his own. It was precisely right for a young man with courage and vision, attached to the land as was his farming father before him, who saw in the swampland the possibility of a farm, bountiful in fields and orchards. He was promised to the law, and in the course of time he came to practice his profession with distinction, establishing headquarters in Limerick. But the farm remained central to his being, and countless others were to know and remember it, engulfed in the warmth of life that it sustained.

In due time the swamp was drained—by immigrants, one hundred strong, from famine-stricken Ireland, brought by Luther from a sailing ship in Boston Harbor —and turned into a hayfield, with the great hay barn in its center. The large, three-storied, multiroomed house was built upon a stone foundation that stands to this day, though the house has long since gone. Other generous barns were built, orchards planted, and the sown fields stretched away to the ascending hills. He called the place Alderwood, and to it he brought his bride, Sarah Hidden Barker, daughter of Deacon Simeon Barker, of Limerick's Congregational Church, and Almira Boardman Barker, of Newburyport, Massachusetts. The wedding date was June 11, 1846. The bride was twenty years old and the groom twenty-five.

Luther Moore had been born in Newfield in 1821, the son of a prosperous farmer who sent his son to Limerick Academy after he had exhausted the resources of the local school. According to the testimony of one of his contemporaries at the Academy, he "recited his Virgil with distinction and gave every indication of being a first rate scholar." After the Academy, his father sent him to Harvard to study law. But a break in his health made it necessary for him to abandon Harvard, to study on his own, at his own pace, with a prescribed amount of time to be spent out of doors. He returned to his father's farm and read law in Newfield with Nathan Clifford, who was later to become an Associate Justice of the Supreme Court of the United States.

After Luther was admitted to the bar in 1844, he opened an office in Stetson, Maine, but in less than two years he returned to Limerick, established an office there, built Alderwood, brought home his bride, and there he remained for the rest of his days except for his terms in office in the State Assembly. By the time he was thirty he had become president of the Maine Senate and made his influence felt in the matters most important to the state—education and intensive and experimental farming. Later he served as trustee of the State Agricultural College, which was destined to become the University of Maine.

In reading scraps of letters left to his heirs, one feels the presence of a man who was reserved and reticent except in the presence of his family. He must have been an unusual father, with a breadth of view that transcends the limits of a country upbringing. At no point does he seem to have assumed the role of authoritarian patriarch one would expect of the time and circumstance. As for his relationship with Anne, it was little short of idolatry on the part of each. She inherited his keenness of mind, his analytical and logical bent, his stubborn determination and reticence, too, in certain matters. The companionship between them Anne herself has described in scattered pieces of writing that make one wish she might have found it possible to write her autobiography.

I am quite sure that my father had no conscious thought of imparting lessons to me as we drove or walked about the country. It was my companionship he sought, not my improvement or instruction, and his invitations always meant a good time. . . .

When his business was finished he would often say: "Now we will go home another way, a little longer and not as good a road—one of the old roads with a beautiful view. I haven't been over it for a long time." Sometimes he shared with me the pictures memory gave back from the road, more often we drove for miles in "social silence." . . .

On such a day, if it fell upon a Sunday, my father would stroll out of the garden and across the barnyard to the wide-open door of the stable to be greeted by joyous whinnying and stamping. "Quiet, Pocahontas, quiet," he would say as he led the horse from her stall, and if I appeared in the doorway I was greeted with an invitation after my own heart. "There's a man I must ride over to the eastern end of the town to see on a little matter of business. Will you come with me—just for the ride? I should love your company." . . .

I did not care to be read to, except by my father, who read just as he talked and seemed to like the same books and pictures I did. The *Nursery* was his favorite magazine, I firmly believed, not because he said it was, but because he seemed so interested in it. I associate with his reading the most beautiful parts of the Bible, Aesop's *Fables*, interspersed with proverbs, nonsense verses, old songs and hymns, a great deal of poetry, stories out of the lives of great men, and many stories of child life. He had a keen sense of dramatic values, a power of mimicry of animals and human beings, a strong sense of humor, and an intimate knowledge of men in their various forms of social and political organization. Moreover, he possessed the rare faculty of complete identification with the emotional life of childhood in all its stages of growth and change, and the imagination to know when to create a diversion. Since my intuitions have been at all times keener than my powers of external observation, I identified myself in turn with the childhood of my father. I seemed to have known him well as a little boy. That I was like him in certain qualities of mind, I was to learn in maturity; that I shared his emotional life, I knew as well at four or five years old as at his death, when I was twenty.

What infinite pleasure Luther Moore must have had in this child of his late years! He had been fifty when she was born. Moreover, she was his only daughter whom he was to enjoy all through her childhood and to know as a young woman of character. He saw himself mirrored in the small person seated beside him in the Concord buggy, and the sympathy between them ran deep. But the little girl, her gray eyes set far apart, her peaked eyebrows like small triangles set above them as though she were forever pleased and astonished by what she saw— this small person, with her delicate bones and slender body, gave back to him also the reflection of his wife, Sarah Hidden. It was from her mother, Sarah Hidden Barker, that Anne inherited her predilection for diversion, her social grace, and her splendid generosity of self and earthly goods.

Sarah Hidden Barker Moore, Anne's mother, was the second daughter of Almira Boardman of Newburyport, Massachusetts, and Simeon Barker of Limerick, Maine. There is a story behind that name, Sarah Hidden, which bears telling. When Almira Boardman was a young girl, her dearest friend was one Sarah Hidden, daughter of Parson Samuel Hidden of Tamworth, New Hampshire. It was she who had been engaged to marry young Deacon Barker of the Congregational Church at Limerick, and the date of the wedding had been set. When the doctors told her that she would not survive until the day, she sent for Almira Boardman and suggested that Almira assume responsibility for the happiness of Deacon Barker.

It was a plan which, in the face of the inevitable, Almira and Simeon came to adopt. In memory of the Sarah Hidden they both had loved, they gave their daughter her name.

The Barkers traced their beginnings in America to one James Barker, who came from England with Ezekial Rogers on the ship *Desire*, which landed in Salem, Massachusetts, in 1638.

The origins of the Boardman family date back to the boyhood of one William Boardman, born in Cambridge, England, in 1614, who came as a child to New England with his mother and stepfather. The name William Boardman persisted into the eighteenth century, and the record of a William Boardman's wedding to Rachel Wiggin still stands in the books of Newburyport. It took place on Saturday, April 9, 1785, at ten o'clock in the morning. Rachel Wiggin Boardman was Almira Boardman's mother. She lived to be ninety-nine years of age and was the subject of tales and legends in the family, having gone to live with her Great-Aunt Rachel at the age of fourteen, following the death of her mother. Rachel Wiggin Boardman's husband was a sea captain, sailing out of Newburyport in the great sailing days. It was she and her aunt before her who established "Rachel" as a name in the Moore-Boardman-Barker family, and the name persists to the present time.

Doubtless the English origins of her mother's people were responsible for Anne Moore's love of English life and English ways. She was an Anglophile almost to the last drop of her blood. But the Irish strain was there through her father.

The story of the first coming of the Irish into Maine and New Hampshire was ever a romantic story to me, for it must have been they who brought the old songs I loved and the fiddles for dancing—my own ancestor, once fondly though fabulously pictured as Tom Moore, the poet, with his harp, being among them. There is a round-topped hill in Limerick which I often climbed to take a look at the world when spring was coming up the valley. And from this hill I came to see more and more clearly, with no premature vanishing of fairies from mountain or glen—a little procession of hard-fisted, warm-hearted Irishmen moving up the valley with shovels, pickaxes and hoes, turning bogs and rocky pasture lands into green fields and flower gardens and then marching down toward the sea again for fresh conquests.

Whatever I know or feel about poetry and history had its beginnings in romantic associations such as these, and while my sharing of Irish poetry with children has been at all times spontaneous and by no means confined to St. Patrick's day and May Eve it is between these two dates that I . . . feel the Old World spell coming over me and the desire to share treasures that have their roots deep down in the childhood of the world.

"Be glad you're Irish," she once said to Bertha Mahony Miller, that elfin, powerful woman who founded *The Horn Book* and accomplished gigantic tasks of distinguished publishing in the world of children's books. Anne gathered together all of her Irish heritage in a fervor of celebration on each St. Patrick's Day. She followed the parade the length of Fifth Avenue, stopping at St. Patrick's Cathedral at some point in the morning. She plastered paper shamrocks on all the letters that left her hand in the week of March 17, and there were special parties of her own—as well as the feasts of the telling of Irish stories and the reading of Irish poetry in the Children's Rooms of the city's libraries. For her, spring always came wearing a leprechaun's hat.

A good account of a St. Patrick's Day celebration is given in a letter to Virginia King in 1943. Anne was retired, but the pace and variety were typical of The Day as she usually celebrated it:

> Mrs. Durand and I had a marvelous St. Patrick's Celebration beginning with a story hour attended by 300 children and adults at Bruce Branch Tuesday Evn'g—Fire on the hearth—Yellow primroses—the Room looked as lovely as I've ever seen it—Next morning Pontifical Mass at St. Patrick's with the 69th Regiment pouring in after the Color Guard from a misty Fifth Avenue. Glorious music —taps—the roll of drums—a service one will always remember.[2]
>
> Jacqueline Overton for luncheon afterward in the Louis XIV Restaurant—Rockefeller Plaza. Miss Florence Overton kept home by bad weather. We sent her yellow tulips, forgetmenots & a pot of shamrock. We caught glimpses of the procession under umbrellas and then Mrs. D. and I saw *Dark Eyes*. You would love it. . . . We ended the day with broiled lobster at 34th & 3d Ave.[3]

2

ALDERWOOD

There are no satisfactions comparable to a free and spacious childhood with a clear title to one's own good name at maturity.

ACM

To HAVE BEEN the only daughter and the youngest child growing up in a family of seven brothers might well have tempted a small girl to adopt the habits of a tomboy by way of compensation for not having been born a boy in the first place. The concomitant danger of an excess of admiration from brothers and an adoring father might have resulted in an accentuation of femininity, creating a small daughter full of wiles and graces, interested chiefly in dolls and the domestic concerns of a diminutive play-pretending mistress of a home and garden.

The child Anne seems characteristically to have gone her own way, assimilating the best of both masculine and feminine worlds. She was not physically robust (her brothers called her "Shrimp"). The stark realities of farm life and the strenuous activities in which her brothers engaged seem to have left little impression on her. Sheep, lambs, cows, and horses were her favorite animals. All her life she regretted the fact that she had never learned to ride horseback when she was young, but horsemanship was not an accepted pastime, even on prosperous American farms, since the animals were considered mainly in relation to the work of farming or were bred to be good carriage horses. Dogs she loved, though nowhere in her writing does she call by name a single memorable canine character. She abhorred cats and feared them all her life long. Her brothers, when they teased her, threatened to throw a cat on her and held this awful power over her all through her childhood.

But the winter sports she shared with them—all the exhilaration of snow and winter winds. She writes of it in *Nicholas: A Manhattan Christmas Story*. The chapter "New Year's Eve in Maine" gives the full flavor of childhood's remembered winters, besides a glimpse of the house in Portland she loved second only to her own Alderwood.

In the story, Nicholas and Ann Caraway are riding a Pullman coach from New York to Portland, and Ann, who is to sleep in the upper berth, says to him:

When I go up and lie down in the top berth, Nicholas, I'll forget all about New York. I'll see only the White Mountains covered with snow and a lovely old garden with Christmas trees growing all around it and then, far away in the sky, the wonderful Northern Lights will stream down.

And after that I'll begin to see all the boys and girls I ever knew, skating and coasting, first in the daylight, then by moonlight, and I'll see great bonfires blazing on the ice, and then I'll sail away on an ice boat, and the next thing I know, Nicholas, I'll be waking up—not in my old home in the country, but in a city that seemed like a fairy city when I was a little girl because Ben's grandfather and grandmother gave my brothers and me such wonderful times there.

The next morning the two travelers are met with a sleigh. The tale continues:

Ben Star tucked the big buffalo robes about them and away dashed the old sleigh with its jingling bells. Up the steep side of Cassidy's Hill raced the horses.

Morning was just breaking over the city and Ben Star told Nicholas to look back and see the white smoke rising from the freight-yard at the foot of the Western Promenade.

"You can't see the harbor from here," he said, "but there's Cape Elizabeth beyond [Fore River]."

"And there's the old grey house on the hill with the little windows like eyes near the roof, and the cupola on top. . . ."

The toboggan rides were high drama as well as a lesson on the conduct of life. In *My Roads to Childhood*, she gives account of the following experience:

This hill by the Baptist Church marks the entrance to the old burial ground with its beautiful view across the Ossipee Valley to the mountains. It was also the starting point for the most thrilling bobsled adventures of my youth. The slide led straight down the precipitous hill to Main Street with its peril of single and double sleighs, and slow-moving ox sleds. Turning a sharp corner, the challenge was to make three more hills, two of them very steep ones, to "the Factory" a mile distant without going off the road. The way was fraught with danger at every turn. The proudest winter of my life was the one I was chosen to sit next to the steering genius who managed the bobsled. His words of caution, "Don't scream if we do go off the road. Sit tight and expect a happy landing next time," have been worth cherishing for many another adventure.

She was well aware of the life her brothers were leading even though she may not have been an invited companion on some of the outdoor adventures. Her way of wooing their interest was to hoard cakes of maple sugar in the dresser drawers of her doll's bureau, to be produced at strategic moments as bribes as well as gifts of the heart. She followed them about the house, "from library to attic," where in addition to bound volumes of *St. Nicholas, Our Young Folks*, and *Harper's Magazine* they had a cache of *The Police Gazette* and other unfamiliar sources of information, and these she read in sweet companionship with them, especially on rainy days when the drain pipe's tinny music broke the silence and heightened the secrecy and daring.

Whatever the extent of her companionship with her brothers, it was to give her rare understanding of boys and men and to tilt the balance of her sympathy toward the male in any matters of judgment. Her profession by its nature dealt largely with women, but her friendships with men were numerous, encompassing young men as well as her contemporaries. She was, in many ways, a man's woman, having a rare gift for comradeship; feminine, perceptive, gay, and sympathetic, but without exacting a toll of homage and idolatry, which women, in almost every relationship with any male, barely escape expecting to some degree. Every aspect of her personality was delicate and feminine, but her processes of thought were direct, logical, and decisive. She reasoned with masculine strength and spoke out without regard for consequences. Her colleague and friend Anne T. Eaton, that inspired librarian of Lincoln School, at Teachers College, Columbia University, has well described the quality of the mind of Anne Carroll Moore. "I knew I could go to her for advice and get it. I loved the way her mind worked, there was no hesitation, no 'let me think this over.' She knew on the spot what she thought and it was always right. . . ." "The vigorous, critical mind that can purge, stimulate and invite," wrote Ruth Sawyer of her in *The Way of the Storyteller*.

Such surge of life swept through that bountiful house as to absorb a child's interest in all manner of incidents and people. "Beyond the White Mountains lay the world," she writes of the time in retrospect, "but I felt in no haste to explore it, I was too fearful of missing something vitally interesting at home." Her older brothers had already left home when Anne was born. As she grew up, they returned for visits with wives and children. Cousins on both sides of the family from Newfield and Portland came for visits and parties. Anne's nieces, Rachel Moore (Warren) and Margaret Moore (Bedell), the children of Anne's brother Harry, remember from their childhood the look of the place. They tell their children and grandchildren the inconsequential tales that echo the tone of life there and are the stuff of legend: how Anne's mother deplored the habit the boys had of waiting until food was on the table before they bethought them to go to the barn to feed the horses. Her most vivid memory of her sons, she said, had been their departing backs as she stood at the doorway to call them to dinner. "Harry, Walter, Luther—whatever your names are— come back—food's on the table"; the story of Aunt Carrie shouting out, "Come quick, Harry's swallowed the sugar bowl" (it was in reality a small decorative knob on the lid); the remembrance of Aunt Ann Eliza, who had a genius for cooking and insisted on carrying on even when her sight began to fail, until the day when the dish rag was served up at the table as part of the main course. It was she who sang as she worked, and filled the house with the measured sound of old hymns; the account of Cousin Alice arriving from Portland for a visit, behind a span of white horses. The steeds were mud-splattered and in need of grooming. Emissaries were sent throughout the town in search of lemons with which to whiten and cleanse them, to the astonishment of the natives.

The house in Portland, Maine, was the home of the most cherished cousin, Alice (Storer) Lunt, ten years older than Anne, who was, on Anne's own confession, "dearer to me than any sister." Anne looked up to her in the years when the difference between ten and twenty was great and claimed her as beloved friend and confidante in terms of equality in the years after sixteen, at which time the decade between them shrank into oblivion. Alice's sons, Dudley and Storer Lunt, and Dudley's children in their turn, were destined to give Anne long devotion that bridged the generations and the vagaries of fate and fortune—a regard that transcended family loyalties and the responsibility the young may feel for the elderly. Day by day and year by year, to the very last, when the years of Anne's life numbered close to ninety, it was the Lunt family who renewed her commitment to the present and kept fresh and vital the interests that bound her to the contemporary scene. Even though Anne was by character and endowment an ageless person, it was their companionship that kept the banners of her spirit flying to the end. The home of the Dudley Lunts in Wilmington, Delaware, was in the later years the natural base for the celebration of traditional holidays. In the comradeship of Storer Lunt, for many years the bachelor of the family and head of the noted publishing firm of W. W. Norton & Company, Anne found an ongoing fervor for books and reading that matched her own and a mind honed to the sharp edge of argument and debate in matters of critical opinion. It was Anne who had persuaded him in the first place to enter the field of book publishing.

In their youth, Anne was to Storer and Dudley an exhilarating comrade whose judgment, advice, and common sense proved trustworthy over the years, whose gaiety and perception colored their own reactions to the business of living. In Storer's case, the relationship came full circle in the years of his maturity, with Anne the recipient of counsel, succor, and endless felicities.

It had all begun at Alderwood with frequent visits between the families of the Barker sisters, Mary Thomas Barker Storer of Portland, and Sarah Hidden Barker Moore of Limerick. Alderwood was the focal point in the lives of "The Barker Girls." There were six of them altogether, three of whom lived at Alderwood and one, Almira, who was married from that house in an apple-green corded silk dress which she left to Anne in her will. It served Anne as costume and ceremonial well nigh all her life. She wore it on state occasions of her own and for appropriate public appearances. When the New York Public Library celebrated its fortieth anniversary in 1935, there appeared in various newspapers throughout the country a picture of Anne in Almira's apple-green dress, with her classmate from Pratt Institute, Mollie Leavitt, also on the staff of the New York Public Library, dressed in the grandeur of forty years past.

The house was also blessed with the presence of a grandmother, Sarah's mother, Almira Boardman Barker. Anne writes of her in *My Roads to Childhood:*

> Always my grandmother remained a city-bred lady of great personal charm. I was twelve when she died at the age of eighty-four. Quite unconsciously she set a standard, for I have never met anyone who grew old so graciously in the homes of her children. Everything she did, whether it was fine needlework or the dipping of her laces in a

china bowl filled with gum-arabic water, was done in such a fascinating way. That she had been a beauty in her Newburyport days was still evident. As for her stories of Lord Timothy Dexter with his strange doings, his mock funeral and his speculations in warming pans for the West Indies, they were a source of unending delight to my brothers and me.

It was our grandmother who read *Uncle Tom's Cabin* aloud to us while we listened, spellbound. My father adored her (his own mother had died when he was sixteen) and she returned his affection and confidence with a single exception. She did not approve of divorce. How often I heard her say, as he was leaving to attend court, "Promise me that you will not divorce anyone this time."

The real strength of Alderwood and the life engendered there lay in the relationship between Anne's father and mother. A handful of letters written by Luther to his wife when he was at Augusta, the state capital, or when Sarah was off on visits to relatives in Boston, one or two of the children tagging along, reveal an equality of judgment shared between them, as well as the love honestly and tenderly declared. Luther showed no hesitation in discussing with his wife details of trials and courtroom procedures, nor of any other matters which concerned him. Among the earliest letters extant are several written from Augusta in the spring of 1854, when Luther Moore was, at thirty-three, president of the State Senate, struggling to gain support for academies of the state, especially the one at Limerick. Their eldest son, Charley, was six years old; a daughter born in 1852 had died within a week of her birth, and Sarah was to have another son in July of that year.

Augusta Sunday Aprl 9th/54

My dear Sarah.

Yours of the 6th was rec'd yesterday morn & I was rejoiced to hear that your father was so comfortable. hope it will continue so, but I fear the warm weather will tend to weaken and reduce him. Remember me to him & tell him I hope to see him better when I get home. It is a dark, rainy, gloomy day here & as I have a slight cold I've concluded not to go to church today, thinking it would be quite as well to keep in. I am lonely enough here. Such a Sabbath as this & can only sit and think of that *home* which is *so dear and precious* to me. What an unhappy man should I be without such a home. When I think of it, I *see & feel how much* I am indebted to you *my dear wife* for my happiness & I hope I may be truly grateful to the great Author of all good for the blessings I enjoy. I've no doubt you are sitting and thinking of me today—how I wish I was with you & Charley. I never wanted to see you both more than now. The time is rapidly passing away & I shall soon be home to *remain* as you say you wish me to. We are turning off the business quite rapidly. Members are getting anxious to go home & I've no doubt we shall adjourn as early as Wednesday of next week. My duties are growing more laborious, tho' I think I feel better the more I have to do. Next week we shall have two sessions a day. We meet at 9 A.M. now instead of 10. Most of the Committees have got through the business referred to them & reported finally. The Committees on the Judiciary & Education are about all who have not reported. The Com. on Education will report finally on Tuesday morning. Mr. Abbott told me last night that they would report in favor of Limerick Academy a half township of land. It will be a desperate struggle to get them tho'. but I think it can be carried. I shall spare no pains or *means* that will insure success & I think I can manage to save 2000$ clear out of it for the Academy but of this I am not certain—the whole thing may fail. If the Dr. inquires about it you may tell him what I've stated about it. . . . I am sorry to hear that you don't feel any better—fear you don't take proper care of yourself. Hope you are well by this time. Charley seems to have got into the notion of writing again—am glad of it for it does me good to see the marks his dear little fingers have traced. I'm afraid Lorenzo will have some trouble about hay to last till I get home. I did not say anything about it in *his* letter. Mr. Bangs has not returned. If it was important for him to be here at all it is now I should think. Quite a number of ministers have gone for good. It don't rain this P.M. & I'm going to church.

I suppose you'll expect this tomorrow night, so I'll mail this P.M.

Give my love to all the family and believe me as

Ever *your own*
Luther

Trouble, anxiety, and the vagaries of human behavior must have existed in so large a family, but there is small echo of them in the letters that are extant. A disastrous libel suit involving Luther Moore is known to have been a matter of concern. He was completely exonerated by the courts, but the cost must have been great. Sarah considered the desirability of leaving Limerick after the suffering and notoriety, but Luther held for staying, knowing the allegations to be false no matter what the decision of the courts might have been.

It was probably this case that marked the beginning of a continuing and nagging worry over money. The maiden sisters in the household moved to Boston, found a house on Blagden Street right behind the Boston Public Library, and maintained themselves as managers of an excellent rooming house. Anne and her mother were frequent visitors there. Letters from Luther to Sarah during those years bespeak the generosity of the man. No matter what the state of the family finances, he could not deny Sarah her extravagances of dress.

Limerick April 25, 1878
[Anne was nine years old]

My dear Wife—

Your letter is rec'd & we are glad to hear from you & Annie. We are all well and you need not worry about any of us. . . . Now as to your dress I think you had better get it & have it made up while you are there. You must not worry about the cost. It is my wish that you get it. . . . I want you to write me Saturday what day we should meet you next week. Whether Monday, Tuesday or Wednesday. Loran wants you to come home—wants to see you & Annie & so we all do. The other boys are doing well. . . .

Give Annie good kisses for me—

Yours
L.

I have just sent Arthur 16$ that he asked for.

In October of that same year, Sarah was once more in Boston, this time without Annie. Luther never complained of her absences beyond declaring his loneliness, which is rebuke by compliment rather than by acrimony. In a letter from Limerick, dated October 17, he reports on the crops: the apples picked, 700 to 800 bushels, the corn husked, the boys well pleased with their crops, and the corn house full. He continues:

Everything goes on nicely, only it seems so odd and lonesome without you. Margaret says she can stay as well as not next week, and so we have talked it all over and we all think you ought to stay until you have made all your visits and seen all you wish to. It has been 27 years since you and I were in Boston and as you will be too old to go 27 years hence you had better make the most of the present opportunity now you are there—Annie is just like a little kitten as good as can be only she wants to see her mother Write often.

As ever   Luther

On June 11, 1881, when Anne was ten, she and her mother and brother Luther, Anne's senior by two years, were away from home, whether in Boston or some other place is not clear in the letter, but obviously it was after some tragic circumstance in the family had occurred. Luther Senior wrote on that day. It was the thirty-fifth wedding anniversary of Sarah and Luther, and he comments on that fact:

Limerick, June 11, 1881

My dear Wife.

I rec'd your letter & was very glad to get it. . . . I hope you are all well & will keep so. I want you to use what money you need & I will make up what you have to borrow when I come in. I realize how lonely it is there now —it seems to be something you can feel in every part of the house. There is a great void—the light of that household has gone out. Am glad Annie and Lu are happy & contented. Kiss them for me & tell them how much I miss them. We are all getting along nicely so far have all been in & abed before 10 o'clock. Arthur seems to take a great deal of fancy to Mary & is very attentive. She is happy & contented I don't want Aunt Sarah to trouble about her. And so far I am glad to say there has been peace in the household We shall work on the road Monday & Tuesday —I have watered everything in the Green House & will look carefully after it. I have been thinking a good deal today & this evening about this day 35 years ago & what changes have taken place— It does not seem so long it has run so smoothly that we have hardly taken note of time, & but for the fact that our children have grown into men we could not realize it— Shall we see 15 yrs more together? I hope so, for I have a great desire to see all the boys settled in life. I shall write Galvin this evening so if anything new occurs I can write it, but give yourself no uneasiness about us as we are all doing well—

Yours as Ever
Luther

Among the varieties of people, with all the tangential relationships they brought into the household, Anne was given time and space in which to grow. She was not sent to school until she was past seven, and at ten she was precipitated into the Academy to make what she could of it. In a letter to her niece, Rachel Moore Warren, written in 1924, covering these matters, she said:

It took the courage of conviction to keep the child I was out of school until past seven, and when elementary teachers were of poor caliber to send her ahead of all her companions to what was virtually High School at ten. I didn't want to go but the case was not open for argument. I was told to try it. Looking back, I think that it was remarkable that any Mother with limited school education and in the midst of all her cares could see so clearly the essentials to be grasped, that she recognized so immediately the people qualified to supply them, in some measure, at least, and cared not a rap not a button for what masqueraded as school systems in her day.

At the Academy she found herself once more in the minority, there being a predominance of boys among the students. The practice of reciting aloud was in force at that time, and Anne listened eagerly, acquainting her ears with the sounds of Latin and Greek as well as the poetry and prose of English masters. Northrop Frye, in his book *The Well Tempered Critic*, describes the results of such educational procedure as the Academy sustained in terms so applicable to Anne as to seem to have been written about her:

> Literary education of this kind, its rhythm and leisure slowly soaking into the body and its wit and concreteness into the mind, can do something to develop a speaking and writing prose style that comes out of the depths of personality and is a genuine expression of it.

No doubt it was the Academy that gave Anne early control of a lucid style in speaking and writing that was to make her a distinctive critic and essayist in her day. She herself gives account of her discovered pleasure in the study of Latin and of the young teacher who made it possible:

> My own most vivid remembrance of entering the teens is of beginning the study of Latin. Up to the age of thir-

teen I had held out against Latin, chiefly because a brother
two years older than I denounced its uselessness with such
eloquence.

"There's no use in Latin. Just a waste of time," he
would say, inviting hours of argument with a brother two
years older than he, who maintained that no one could be
educated without the study of Latin, and no one would
want to be who had once mastered the technique and was
able to read Virgil, Cicero, and Horace just as he read
other books.

And while the battle over languages—dead and living—
was still raging, came a new principal to the old academy.
He it was who persuaded me to begin the study of Latin.
"Why not give it a fair trial?" he said, and proceeded to
make the first year of Latin so delightful that it remains
the most potent influence upon my outlook during those
impressionable years.

Less skillful as a teacher of all things to all types of
minds than his predecessor in this old New England academy, the new principal was an ardent lover of literature
and language, with a charm of personality which gave him
place at once in the life of the village.

To him the year of teaching was an interlude between
college and a professional school. He shared both generously and acceptably his love of Latin for its own sake. I
do not remember that this young man in his early twenties
ever made a direct suggestion to me to read a book. The
invitation lay rather in his own personal habit. Along with
the newspapers, magazines, and books of the day, he
seemed always to be reading some classic as well, and since
he was a member of our own household for the year and
left his books lying about, I made my first perplexed acquaintance with Dante that winter and began to read
Shakespeare with new eyes after listening to some admirable reading of his lines by members of a Shakespeare club
to which I was too young to belong. I had previously read
through a one volume Shakespeare in very much the same
mood and temper as I had read the Bible through—to see
what it was like and to say that I had done it in a company
of my peers.

All the days of Alderwood! They were, for Anne, the ultima Thule. Because she had lived at the start of life with intense joy, in a world where grace, trust, and love were the accepted norm, the search for home need never again be undertaken. Most women on their own in life strive to possess themselves of a permanent dwelling place. Not Anne. She was free to move about the world. Like the opera singer in Gilda Varesi's play *Enter Madam*, who created a home in any place with the deployment of certain scarves, shawls, and draperies, Anne needed only a clutch of symbolic possessions to feel safely rooted anywhere.

In New York she lived in countless places: rented rooms, clubs, hotels in neighborhoods she found congenial, studio apartments. In one such she asked the landlord for a mousetrap, troubled as she was by a small beastie. He said he had no mousetrap, but he offered to lend her his cat for as long as might be necessary. Greenwich Village and Gramercy Park were favored haunts, and she found an apartment greatly to her liking in one of the old houses of Chelsea, set back from the street, with wrought-iron balconies and balustrades, dispirited ivy on display, and scraggly flowers dauntless among old bricks. The degree of comfort, elegance, or lack of it mattered little to her. At the peak of her career she holed up for a time in a dark back room, looking out on a brick wall, at the old Woodstock Hotel on Broadway, the better to aid financially a young grand-niece in her year at library school. Because she possessed Alderwood and was in turn possessed by it, "all places were alike to her." Except "The Balcony." That was yet to come.

In a birthday letter written to her goddaughter, Alice Campbell King, from Berkeley, California, in 1942, she speaks of the subject of birthright:

I love San Francisco and I feel very happy to be here for a time but I can never love any city as I love New York, nor any real countryside as I love New England and Old England, just as I fancy you will never love any part of our dear country as you love the South where you first saw the light. But it is something to take with you through all the birthdays to come that you never lose your birthright even when you are living somewhere else and that I think makes life wonderful at all times and in all places and assures a welcome wherever we go.

"None of us ever escape the first few years of our lives." It is not Anne who speaks but Lizette Woodworth Reese in her book *A Victorian Village,* which Anne revered and quoted in her review of it in the New York *Herald Tribune.* The quotation continues: "They make a mold into which we are cast, and though it may be broken, and we be turned loose, some remnant of it, some intangible evil or lovely thing, or both, will remain with us, like the odor to a flower or the smoothness of a piece of ivory."

The mold in which Anne was cast predisposed her to expectancies of joy and triumph. ("Admit to no discouragement" was her initial advice to her immediate successor at the New York Public Library.) That she considered disappointment, tragedy, sorrow, and woe almost as matters of personal disgrace to be borne privately and in silence was due in large measure to the tone and flavor of those first years. It was not that she denied the existence of tragedy or attempted to soften or explain it. She knew it well, having ample share of it in her lifetime. Her awareness of it increased through her sympathy with all those whom she cherished. Countless people confided in her their utmost sorrow. She never betrayed them for the sake of tales to be told, but held their woes in secret as she held her own. No one made better comrade in sorrow. She voiced no wisdom or advice, gave no homilies of consolation. She was there if needed, her presence testimony to the larger harmony she could never deny, having experienced in her early years a world beautiful in its proportions, peopled by men and women intent on giving life itself the delineation of intuitive art. In one of the most memorable biographical passages that occur often in her discussion of books, she writes of the first decade:

> I was not a bookish child, I discovered, although I had always cared to read. I have no recollection of any process or method by which I learned to read, but I hold a very vivid recollection of the first book from which I read. It was a large print edition of the Gospel of St. John. The time was early evening, and I went to bed thrilled with the discovery and the beauty of the words. I told no one until I could read well. I may have been five or even six years old, I have never been sure, but I recall very definitely that I brought to the reading of poetry, the psalms and the prophets strong impressions of the beauty of the country about me. Beyond Mt. Washington lay the world, just out of sight, and beyond the low horizon line to the southeast lay the sea. I had seen the sea, but I had not seen the world, and I was always wondering about it.
>
> This sense of wonder and mystery, the beauty of nature, the passing from night to day, the speaking voices of the people about me, the sound of music, are present in my earliest recollections. I had a keen interest in pictures and I was always seeing things in pictures. I had no gift for drawing, and the mechanics of writing was extremely difficult for me. I shall never be able to unearth a manuscript written before the age of ten. My early literary compositions were all scribbled and dispatched by post. I never had a doubt that what I whispered as I scribbled was read by the cousin or brother to whom it was sent. Writing, like going to school, was a social experience full of news of people and of what they said and did. Never did

I write out of deeper emotions. I hated goodness in books, and the tendency to get everybody to behave alike, in life or in books.

"Are you a citizen of New York?" a Cockney lad asked Anne at the David Copperfield Library in London, the year 1922. The first two chapters of her book *New Roads to Childhood* tell the story of that library. The lad could as well have asked, "Are you a citizen of the world?" and the answer could have been the same, "I am." Work with the children of New York and their parents made Anne a world citizen. She responded to the diverse cultures and convictions with characteristic eagerness. Her regard and respect was never vitiated by pity. She understood the million variations fate composes upon the theme of existence, and welcomed entrance through every door her work opened to her. Here again it was Alderwood that had prepared her for all that was to come. In one of the most eloquent passages she ever wrote, and perhaps the most quoted, she tells the truth of it:

> Nearly everything that happens in novels had happened in the village where I grew up. Here were romance and mystery, beauty and terror, here lived cowards, liars, thieves, and adulterers, as well as men and women of character and definite achievement. I had seen with my own eyes, heard with my own ears and felt with strong feelings of my own the human drama in which I was playing a part long before I was fifteen.
>
> A frank determination to know all that can happen to human beings in books or in life is quite different from a prurient curiosity. Feeling under obligation myself, I have never been shocked to find other boys and girls, similarly impelled to find out all that they can.

Those Sunday-morning rides with her father had taken Anne among foreigners, the poor, the workers in the woolen mills, so that her experience of life, even in Limerick, lay beyond the boundaries of her schooling and the social life of a small New England village. Lawyers, like doctors, know the crooked and the straight of life. Anne must have listened and observed with that rare degree of intensity she brought to bear upon every action of her life.

The breadth of view, the courage and compassion did not derive from the heritage of her father alone. In the plot of the Limerick cemetery where the Moores are buried—"planted," Anne would have said, a New England term that pleased her, bold statement of fact that it is yet holding promise of transfiguration—in that place stands a small headstone marking the grave of a young woman, a minister's wife who had run off with her lover. After a time she returned, with her child, to suffer such scorn as to bring to mind the anguish of Hester in *The Scarlet Letter*. When she died soon after, no one would give her Christian burial or space in any hallowed ground. It was Sarah Hidden Moore who insisted that the Moore plot receive her to lie for the ages under winter snows, among summer's lilies of the valley, black-eyed Susans, daisies, and wild honeysuckle that tangle there with indiscriminate beatitude over the graves of the Moores and the young, passionate outcast.

3

BRADFORD

I was brought under the spell of historical perspective in the midst of natural phenomena. . . .

The plain truths of today are discounted by the amazing discoveries and inventions of tomorrow. We may as well take on trust that there is a truth of emotion as well as of fact.   ACM

$\mathcal{B}$RADFORD, MASSACHUSETTS, is one of the villages clustered in the northernmost and narrowest corner of the state, lying among benign hills, the Merrimac curving through the region to the sea and the transcendental elms of New England reaching skyward. Rowley, Bradford, Haverhill, and Boxford—stout English names that rumble on the tongue like the old refrain "Rowley, powley, gammon and spinach."

The Haverhill *Observer* of April 27, 1803, announced the founding of a new academy erected in Bradford "half a mile from Haverhill bridge":

> under the care of the best instructors; and will be opened on Wednesday the first day of June, which contains two apartments, one for the Males, the other for Females. In the Male apartment will be taught the English, Latin and

Greek languages; Reading, Writing, Geography, Arithmetic, and all other necessary branches of School Education. In the Female will be Embroidery, and all other forms of needlework together with Drawing and Painting. The tuition will be placed on so low terms as barely to defray the necessary expences with the help of the Interest of a Considerable Fund appropriated for that purpose. Boarding will also be very low, and every attention will be paid to form the minds of youth to virtuous and religious habits, and secure them from every kind of immorality. Such as are disposed to commit their children to their care, may depend upon their punctuality, and every favor will be acknowledged.[1]

Academies were indigenous to New England. The difficulties of establishing state-supported schools were manifold even when laws were passed for the maintenance of them and fines imposed for failure to conform to the law. The academy made certain that some form of classical education was established in community after community. Funds were raised among the citizens by various means, sometimes by lotteries or by land grants from the state. "Academies were never 'free' in the sense of admitting students without the payment of tuition, but they were free to all who could qualify for admission and were never operated for private gain."

Hard work on the part of a few families of Bradford had preceded the appearance of the announcement in the *Observer*, including the adoption of rules and regulations, drawn up by committee. The by-laws were comprehensive, covering points of procedure as well as rules of conduct for the students. Consider the qualifications set forth for the choice of suitable persons to conduct the school:

Art. 1. The immediate care of the Instruction of this Institution shall be committed to a Preceptor and Preceptress appointed by the Proprietors of the Institution.

Art. 2. The instruction in the female Apartment may be suspended whenever the Proprietors Judge necessary.

Art. 3. No person shall be appointed Preceptor of this Academy who has not received a publick education who does not Sustain a good moral charictor and reputed a Gentleman of good abilitys.

Art. 4. No young lady shall sustain the Office of Preceptress who is not a Reputable person well versed in the Science of Belles lettres, Embroidery, and all kind of fine needle work.

Article 2 allows rather comfortably for the suspension of female education. The ironic fact remains that from the beginning the female students outnumbered the males, and in 1836 all attempt to educate the young male was abandoned. The school became the Bradford Academy for Women and exists to this day as a junior college for women.

By the time Anne Moore entered Bradford in 1889, the school had attained a position of leadership. Anne E. Johnson, a woman of considerable intellect and character, was nearing the end of her nineteen-year period as principal. In her time she had established stringent scholastic standards for those who hoped to acquire a diploma at graduation. Latin, science, mathematics, logic were required, and, in the senior year, metaphysics and theology were added. Many of the students attended the academy as "specials"—"The giddy, giddy specials," as they were known—taking such electives as appealed to them with no thought of a credential of any kind. The rigidity gave way somewhat under the influence of Ida C. Allen, who became assistant principal in 1888 (later she was to succeed Miss Johnson), for she supported greater freedom of choice in the matter of courses available to those who hoped to graduate, and by her own enthusiasm for art as a fact of everyday life as well as a subject of study she was to enhance and enliven the actuality of school life.

Anne, with the credentials from Limerick Academy behind her, was able to encompass in two years the courses necessary for obtaining the diploma, graduating from Bradford in 1891. The experience of Bradford was pivotal to the life of Anne Carroll Moore. Its progress through the decades of her lifetime, its hold upon succeeding generations of young women were matters that commanded her ardor and devotion. She loved the place. She noted every change in the landscape, rejoiced in the new buildings—the President's House, the distinctive chapel, designed by Charles Stone, which seemed to have grown from the pines that surrounded it. Successive presidents and alumnae secretaries came to know her friendship, and she returned to the campus for special celebrations in the life of the school and particularly upon the graduation of two young women who had chosen Bradford because of their association with ACM. Anne Lunt, daughter of Dudley Lunt, was one; the other, Alice Campbell King, the daughter of Virginia Bowman King, once a children's librarian in the New York Public Library for whom Anne bore great affection. The college recorded through the pages of its alumnae bulletins the succeeding honors that were heaped upon ACM in her lifetime and crowned these garlands of laurels by bestowing upon her the Jean Pond Trophy (June 2, 1956), whose only other recipient had been Jean Pond herself, the beloved teacher, assistant principal, and vice-principal of Bradford.

Anne's memories of Bradford and tributes to her years there were recurring subjects in her speaking as well as her writing. Among the scraps of notes salvaged from the tangled conglomeration of her papers there emerged an early talk written in 1900 (she was twenty-nine years old), when ACM was midway in her career at the Pratt Institute Library and nine years distant from the Bradford graduation. It is not known for what occasion the talk was created, but the topic to which Anne addressed herself was: Is There a Place for Bradford Academy among the Educational Institutions of Today? Such parts of it as reflect the life at Bradford in her day are included here:

Before attempting to give answer to this question, it has seemed to me necessary to go back to the years of my own school experience and in the light of subsequent events, to mention some of the characteristic features of the school as I knew it in the years 1890 & 1891.

First of all, I should mention its *social opportunity*. Among the students, numbering 150 or more, of those years there were girls from Western cities and from New England farms and villages, from southern plantations and from northern manufacturing towns, from foreign missionary fields and from Back Bay in Boston, from the plains of Texas and from Fifth Avenue in New York. These various elements mixed and mingled in one great homogeneous life—some of them becoming friends for a life time while others merely enjoyed pleasant acquaintance for the time or perhaps did not care for one another at all but learned, notwithstanding lack of personal affection, to respect character and a certain wholesome disregard for the false and the pretentious. The assimilation of such a social experience distinguishes in later life the woman who is able to get on with all kinds of people from the one who is confined to the narrow range of her native town or the town of her adoption or to a certain section in a large city. (There is quite as much of provincialism existing in our large cities as in out-of-the-way country districts.) . . .

The course of study as I knew it was as strong in the essential features of metaphysics, English and American literature and general history as the work in most women's colleges of the time. . . .

In the subjects I have mentioned I feel that I owe to my

teachers a lasting debt of gratitude. The course in literature was then given by Miss Allen, the present principal,
whose love for the subject was communicated to her pupils in a marked degree. The history was given by Miss
Pond, a true disciple of Miss Annie E. Johnson's mental
and moral philosophy: Paley's *Natural Theology*, Fisher's
Evidence of Christianity and, shall I add, a philosophy of
life which has been a blessing and an inspiration to every
girl who is privileged to receive her instructions.

These were Anne's beliefs in 1900. Half a century beyond—in 1952—she wrote of Bradford once again: "I
owe a lasting debt to Bradford of the nineties for whatever I have been able to contribute to my profession of
librarianship."

ACM was no seeker of office, but she served as president of the New York Bradford Club for two terms
(1916–1920) and was class recorder in her own right and
as aid to her erstwhile roommate and lifetime friend, Alice
Gale Hobson, whose house and hospitality at Little
Boar's Head, New Hampshire, was a continuing pleasure.

Her devotion increased in the latter years, especially
subsequent to the coming of Dorothy Bell as principal in
1940. Miss Moore's letters to her, to Jean Pond and Jane
Runyan, alumnae association secretary, reveal an almost
childlike reliance upon their pride in her accomplishments and in the honors heaped upon her. Bradford
became a substitute for the lost parents who could not
know how far-reaching was the heritage they had given
her.

476 Fifth Avenue
New York
May 22, 1932.

Dear Jean Pond:
   It now seems certain that I will not be able to celebrate
the fortieth anniversary of the class at Bradford. Since I
began celebrating it nearly a year ago in California with

Winnifred [Winnifred M. Lyman] and continued to do so throughout 1931 it is not far from my thoughts. Until very recent events changed my vacation plans I had hoped to be with you. One of the events, which may not be told until June 8th, is that the trustees of Pratt Institute have asked if they may confer a "Diploma of Honor" upon me and have requested that I be there to receive it in person. I'm really very pleased to have that form of recognition of my work after twenty six years across the river. There's a reality about it often missing from an honorary degree. . . .

I was at Simmons for a lecture last Monday and spent the night with Grace [Grace E. Goodwin], and after seeing how impossible it would be for her to be away from home I am the more reconciled to holding over our reunion. The last one was too perfect to take chances. . . . We all missed you at the New York luncheon.

With love and millions of good wishes for the coming days.

Anne Moore.

3 Mitchell Place
June 10, 1932.

Dear Jean Pond:

You may like to see the Citation even tho' I may not let out of my keeping the Diploma of Honor itself. It's a beautiful one and for the first time I feel like having it framed since it means so much.

It was given for the first time last year to a man who has done remarkable things with Radio. Apparently I'm the first woman to receive it and it was a complete surprise to Miss Rathbone, the head of the Pratt Library School. In short, a direct act of the Trustees which is a triumph for the children and their books to be thus recognized. The Academy of Music was packed and Dean Gauss of Princeton gave a very fine address. Mr. Harold Pratt proved a delightful shepherd to guide my steps to the front row on the platform. Mr. Frederick Pratt, now the President, and probably responsible for my appearance was highly pleased that strict confidence had been kept and that Pratt Library Staff were speculating as to why I had come until they looked at the program. . . .

The one regret I felt was that Miss Plummer could not be there to see the work with children chosen out of the whole library field for this recognition. She was the first to accord it departmental status on equal terms and on its own base rather than as an appendage of a circulation dept. "You can do with it whatever you have it in you to do," was all she said in starting me off.

I hope the girls didn't freeze at Commencement and that it was as always a great success. I wish I might have been there but you can see I'm sure that it was the year for Pratt Institute and now I'm working at top speed on *Nicholas and the Golden Goose* which is to be published this fall.

Officially, I'm away on vacation—actually at the Panhellenic until I can turn over the ms. It's a great life after you get your second or third wind.

With greetings to your sister and my love always
Anne Moore

Twenty-three years later, in 1955, Pratt Institute honored ACM once again, and once again Anne reported the matter with pride, this time in a letter to Miss Bell:

35 Fifth Avenue
New York
May 21, 1955

Dear Miss Bell:

May has been such a heavenly month that I've been on the wing from its first weekend with dogwood and azaleas in Wilmington to Float Night with the whole campus in bloom at Smith the past week. I was contemplating Bradford commencement when the President of Pratt Institute telephoned me to say that the trustees had voted to confer a Litt.D. on me as one of the first group of Alumni to be given honorary degrees. Needless to say I was surprised and unbelieving until a confirming letter came next day. So I'll be going to Brooklyn to receive it on June 3rd instead of to Bradford. You may be sure that I'll be taking Bradford memories along with me and thinking with deep pleasure and satisfaction of your welcome to the new President's House. What a relief it must be to you at all times. With my love and good wishes

Anne Carroll Moore.

Every visit to Bradford campus invigorated her spirit and gave her fresh impetus and vision. In 1950, when she was in the last stages of recuperating from a vicious bout of pneumonia, she insisted on going to the commencement at Bradford. With the consent of her doctor, Anne took off. It was understood that she could be scheduled for no gatherings, free to go or stay as she pleased. She reported to Maria Cimino, in the New York Public Library's Central Children's Room, that some of the students came to call on her early one morning, unofficially and unannounced. They were eager to meet a graduate of 1891, they said, and to see what she was like. Anne opened the door to them, her hair in curl papers, saying, "Well, you see she is still vain enough to care how she looks." If she were following her customary procedure, those "curl papers" were scraps of pink tissue paper peculiar to packages originating at Lord & Taylor of New York.

Seven years later, in 1957, when ACM was seventy-nine, she went once more to a Bradford commencement, Storer Lunt simplifying the intricacies of travel by driving her there. A letter to Jane Runyan tells the story. The words and music are familiar, a variation on ACM's repeated theme of triumph and exaltation.

The Grosvenor
35 Fifth Avenue
New York

May 7, 1957

Dear Jane Runyan:

Before the Commencement Announcement came I was about to write and break the news of my new lease of life

—fairly bursting with health the past two weeks and eager to see the President's House and to tell the rest of the Alumnae how much I'm enjoying the Jean Pond trophy. Having seen Round the World in 80 days and The Waltz of the Toreadors (with Sir Ralph valiantly playing his part in spite of his larynx) I feel up to anything that doesn't involve standing or much stair-climbing. If a bed should be possible at the Infirmary it would be wonderful. If not, perhaps you will find one that doesn't involve too much "to and fro" so I enclose the card. I would even like to arrive on Thursday to avoid the crowd and have a bit more time but I'm not yet sure how I'll come whether by train or motor.

After a winter of hibernation it is marvelous to feel and I'm told, to look as I do. My love to Miss Bell. I thought of you both especially at Easter—it was a very beautiful one here and after 8 o'clock service at the Church of the Ascension I had the two King girls for luncheon here with primroses from their Mother's garden in Biltmore [North Carolina].

With love and anticipation

Anne Carroll Moore

No continuing relationship could have been happier for Anne than that which Bradford afforded, symbolizing by its very nature the polarization of her life: her intense attachment to the strengths and traditions of the past, her eager commitment to the future with its ongoing promises. But Anne herself revealed the deepest core and cause of the matter in a letter to Miss Bell, written on May Day, 1953. There she disclosed that her graduation day, June 11, 1891, which her mother and father had celebrated with her at Bradford in great pride, had also been the forty-fifth anniversary of their wedding. Anne was to hold to that day forever because it was destined to be the last such family reunion she was to know.

As for Anne's days at Bradford as a student, there are extant none of her letters to her parents, but the few existing letters that they wrote her show Anne to have been a somewhat strong-willed and stubborn young lady, suffering the complaint of most young people—namely, a certain dereliction in acknowledging receipt of funds and a never-ending need for money.

Alderwood was a lonely place for Sarah Hidden and Luther Moore, with Anne, their youngest child, gone from home. Anne's father arranged frequent visits to Bradford and sent apples from the orchards of Alderwood for midnight eating. He and Anne made plans to go to Boston together, but the plan came to naught, as is revealed in the following letters.

Limerick   Oct. 16, 1889

My dear Annie:

I shall leave here tomorrow & take the P.M. train for Berwick & stop at Harry's all night and Friday AM go to Bradford by the train you spoke of last week as due at 12 & then take your 2 o'clock train for Boston, hoping to have your company. I see no reason why we can't go this time. I shall put up a box of apples express and take with me to the depot and send along by express. You had better not open until your return from Boston. The box will get to you before I do I suppose. I suppose there is some man about who can take it to your room.

As ever Lovingly.
L. S. Moore

Limerick   Oct. 20, 1889

My dear Annie:

Your good letter was received. I am sorry that I am not feeling well enough to go to Boston tomorrow. My cold has been very bad & I cough a good deal, but am getting over it. I want to feel well when I go or I do not enjoy it. So I have concluded to defer my visit for a week when I hope the weather and other conditions will be more favor-

able. Should I not be able to go then I will send you some
money so you may go to Boston yourself and get your
books. I enclose one dollar for pin money. Until then—

Affectionately yours
L. S. Moore

Boston was a temptation for Anne. She went for
Thanksgiving in 1889, apparently ignoring her father's
disappointment in not having her at home.

Limerick   Nov. 11, 1889
My dear Annie:
    Your good letter is received & is none the less welcome
because of the request for money. I know you cannot live
without it. And I am sure you will not waste it. . . . I
send you enclosed five dollars of which please acknowledge receipt. As soon as it comes to hand. We are all well
& would much enjoy your being with us Thanksgiving
Day, at any rate you have a cordial invitation. I know you
will not come, but it does really seem that you ought to be
here. We will have to have our turkey for a week.
    Write me how much money you will need for your trip
to Boston for you are bound to go I very well know not
withstanding your invitation here. . . .

The girls at Bradford had somewhere heard a lecture
by Sir Henry Morton Stanley, the rescuer of David
Livingstone in Africa, as Luther's letter of January 21
reveals.

Limerick   Jan. 21, 1891
My dear Annie:
    Of course I was delighted with your letter. It was so
good, so entertaining and withal written so plainly that it
more than satisfied. Your description of Stanley's return
was at times almost an impersonation, I would have been
glad to have heard & seen him, but when in Portland, the
weather was so bad that I did not think best to risk the exposure. I am glad you had the opportunity. I see the girls
at Wellesley had a great time with Mrs. Stanley. Too bad

you could not have seen her. Should like to drop in and
surprise you some day. I suppose the thought that money
may be needed ought to occur to me without suggestion so I enclose five dollars but don't be surprised and
think that any radical change has taken place in me, for
this is only a freak, but I hope you won't take it as an indication of mental unsoundness. Let us know you get it.

Yours as ever,
L. S. Moore

On February 15, 1891, Anne's mother wrote a letter
that began in contemplation, for she was mindful of the
fact that her eldest son, her first child, Charles William
Moore, dead at twenty-five, had been lost to her for
eight long years.

Feb 15: '91

My dear Annie:

I must say a few words to you tonight. It has been one
of my hard days [the] anniversary of my dear Charley's
leaving me. It did not seem then that I could live without
him. . . . How I have missed him, no-one can tell. . . .
He never seems very far away from me. He was so fond of
you . . . [and] never so happy as when you were about
him. You were doubly dear to me then & ever since. . . .

Your father had a great time over your letter. Thinks
you write the best letters of anyone—so natural & easy.
[He] says you are the brightest of any of them. Now he
has done it, has he not! Do not let it lift you up too much
. . . I hope you will succeed with your essay & that you
will attend to it right away before you get any more
popcorn feeds. Do not think that will strengthen you
much. . . .

I should have enjoyed seeing the camellias. I do think
them so beautiful. Have tried hard to raise them. Mean to
try again some time.

Miss Allen is very good to give you so much time. Talk
with her as you have opportunity about your future studies for I do not expect you will be willing to stop where
you are.

We go on the same old way. [I] am looking forward to
your coming home. Now what should we do were it not
for anticipation. . . . I suppose you didn't have any Valentines. Do not worry about the dress it will come right
somehow. I must stop now so this can be mailed. Be sure
not to get sick.

Your loving Mother.

At Bradford it was customary to award each year to
two members of the graduating class a prize in the
amount of twenty-five dollars, one for "the greatest
progress in culture and scholarship" and the second for
the best essay. In the class of 1891, Miss Almira D. Locke
was deemed to have made the greatest progress, and
Miss Irene Tyler won the prize for the best essay. But
Miss Annie C. Moore had submitted a paper on "Birds
of History and Literature" which so stirred the judges
as to necessitate their breaking with precedent to the
extent of awarding her a special prize of twenty dollars.

"All along the fields of literature," it began, "fresh
avenues of thought are opening not only fragrant with
perfume of flowers, but musical with the song of birds."
Two portions of that paper dimly foreshadow certain
interests in Anne's future. One, a reference to Hans
Christian Andersen: "Thanks to Hans Christian Andersen, other birds will always hover about our childhood;
no purer moral was ever taught than by the story of The
Ugly Duckling, yet the childish mind receives its im-
press all unconsciously, years after the story comes again,
its beauty in no wise impaired by the teaching now so
plain."

The second is a small tribute to owls, "the most pic-
turesque and human of all birds," a trio of which were
to head up her pages of criticism of children's books in
the New York *Herald Tribune* "Books" and *The Horn*

Book and to give title to the three subsequent volumes of essays, *The Three Owls*.

Anne left Bradford, knowing well that her formal education was at an end. She longed to go to Smith, as she confessed years later in a letter to her niece, Rachel Moore Warren, but she knew it was a financial impossibility.

Two professions were generally open to the unmarried woman of that era. She could become a teacher or a missionary. Bradford, with its traditional sympathy for the mission field, had no doubt exposed Anne to the possibilities of such a life. As for teaching, Miss Allen had assured Anne of her ability to teach should she wish. But Anne was drawn to neither pursuit.

After the festivities of graduation, Anne went to Boston to visit the aunts and to have as gay a time as possible. When she returned to Limerick she announced that she was going into her father's law office to read law. In light of the fact that opportunities for women lawyers were all but nonexistent, it was a decision that was hardly practicable. But Anne was adamant in her choice.

Part of ACM's fascination lay in her audacity. She was no rebel, no nonconformist. Custom, propriety, and, above all, a certain style and elegance were greatly important to her, yet she was capable of spurts of outlandish behavior. Sometimes it was no more than an act of spontaneous mischief, such as she perpetrated in Los Angeles when her friend "Cousin Oscar," [2] Althea Warren, director of the Los Angeles Public Library, Gladys English, head of work with children in that library, and several others met her at the railway station early in the morning. They were all invited to breakfast at the station restaurant, a pleasant place then in the heyday of

Fred Harvey's reign as restaurateur. As the group was being ushered to the table, a waitress passed them in the aisle carrying a large tray with glasses of fresh orange juice. Anne, as she walked, scooped up a glass in each hand without a moment's break in her tread and joined the others. At times high-handed arrogance took command, as when in St. Paul, Minnesota, she ordered the hotel management to clear her room of its abnormally overstuffed plush furniture and replace it with something simple and less conducive to nightmare.

Inventiveness was part of that audacity, as when she lit upon the scheme of extracting money for the Bradford Endowment Fund, not from her classmates and other alumnae but by addressing her pleas to their grown sons, who were thus invited to honor their mothers. She would "undertake gigantic tasks for honor's sake," eschewing common sense to work with no resource at her command other than her own strength and imagination. Such was her achievement of organizing and managing a lecture series in New York for Marie Shedlock of England at the time of the First World War. The determination to read law with her father was an early indication of characteristically absolute and independent action. Her audacity was destined to bring her grave encounters as well as gay and inconsequential ones, and in one instance her action bordered on the heroic.

Six months were allotted to the Moores, father and daughter in "partnership," from July 1891 to January 1892. Four months before Anne's graduation from Bradford, her father had written to her as follows:

Limerick, Feb. 3rd. 1891

My dear Annie:
  Your good letter just received and I hasten to comply with your request as I can as well spare the money now as

later and I don't want you to have to count the few coins you have like a devout Catholic his beads. I enclose five dollars which acknowledge as soon as received. What shall we do with you when school days are over? I think we will keep you a while ourselves. Though I wish we were able to give you as good privileges as the country affords. Its growing dark and I must go home. All well.

Aft. yours.   L.S.M.

"Its growing dark and I must go home."

The winter of 1891–1892 was severe beyond memory. An epidemic of influenza raged through the countryside. Luther Sanborn Moore died of it on January 14, 1892. Two days later Anne's mother, Sarah Hidden, succumbed to the scourge. The years of being the cherished only daughter had come to an end and Alderwood was all but gone.

4

PRATT INSTITUTE: THE STUDENT YEAR

Librarianship offers release for creative, intelligent social relationships which know no geographical boundaries—freedom to enjoy and share the books one loves.

ACM

*N*OT UNTIL four years after the death of her father and mother did Anne discover the direction her life was to take. She stumbled through the first dark year with the help of Alice Lunt, who came immediately from Portland at the time she was most needed. When word of the double tragedy reached her, she got out of her own sickbed and drove by sleigh the fifty miles to Limerick to help the distraught household. Anne's elder brother, Harry Moore, meanwhile, had become principal of Limerick Academy. He and his wife, whom Anne held in great affection, and their two little girls, Rachel and Margaret, came to live in Alderwood and filled the echoing rooms with new life. Anne weighed the possibility of teaching at the Academy with her brother. Before she could undertake it, the cherished sister-in-law died in childbirth, and Anne found herself mistress of Alderwood, with the responsibility of caring for two children, aged five and seven. For two and one half years she was immersed in the tasks and cares of a household and a family, neither of which was hers in actuality.

If there was in Anne's life an all-encompassing romance, she kept it well hidden. Nowhere in her correspondence—and letter writing was for Anne a plenary and endemic necessity—nowhere does she give any hint of having known the troubled joy of being young and in love. Nothing less than the grand passion would have sufficed. In everything she accomplished, in every encounter with people or circumstances, extremes of intensity governed her reaction. It was all or nothing, acceptance or rejection, with small room for compromise and little patience with the shading of "yes and no."

"I don't suppose you got any Valentines," her mother had written when Anne was at Bradford, as though it were too much to expect of her. The matter of marriage seemed never to have occurred to her father. "I do not worry about you," he said to her when she came out of Bradford, "because I feel sure you will always be rich in the love of friends." There was a legend in the family, known to Constance and Ruth Moore, the daughters of Anne's brother Luther. Their version of the tale was that Aunt Annie had once been engaged to a young man. She appeared at the breakfast table one morning and announced to the assembled family that his name was never again to be mentioned by anyone. Furthermore, Dudley Lunt remembers that once in his young manhood Anne hinted at a love affair that she brought to an end without the consolation of having shared with anyone the strain and anguish it entailed. These are stories told and dimly remembered, but the nature of legend and myth is to disclose truths of feeling and response that transcend the actuality of fact.

Certain pictures show Anne lovely in her youth with ethereal beauty. Tall, graceful, and slender: "jimp" is the word for her, borrowed from balladry, encompassing delicacy in its meaning, as well as grace and elegance. She had ample opportunity for meeting young men, with seven brothers in the house at one time or another offering her the friendship of their companions. In a letter written to a friend in 1943 she refers to a possibility of marriage.

> I hope you had a happy Thanksgiving Day and that we may soon meet again or "together" as Nancy Bedell's mother [Margaret Moore] and her sister expressed it when they felt I might marry and leave them. That was long ago and far away. . . .

At a time of crisis when she felt called upon to explain certain matters in a letter to Franklin Hopper, the director of the New York Public Library, she again intimated that a proposal of marriage had come in that period when she was absorbed in the care of her nieces and implied that she had chosen the children as a matter of duty. Whether she was motivated in her choice by her New England conscience, her devotion to the children or whether the children afforded a welcome escape from the possibility of marriage must remain a matter of conjecture.

In the fourth year of the interim period at Limerick, Harry Moore married a second time, choosing for his bride a classmate of Anne's from Bradford, for whom Anne never felt the degree of affection she had given to her first sister-in-law, though she befriended her in generous fashion.

Somewhere Anne caught the rumor of librarianship as a profession for women. Public libraries were in their first period of ascendancy. She learned that the New York Regents' examinations for entrance to library school were scheduled to be given in Boston, and she decided to try them. Off she went, telling no one of her intent, facing, as was customary with her, ordeal or dubious adventure in secret and silent encounter.

In a long, revelatory letter to Miss Bell, Anne gave her own account.

Six weeks or more later I received a pass card and with it a letter stating that admission Board at the State Library School at Albany had made a ruling to admit only college graduates. A circular of the Pratt Institute Library School was enclosed. A church centennial was being observed in Limerick and a young minister who became later the minister of the Park Street Church in Boston, made the chief address. I decided to consult him knowing that he had had a church in Brooklyn. He said very frankly that he knew nothing about library teaching—very few people did in the nineties—but that a year in Brooklyn and New York City would be worth far more to me than a year in Albany. My father had been of great help to him when he had his start in Limerick and he was determined that I at once begin a life of my own for my father's sake as well as my own. He lost no time in writing to Pratt Institute that very night [stating] that I should be admitted on the Regents Examination record and told me I would embarrass him very much if I didn't do likewise. It gave me just the push that was needed.

Pratt Institute first opened its doors to students in 1887. Founded by a family of successful industrialists, eager to make a contribution to the city and the neighborhood in which they had prospered, Pratt was envisioned as a technical school, designed to offer courses to young people for whom college was not a possibility.

Architecture, art, engineering, home economics, and library science were the subjects that comprised the early course of study.

Anne entered Pratt in September of 1895 and moved for the first time beyond the environs of New England. She was twenty-four years old. The century was turning upon the axis of its last five years. An air of hope and the promise of expansion characterized the period. Brooklyn streets were in a state of eruption, a subway under construction beneath the cobblestones, and Pratt Institute on Ryerson Street was itself undergoing a change and signs of growth, a new library being well under way by the time Anne arrived.

Many of Anne's recollections of Pratt are preserved on a series of "P" slips she assembled as notes from which to speak at the fiftieth anniversary of her class in 1946.

Why is it that in all library literature there is no research into the origin or etymology of that ubiquitous piece of paper, measuring five inches by three, called a "P" slip, without which no library can function? The computer can hardly hope to equal its usefulness. The librarian's dependence on it often becomes a lifetime habit. So it was with Anne. If none were at hand, she created a similitude by cutting stationery down to size.

The talk ACM gave at the fiftieth anniversary of her class appears in the Pratt Graduates' Association *News Letter*, February 1947, but the "P" slip as source material is used in the following instance.

Having accounted for all twenty members of the class of '96, ten of whom were living, Anne began by saying that she intended to show "the reasons why our relationship to Pratt Institute has endured for fifty years."

There follow then quotations from the letters of absent classmates, the introduction of some of those present, chiefly Mollie Leavitt, who in 1946 had only recently retired from the New York Public Library after forty-two years in charge of Gifts and Welfare. Then vignettes of faculty and students peel off the packet of "P" slips, the order of their coming unpredictable since the slips are unnumbered. Here they are in part.

Mary Wright Plummer. Of all American librarians of her time she was the one who made the strongest impression abroad. Her professional papers were read by librarians in all parts of the world—of the 1890's & early 1900's. Linguist and poet and a natural student of the literature of other countries Miss Plummer was chosen as the United States delegate to the International Congress of Librarians held in Paris in 1900. For 2 months she was in charge of a graphic Exhibit at the Paris Exposition printing two papers in French. One on cooperation between public librarians & public schools in the U.S. The other on Bibliography. Miss Plummer's clear perception of international relationships and her warm friendships with European librarians and writers contributed definitely to the cosmopolitan atmosphere of the library and of the whole Institute. Educators from all over the world were visiting Pratt Institute for new ideas in demonstrable terms & the free library, thanks to Miss Plummer's interpretation, proved one of the most interesting of those ideas.

Mildred (Collar) Gardner, a director of The Redwood Library of Newport, R.I., whose interest in civic affairs has been continuous from her resignation as a librarian to be married in 1911.

Mrs. Gardner as a student had the temerity to challenge the instructor in cataloguing at every turn. She had no respect for a model catalogue as such. She brought an incisive scholarly mind to bear on every problem and was at once the admiration and the terror of an instructor who had accepted rules without allowing for exception.

Caroline Weeks, Registrar of Pratt Institute 1895. A genius in human relationships and the most selfless person I have ever known. We met in a boarding house on Ryerson Street in the latter half of my student year and achieved a rare friendship.

Mary L. Avery, Lecturer, Editor of *Pratt Institute Monthly*. Severe in manner, outstanding—when speaking of books, she said, "You must at least hold these books in your hands with a realization of what they are."

Pratt Institute was only eight years old when we took our course in the old class room across the street. The School of Domestic Science was on the floor above and beaten biscuits were literally pounded out over our heads. . . .

The ironic truth of the matter is that, while at Pratt, work with children interested Anne Moore very little. At first she was drawn to the fascination of research and reference work. But the ultimate appeal lay in the new concept of County Library Service, under the directorship of the State Library. Soon after she graduated from Pratt in June 1896 she set out for Augusta, Maine, to see what the prospect might be. But Maine was then far from a beginning in state organization. The best the State Library could offer was an invitation to return "some day" to address the State Legislature on the advantages of a statewide basis for library service.

Meanwhile, Anna Barnard White, Anne's classmate at Pratt, with whom she had shared the office of class president, accepted Miss Plummer's offer to head up the new Children's Library of Pratt Institute. The work was hardly begun, a matter of two or three months, when Miss White resigned. Mary Wright Plummer wrote to Anne, inviting her to return to Pratt, this time as a member of the library staff, to direct the work of the Children's Library. Anne was there within four days.

That was in the fall of 1896. On February 23, 1897, Anne sat down to address herself to the task of writing her stint of a round-robin letter to the classmates at Bradford. "Dear Birdlings," it began, and after explaining reasons for her desultory past she regaled them with the following account:

> Oh girls. I've got so much to say I don't know where to begin. If I stopped to think I might be chilled by the fear that you would not be interested in everything. . . .
>
> One of my classmates who had been taken on the Library Staff after graduation basely deserted the profession but opened the door of my future and here I am in Brooklyn. . . . [On] the nineteenth of June I became possessed of another roll of parchment. Two weeks before commencement I received a letter from the Superintendent of Schools in the State of Maine asking me if I would deliver a series of talks upon "Library Methods of Study" before the Summer School to be held in Saco. Having long before determined to undertake the first piece of work which presented itself I saw no way of escape though I had no more idea how it was to be accomplished than a babe in arms.
>
> People were so comforting. "It will be such good experience," they said. . . .
>
> I had undertaken library work because it seemed to present a quiet congenial life with the seamy side underneath and [now] at the outset I must appear as a *female lecturer* in miniature.
>
> There was little time to "reason why" and I fell to collecting material to take home with me.
>
> In the midst of it my brother was married in Philadelphia and I appeared as bridesmaid for the last time.
>
> I left Pratt with some reluctance for I had grown to care for the place and the people though I've no affection for Brooklyn.
>
> On my way home I visited libraries in Hartford, Worcester and Boston, picking up lists and "Brillianti" for my lecturing. I reached Limerick a day ahead of the bridal pair, opened the house and tried to blazon welcome on the family shield. The next three weeks were busy enough. I initiated my new sister into the mysteries of

house keeping, made jelly, preserves, did everything but sew by day and worked up my papers at night.

Fancy, girls, any one of you seated on a *platform* while a man introduced the next speaker as "Miss Moore from Pratt's Polytechnical Institution, Brooklyn, New York." I was scared but I made up my mind to one thing. I would interest those people in something even though I sent my notes to the winds and after the first morning I used them hardly at all. I found a very pretty little library in the school building, where the Summer School was held. Here I displayed lists, books, all the illustrative material I could gather, and here people came to talk after the more formal talk down stairs. I really enjoyed it very much especially the "side talks." . . .

I spent ten days in Portland after this. Visited the State Library in Augusta on invitation of the Librarian. The poor man was quite taken aback when he saw me. We had had some correspondence and he evidently thought me on the shady side of "somewhat."

"There—there's a circus in town today," he stammered. "Wouldn't you like to see the parade?" Of course I would and did. When luncheon hour came I was delivered into the hands of a young assistant who had previously been summoned to entertain me by showing me pictures.

We went not to a hotel nor yet to a restaurant but to the young man's house where I was warmly welcomed with "We're always glad to see Ernie's friends even though they are library cranks."

Time forbids a description of the visit and how I was entertained. Ernie drove me out to the Insane Asylum in the afternoon and facetiously introduced me to the librarian of the City library as "a young lady we hope to have speak before the legislature this winter." He suggested my spending the last of August at Popham Beach where he was to spend his vacation. The family objected to the same as open to misconstruction and I decided to take a journey to Cleveland instead. This is not a letter of travel but it might easily become crowded with incident should I describe that trip to the edge of the west [Cleveland], my first journey beyond New York. I left Boston with a party, names of whom were well known to me at the start, but I cannot call up the figures of some of them, notably the elephantine soul who occupied the lower half of my section, without a rush of something like tears.

We had one common end in view, to attend the annual meeting of the American Library Association held in Cleveland from Sept. 1–4, 1896. Arrived in Cleveland, we found the Hollander, our headquarters, swarming with a Bryan Convention. Alas, for the solitude of my own apartment, engaged two weeks before. I was forced to share with a gaunt female from the State of "Ioway." My first impression—she in red flannel petticoat attired, one or two other nondescript articles of dress not to be mentioned in these pages—was not conducive to *Sisterly* affection. I love the human race but when it comes to sleeping with them promiscuously, I am reluctant.

She was State Librarian by the way, got in through a political pull for she is no more fitted to care for the interests of a state institution than—words fail me. There was a reception at the Hollander that night and I met many delightful people. When at last I sought my chamber I found "Ioway" in nightly attire, hair in leads, *chewing* gum.

"Now you never suspicioned did you, that I was a married woman." I certainly never did, I rejoined with a glance of relief at the cot in the extreme corner. I was not to sleep with her.

"Yes, I've got two grown girls." "You, you must have been married very young," I faltered. "A good deal younger than I mean the girls to be," with unction. "Are your daughters engaged in library work?" "No, they isn't as yet, one's been taken' lessons in physical culture 'n the other in Elocution but just as soon as they get rested up I shall set them to work on travelling libraries. The bill passed our legislature last spring." . . .

On the way home, I stopped at Buffalo and had a lovely day at Niagara. I was winding up with a very good time in Boston, seeing everybody and [buying] a few things when I received the letter which put an end to my wanderings and brought me back to Pratt.

I had a very short time for goodbys. It is better so—

only three days in Limerick.

And now for my work which is all engrossing.

Our new library was opened last June and here in a big room, flooded with sunlight on bright days and crowded with children on grey days, I am living some of the most satisfying days of my life. . . .

I have all nationalities common to large cities. The majority of the children are of the poor middle class but there are many extreme cases. There are some children from the best families also and from them all it seems to me in time one may gain a fairly composite idea of child life. . . .

I dissipate by going to New York. I have all day Tuesday to go where I please. I learned to ride a wheel in the fall and enjoy it immensely though I'm not as secure as I might be and hope to be.

Just now I'm attending some art lectures on Wednesday afternoons. There are a thousand things one sighs to do at Pratt but my hours are long and I have to be careful. I have spun out a long thread. . . .

Congratulations to them as fits to 'em. . . . Whenever a body comes to New York do let her sound her trumpet.

With the best of good wishes

Yours at last.

Annie Carroll Moore

Certain distinctive traits of mind and temperament are revealed in this letter: the quick eye to mark details; the ear, tuned to dialogue and rhythms of speech; the decisive judgment of people; the prejudice against the Middle West which never quite left her although it was later mitigated by her association with the university at Ames, Iowa; the energy which led her to encompass multiple tasks in a day and enabled her to pursue proffered opportunities for adventure to the limits of her physical strength.

5

PRATT INSTITUTE: THE PROFESSIONAL YEARS

> *Out of this vivid sense of the reality of the Andersen stories that I loved best and their association with the affairs of my own everyday life I stepped into the children's room of a public library and found there an ideal spot to continue my celebration of Hans Andersen's birthday, for a children's room is more like a garden than any spot I know.*   ACM

*I*T WAS high good fortune that brought Anne Carroll Moore and Mary Wright Plummer into partnership at a time when education for librarianship was at its beginning and work with children seething to discover its definitive form and philosophy.

Miss Plummer had been given full responsibility for planning the library building at Pratt and for determining the scope of its work. Two far-reaching innovations were the product of her imaginative approach: one, a room designated as a library for children, not as an afterthought but initiated on the drawing board of the architect; secondly, an art reference library for general use, including in its collection slides and prints as well as books.

In the person of ACM these new directions were to find a single focus. Children, books, and pictures—these were for her a major triad. She made good use of the art department at Pratt, enkindling in the children a response to the whole spectrum of art, through the exhibitions they saw on the walls of their library and through the illustrations in their picture books.

When Anne went to Pratt to head up the children's library, her knowledge of children was limited to the all but total recall of her own childhood, to chance accounts of childhood she had encountered in her reading, to the direct experience accrued to her through her care of and devotion to her nieces, Rachel and Margaret Moore, and to the association with her brother Luther's children, Constance and Ruth. As for her knowledge of children's reading, of the books they chose on their own or of those available for them, she had only the remembrance of her own reading ready at hand as aid and understanding. At this precise point of ignorance Anne Moore showed a proclivity that was to give her wisdom all her life long. Whenever she hungered for knowledge of any subject she straightway sought out the deepest origins of the matter. More than thorough study and research were involved. What she pursued was living proof, the very headwaters of accomplishment and personality. The vitality of that distinctive list, "A Choice of a Hobby," which she made for Compton's Pictured Encyclopedia in 1934 and revised from time to time, was due to the fact that she consulted first off not the literature of the subject but the men and women, the boys and girls, whose hobbies were vivid in their lives. The

circus chapter in *Nicholas: A Manhattan Christmas Story*
derives its validity not from her years of attending circuses, circus buff though she was, but from hours spent
behind scenes, an actuality she brought off with the help
of Mr. Edwin Norwood, for long years the publicity
director for Barnum & Bailey. She talked with clowns
and knew the giraffes by their given names! As for riding on the back of the great tortoise at the Bronx Zoo,
a feat her hero Nicholas accomplished easily, being eight
inches high, she herself essayed the adventure, the better
to catch the feel of it.

Her judgment of current books was never an isolated
factor performed within the limits of the time in which
she chanced to read them. Whenever she was elated by
book or illustrations, stirred by the intensity of the writing or captivated by signs of freshness and originality,
she set about to discover the roots of the inspiration by
seeking to know, on her own terms, the authors and
artists as well as editors and publishers, whom she held
accountable for format and design. Consequently, her
criticism was illuminated by a sense of kinship with those
secret inner wells of being that give artists and authors
their power and their distinctive coloration. As for the
writers dead and gone, she delved and dug for every
scrap of information about them, biographical and critical, read their books in toto with the zeal of an avid
scholar, and in her travels trudged the country paths and
city streets they had walked in their lifetimes. She re-
trieved them from the dead past, presenting them as living personalities, breathing, palpable, and relevant, in her
lectures to students at Pratt and later to the staff of the
children's librarians in New York. George MacDonald,
Laura E. Richards, Washington Irving, Sarah Orne Jewett, Julia Horatia Ewing, Henry Longfellow—what gifts

she made of them!

At the Pratt Institute Free Library, in 1896, the first subject marked for investigation in the mind of ACM was childhood itself. The children's room had been functioning for only a few months when Anne took charge of it. Neighborhood children came in large numbers, the novelty of the adventure of taking one's own books off the shelves still bright and exciting, and there were crowds of children of diversified backgrounds demanding the services of the new librarian. But ACM was not content to observe only the children within the environs of the library. She was determined to know all she possibly could about childhood. She went where the children were: to the schools, the settlement houses, and the streets—New York as well as Brooklyn, the area of her investigation.

Chief among the innovations in education at that time was the kindergarten, first recognized as a part of public education in the United States in 1873. The movement, predating nursery-school programs, was based on the philosophy of its founder, the German educator Friedrich Wilhelm Froebel, who held that the education of young children between the ages of four and six should derive from the natural instincts and activities of the children themselves. Play was the keynote of the schema. The profession attracted numbers of teachers who by an excess of enthusiasm created a stereotype of the kindergarten teacher as a person dedicated to the service of children but often sentimental in her approach to them.

The settlement-house movement in America, an outgrowth of a philosophy of social service originating in England in 1884 with the founding of London's Toynbee Hall, was initiated in New York in 1886, when the Neighborhood Guild Settlement House was established, later becoming the University Settlement. Jane Addams' famed Hull House in Chicago came into existence in 1889. The turmoil of the industrial cities that swallowed up the great migrations of people from Middle and Eastern Europe in the years spanning the nineteenth and twentieth centuries was alleviated and given a modicum of order through the work of the settlement houses with their programs of athletics, drama, informal education, their social clubs, and their concern for the Americanization of the hordes of seeking people.

From her first exploration of these haunts of children, Anne acquired a knowledge of child psychology and behavior and studied at the same time the varieties of approaches to children on the part of the adults who worked with them. Her mind was so honed to the differentiation between these concerns with children as to give her own liminal profession—Library Work with Children—distinctive form and clear direction.

The reports of Miss Moore's decade at Pratt, together with certain articles she wrote for professional journals, reveal the sunrise of her vision "a ribbon at a time." A portion of the first annual report, ending June 30, 1897, runs:

> The order of the room has constantly improved, and certain of the older children have been of much assistance in making the social atmosphere of the room what it should be.
>
> Nevertheless, there is nothing of the school about the Children's Library. As one boy expressed it, "It's better'n any school 'cause you don't have to learn anything if you don't want to." Our part is of course to lead them to "want to," and to make the caring as easy and as agreeable as possible by providing quiet and ready assistance and the best books.
>
> For, after all, the library should not forget that its true

function in the work of education is to provide the means found in books and instruction in their use. Let us use kindergarten methods as far as they help us to this end, and by all means let us have the kindergarten spirit; but let us not turn the Children's Library into a kindergarten, a creche, or a club. Clubs may easily grow out of the Children's Library, and it is most desirable that they should; but the Library itself should be sought as a mental resource, it seems to us, and if we can educate one generation of children to regard it in this way, the problem of self-education is not far from being solved. . . .

Our whole doctrine, in fact, may be summed up by this: Make routine subservient to the gaining of the main object, and take time to judge when it is proper to make exceptions to the rules. Of course we are liable to the feeling of over-much responsibility that all sociological work brings to the worker; but we try to preserve patience and serenity and to realize that the books themselves are accomplishing much. . . .

The report of 1898 reveals the first appearance of the pledge which later became established practice in the New York Public Library. To this day, every child, on receiving a library card in the New York Public Library, writes his name beneath a pledge in an impressive, large black book. The Pratt version read as follows:

> By writing my name in this register, I pledge myself to take good care of all the books I draw from this library, to pay all fines and damages rightly charged against me, and to obey all the rules of the Children's Library and Reading Room.

The ceremony of the pledge proved to be one of the strongest psychological bonds between children and their libraries. By the time ACM inaugurated it in New York, she had perfected the wording. The matter is told with simple dignity, omitting any hint of punitive action:

When I write my name in this book I promise to take good care of the books I use at home and in the library, and to obey the rules of the library.

The staffs of the children's rooms in the New York Public Library were admonished to remember that for most children library membership is their first independent act of citizenship. As such, it involves a reciprocal responsibility: the granting of a privilege and the obligation to abide by the rules that make the privilege possible. It was good to come upon confirmation of her theory as recently as 1969 in Philip Roth's tribute to the Central Library of Newark, when the existence of that library was threatened. He wrote in the *Wilson Library Bulletin* of April of that year:

Why I had to care for the books I borrowed, return them unscarred and on time, was because they weren't our property alone, they were *everybody's*.

This idea had as much to do with civilizing me as any idea I was ever to come upon in the books themselves.

The assistants in charge of registering children at entrance desks were instructed never to treat the signing of the pledge as mere routine. Time and attention were to be given to each event, with full awareness of what that moment meant to the child, no matter how long the line of children waiting to come to grips with the pledge, the pen, and the hard precision of setting one's name on a given line.

"There's something about writing your name in a big, black book that is remembered," ACM said. She lived to know the truth of it. During two world wars more than one soldier on leave or returning home from the war sought out the branch children's room of his boyhood and asked to see his name written in the book when he had first joined. What they sought—their lost child-

hood, some symbol of the past, some token of identity—
wise librarians did not seek to know but gladly dug in
basement files to find the book recording the long-gone
year.

The Children's Library at Pratt was open in the evening for the use of older children. Because of the prox-
imity of the Adult Department, circulation of books to
children with the resulting hullabaloo was not permitted
in the evening hours. Anne observed the pleasure these
children found in a place sacred to desultory reading as
well as to the serious business of "looking up things."
She resolved to reserve some corner of the library for
such pursuits during the daytime as well.

When in time the idea was translated to the New York
Public Library, increased benefits accrued from it. The
"Reading Room" of each children's library proffered
reference books, to be sure, but offered for display small
collections of costly books, rich in illustration, books
bright in their original bindings, escaping the conform-
ity of library buckram and the ignominy of pasted book
pockets and date slips. All this was before the great plas-
tic-cover revolution! Children were free to explore fine
editions on their own and to read the pivotal books of
the years as represented in these non-circulating collections. The books were immediately available also for exhibitions, for classroom visits and book talks, or as sources
for the storyteller.

When book budgets were cut to the bone, as they
were during the 1929 depression, a token copy of the
new titles was available in reading-room collections. It
was no uncommon sight in the thin days of the thirties
to see varicolored pieces of paper o'ertopping the edges
of books on the shelves, each with the name of a child
on it, marking the places of itinerant readers. Over the

years each children's room acquired a nucleus of distinguished books. When the Second World War swept thousands of titles into the limbo of "out of print," a record of the years existed in these reading-room collections, a living, continuous history of children's books in the twentieth century.

For a person who never confessed to boredom, Anne Carroll Moore held a curious concern lest children suffer from it in their reading as well as in their often cramped and meager lives. She knew that a sustained habit of monotony can destroy the curiosity of a child, dull his powers of perception, and cripple his ability to respond to wonder and delight. The threat of dullness and disinterest she circumvented not by heaping one excitement on another but by creating a variety of events in the life of the Children's Library. Exhibitions were a continuing source of renewal, and Anne became expert in the choice of their subject matter and the manner of presentation.

> We have found it a good plan to show natural objects in the room and interest the children first in these, then in books about them. In this way the books and pictures "come real" as a little fellow expressed it.

So reads an early report.

The calendar of the year—seasons and holidays—was a natural incentive for the building of exhibitions and offered an opportunity to create appropriate and inciting reading lists. No matter how elaborate or ambitious the exhibition and the special occasions staged around it, the objective of reading was never forgotten. All activity was subservient to that ideal and served only to enlarge and heighten the private pleasure of the book.

The scope of the exhibitions grew with the years and came to include the interests of the librarian as well as those of the children who thus found themselves involved in such matters as *Queen Victoria and Her Reign* and *Japanese Prints and the Art of Japan.* The exhibition of Japanese prints in the Pratt Children's Library turned the minds of all observers to Japan. Mr. A. M. Kashiwa, whom Anne had consulted as authority, visited the room often, enchanting the children with the formality of his friendship and the grace and ritual of his bows.

The Spanish-American War was foremost in the minds of Americans in 1899. The hard fact of war Anne translated into an exhibition on heroism. For the climactic event, which she often introduced midway of an exhibition, she invited Dr. C. Hanford Henderson, director of the Pratt Institute High School, to speak to the children on heroism. The boys and girls discussed the subject among themselves, and some expressed themselves in writing. Certain statements, deemed by Anne to be significant, were preserved in the chronicles of the library.

One lad of fourteen, an ardent reader at Pratt since his eleventh year, commented on the subject in this fashion:

> In ancient times a brave man only was a hero but now, in modern times, a hero has to be both brave and good morally and virtually.

His interest in the Children's Library outlived his childhood. When he had gone off to college at Cornell and later to Germany to study, he asked that the plant he had once given his mother as a birthday gift be taken to the Children's Library. There it stood in a southern window, overlooking the playground—a living reminder of that shy and serious boy who named the toy boats he sailed in Prospect Park after characters from the *Leather Stocking Tales.*

These "innovations" are not outmoded. Certain immutable truths emerge from a long perusal of the reports of ACM's decade at Pratt. They are pertinent to the world today, even necessary as counterattack on the dilemma of the overstimulated, "outer-directed," fast-paced, increasingly mechanized life of the contemporary child. The need for a place of one's own in a public institution still exists for children. The chance to see and hear interesting adults in the reality of flesh and blood, to meet them on terms of equality outside the instructional environment of home and school, without the interruptions of commercials—this remains for children an experience that dignifies them as persons and touches their imaginations with quickening immediacy.

As for the art of making an exhibit, ACM was to write on that topic with verve and solid good sense in one of her lead editorials for her page of criticism—"The Three Owls" of the New York *Herald Tribune*—in the issue of January 27, 1929. Since it is not included in the three volumes she herself culled from the pages of "The Three Owls," it deserves the permanency of print here.

We hear a good deal about creative reading and writing, creative art and creative education, but we are still too often bored by static and ill-chosen exhibitions of books and prints.

Interested, as I am, in the whole subject of children's books and in the manner of their evolution and production, I am not inspirited by the sight of precious and perishable little Newbery and Isaiah Thomas volumes stretched painfully wide open one against another, lying flat like pressed flowers in black, coffin-like exhibition cases with no point of contrast or living historical association. Neither the collector's instinct nor the cataloguer's meticulous arrangement achieves the kind of exhibition one likes to look at for sheer pleasure of looking—the kind of exhibition that draws one back for another look before it is too late—the kind from which one brings away ideas. Since New Year's I have been five times to see the exhibition of children's books at the Grolier Club arranged by Ruth Granniss, librarian of the club, with the assistance of Mrs. Haight.

As an exhibition of the subject for the special student it is by no means complete; as an introduction of it to the casual visitor, as a reminder to the historian or scholar that children's books have a place in the scheme of things, as a tonic for jaded authors, artists, publishers, librarians or booksellers it is delightfully free from the besetting sins of book exhibitions in general. It is so well placed that it is possible to take in the plan of it at a glance, yet it achieves variety, continuity, color, freshness and contrast, as well as definite chronology stretching from the Gutenberg Bible, and illustrated German and Italian editions of Aesop dated 1480 and 1485, to the Ernest Shepard originals for Winnie the Pooh.

The majority of the books stand up in groups composed of their kind rather than lie down in rows so similar as all to look alike. The standing arrangement is made possible by the deep three-tier cases of glass shelving about the walls of the room. The effectiveness and variety in the presentation of the subject are the fruit of years of experience in the selection of rare books and prints applied to the subject too seldom related to such liberal sources. [Mrs.] Granniss admitted that she had had her doubts about being able to make this exhibit definitely interesting and admitted that it had taken a good deal of time and a vast amount of daily weeding while assembling the material. Any true exhibition has to grow under the eye and the hand until it takes on form and meaning. It is a fascinating form of art, that of exhibition making, whether achieved with a single book or manuscript like this or groups of books in library or bookshop.

Once the Children's Library was established as a focal point in the community, ACM turned her attention to the neighborhood schools, seeking ways of serving teachers and pupils alike within the limitations of the library resources.

In the *Library Journal* of April 1902—Helen Haines was editor of the publication at that time—there appeared an article written by Miss Moore entitled "Visits to Public Schools." It chronicles experience so universal in the lives of children's librarians at one point or another as to be timeless in interest and in the wisdom of its conclusions.

> The subject of co-operation between librarian and schools from the standpoint of the supply of books and methods of circulating them has been admirably presented from time to time by librarians who have been doing organized work with schools for many years. The object of this paper is to present the social side of the most admirable experience in unorganized work with the elementary schools of a large city. . . .

There follow accounts of the number of public schools in Brooklyn, the relationship between Pratt Library and the newly established Brooklyn Public Library and the status of cooperation with the schools, which was practically nonexistent. The report continues:

> We were not prepared to supply school duplicates nor to send books to the schools.
> We were prepared to receive the teachers and the children at the library and to give them every possible means of assistance in connection with their school work as well as in their general reading. Our problem then was to make children and teachers really want to come.
> We wrote letters of invitation to school principals and teachers, telling them that the library would be glad to lend assistance in various branches of the school work, particularly in the study of English, in nature study, history, geography, etc. The letters sent to school principals received little more notice than a general circular. They

were usually read at the opening exercises of the school and were sometimes passed about among the teachers. The letters sent to individual teachers brought more satisfactory results. Many of them visited the library and procured application blanks for their classes and teachers' cards for themselves.

In order to get a better idea of actual conditions in the schools and a better knowledge of the reading ability of the average child in a given grade, it was decided that the children's librarian should visit five representative schools noted upon our list. Out of the 130 schools 50 at least have been represented in our records.

The school visits began in the principal's office, where half a precious morning was sometimes spent before an opportunity of speaking to the chief functionary could be granted. The visitor was invariably treated with great politeness, the library was spoken of as an important part of an admirable institution doing noble educational work, but there was no apparent desire on the school side for a union of forces. The request to visit certain classes was readily granted, and the principal frequently offered to conduct the visitor through the building. One such visit, at the very beginning of the work, filled her with great awe of the "system." The tour of the building was made in breathless haste, and there was no time for visits to the class room. We simply rushed through the rooms. How might one hope to penetrate walls of apparent impenetrability and really come to know the inmates? That even such a visit might have results was a great surprise but was evidenced by the return of one of our old boys with several new ones, who were introduced after this fashion:

"These fellers here want to join. I told 'em about the lib'ry. I left my card here and forgot all about it. When I saw our principal *chase* you through our school yesterday I thought I'd like to belong again. I told the teacher you was from Pratt's, and she said she guessed she would come to the lib'ry some day. She's never seen it." . . .

From this introductory round of visits we gathered a good deal of practical information concerning the conditions under which public school work is done and the various ways of doing it, as expressed by the personalities of the teachers as well as by the attitude of the children. We enlarged our circle of acquaintance very appreciably and found here and there a teacher with the book sense and the child sense so united that her work was an inspiration. . . .

A year later . . . the visitor presented herself at one of these same schools, feeling sure that this time she would be asked to say something to the children.

Vain hope! The principal received her with the most polite expressions of interest and said he himself would take great pleasure in speaking of the exhibition [in the library] at the opening exercises of the school, to which no invitation was extended.

On her way down stairs the visitor, feeling very dubious about ever making what she considered successful school visits, was attracted by the strains of a violin. Looking through the stairway window she saw an old man, with the sunniest smile, standing in the midst of a room full of happy-faced children and drawing his bow across his fiddle as if he loved it and could not help it. Presently they all began to sing, quite naturally and spontaneously. One felt at once, even through dingy glass, that the relations were absolutely harmonious between the children, the teacher, and the old violin player.

A teacher who passed on the stairs was asked if the old man came often to the school.

"Oh, yes," she said, "he teaches the children music and they look forward to his coming with the greatest delight." The incident, trivial though it may seem, was full of suggestion for the matter at hand. It was quite evident, if he had any other business the old violin player had left it all behind when he came into the school room. He came to make music, and he played till the children wanted to sing. While we cannot hope to strike the same chord with library books and library privileges that is reached by a violin note, for the charm of music is more subtle than the charm of books, may we not hope to so master the technique of our subject as to be able to present its essence as the violin player presented his melody, rather than the exercises which have made more perfect melody possible?

Books must seem to us like real life, and human experiences must seem like chapters from unwritten books.

There is a certain technique of library visits to schools which seems to me to consist in taking things exactly as one finds them and adapting one's self so completely and cheerfully to the situation, whether it means sitting in an office, standing in a passage way, rushing through class rooms, receiving polite but immediate dismissal, or having pleasant talks with children and teachers, as to make it seem the most natural experience in the world while it lasts, and to make it the basis for future experiences. Theories, methods, the habit of looking too early for results, and above all, an aggressive or a too retiring personality, must be got rid of at any cost if we are to beget a love for books and win confidence and respect for our ways of giving them into the hands of those who want them, or who may be induced to want them. . . .

Always diligent in her pursuit of the dramatic as a means of increasing the pleasure of children in books, ACM found storytelling a bright promise of rich associative experience for the children at Pratt. From the beginning of her work she had taken advantage of every opportunity to talk to children about reading and to speak to them out of her own enthusiasm and discoveries in the evening when the room was closed to the circulation of books. She often read aloud. A splendid reader she, to the end of her days, the voice alive, alert to every nuance of meaning, paced to perfection, and never a tinge of artificiality in it. She related to them events in her own life and in the life of her father and told them about the boyhood of Frederick Pratt, the founder of the Pratt Institute, and of his childhood spent in the region where they themselves now enjoyed a library. The children's response was immediate. They described such periods of conversation as times of "telling things."

It must be remembered that storytelling as it is known today did not exist in the early 1900s. The mode of the day was something known as elocution, painful in its gaucheries of overdramatization and rampant sentimentality. These were anathema to Anne. She was sensitive too to the difference between telling things and teaching things, recognizing that children resent, particularly in the freedom of the library, any hint of being purposefully and systematically instructed.

With her usual thoroughness, she began to experiment with storytelling and to expand the range of special occasions staged for the children at Pratt. One program was devoted to the subject of dogs, and only boys and girls who owned dogs were given a ticket of admission. At another time Dan Beard, that genius of *The Boys' Handbook* and a founder of the Boy Scouts of America, was the star performer, the audience limited to boys who had known and used his books. She searched among students at Pratt in the kindergarten training class and other departments for people whom she felt might have a gift for storytelling or for talking directly to children of their own experiences with such conviction as to involve the listeners in the intensity of their initial emotion.

Why ACM did not herself attempt storytelling remains a secret unrevealed. She held an uncanny rapport with children, her response to the dramatic was eager and intuitive, and certainly she was endowed with the gifts of a natural storyteller. Perhaps some New England reticence constrained her. That she was dedicated to storytelling and to those who could tell stories to good effect was demonstrated throughout the years of her professional life.

In the *Library Journal* of April 1905 there is her account of the experiments at Pratt, touching on such practical matters as the arrangement of seating, size of groups, the control of the audience by school grade, age, or interest, including consideration of the inspirational heights to which storytellers aspire as well as reporting on the measured and proven results of tale-telling. At one point in the article ACM gives an account of a Christmas story hour to which she had invited a kindergarten teacher as storyteller. The guest performer arrived bringing with her three students in training. All four of them told stories. The brief paragraph describing this incident reveals one source of ACM's fascination, the antithetical turn of her mind. She could speak extensively of fairy godmothers, the lighting of wishing candles or of other small rituals in her private mythology and in the same breath pronounce so solid and so sensible a judgment as to thrust the bemused reader or listener into the cold shock of common sense.

> After the storyteller had gone, the children lingered to say Merry Christmas and I lighted them out at the door telling them they might wish on the candle as they passed under it and that when they had all gone, I would blow out their wishes which they must not tell until they came true. I would not advise inviting more than one person to tell stories on the same evening. It gives to the story hour too much of the nature of an entertainment.

Typical of many of ACM's reports, her conclusions transcend the time in which they appeared.

> Generalization from particular experience is a dangerous thing unless that experience is grounded upon principles strong enough to withstand the shock of change of circumstance or condition. I am fully aware that such a story hour as I have described would not fit every library. If it had been made with that intention it would not fit in the place where it belongs. I firmly believe, however, that

some kind of a story hour is both physically possible and highly desirable in every library where work with children is being done, whether it be a small and poor library or a rich and institutionalized one. The first essential is that someone shall believe in it heart and soul, and since the weight of that belief lies far back in childhood, there is no alternative but to get back into one's own childhood; the next step is to muster all one's resources and prepare to make them tell toward the desired object; and finally, to take all the things one is unable to do personally, find people who can do them and so order the work that it will seem an easy and a pleasant thing to come into it as a story-teller. It need not take eight years to make the start —eight months or even eight weeks might be sufficient in a town where one had lived always and in such relation with people as to know their real gifts and to be able to claim a share in them. I have given emphasis to the presence of flowers, pictures, lighted candles and other things which might be considered non-essentials to story-teller and to children. If to another they seem trivial I can only say "I see it so," for I believe the final test of every story hour will be, not whether the story was perfectly told, but whether it was told in a way to create associations in the minds of the children that will abide with them forever.

The definitive event which was to fix for all time in Anne's mind the image of perfection in storytelling was being staged in 1900 in the fashionable ballroom of Sherry's[1] in Manhattan, put to use in the afternoons as the setting for a series of polite lectures on varied topics and gentle recitals by *artistes*. The impresario of these occasions was a Mrs. Charlotte Osgood Mason, who as early as 1900 had been importuned by Dr. Earl Barnes[2] to present in recital a certain Marie Shedlock of England. He had spoken of her as "an elocutionist," and consequently Mrs. Mason had avoided meeting her as long as she possibly could. The day came when meet her she must. She found herself confronted by a petite and beautiful woman of charming presence whose manner of speech was music to the ear, the accent English with certain intonations that were unmistakably French.

A remarkable woman, Marie Shedlock, who at the age of forty-five abandoned teaching in one of London's most successful public day schools for girls to launch herself in the professional world as a lecturer and to emerge eventually as a performer of rare subtlety and grace. Since she was born in Boulogne of English parentage, educated in France and Germany, hers was an international childhood. Her father's profession made it mandatory for the family to move about the countries of Europe. He was an engineer and at one time was involved in the construction of the first railroad in France, built under the direction of the English engineering genius, Isambard Brunel.

When Marie Shedlock came to America, she had in her repertoire one lecture, "The Fun and Philosophy of Hans Christian Andersen." She told certain of Andersen's stories in the course of her talk, and in this storytelling Mrs. Mason recognized a unique talent. In her small person Marie Shedlock combined the French mastery of precise and polished gesture, a heritage from the Continental theater of mime, with the English habit of literature and storytelling as distinct from dramatic reading. These were the gifts she brought to bear upon the humor, pathos, and poetic irony of H. C. Andersen. Seldom has his genius been as richly served.

"I was completely captivated," wrote Mrs. Mason in her memoirs of the affair, "and felt there could be nothing more beautiful to do for the precise and hide-bound little children of the social set in New York than to have some afternoon at Sherry's with little Marie telling her stories in her inimitable way."

The critics acclaimed Marie Shedlock as well as did

the children. "Every tale of the seven was admirably chosen and admirably told," wrote the critic of the New York *Morning Post*, "simply and with little gesture, but every now and then some delicious little bit of hokus-pokus, worthy of Madam Yvette Guilbert." [3]

From 1900 until 1907, Marie Shedlock toured the United States, going as far inland as Iowa, loving the Midwest and finding herself beloved there.

It was not ACM who encountered Miss Shedlock at Sherry's but Mary Wright Plummer. She lost no time in presenting her as speaker to the trustees and faculty members at Pratt in the year 1902. She came again the following year to tell stories to the children in the Children's Library. In 1906, when Anne was at the beginning of her work in the New York Public Library, Marie Shedlock appeared once more at Pratt, this time telling Hans Christian Andersen's "The Nightingale." Among her listeners was a student in the library school, Anna Cogswell Tyler, who was enchanted with what she heard and decided then and there on the direction her life was to take: she would become a storyteller. She it was who two years later was chosen by ACM to head up storytelling in the New York Public Library. For this reason, Anne was to write in "The Three Owls" in 1927:

> Storytelling in the New York Public Library has its roots in Miss Shedlock's rendering of "The Nightingale" twenty-five years ago.

For this reason, too, the birthday of Miss Shedlock is celebrated in the New York Public Library. On the fifth of May, or thereabouts, the storytellers gather at Staten Island, where there are still patches of green surrounding certain of the branch libraries and even a garden here and there, to hear stories told, one by a gifted experienced storyteller on the staff and others by newcomers to the scene. It is an occasion observed with a tradition and ceremony of its own, marking the end of the winter storytelling in branch libraries and the beginning of the hot city summer when the storytellers take to city parks and playgrounds, heroic troopers that they are, to tell their stories to children.

It is not clear at what point the friendship between Anne and Marie Shedlock developed, but it probably occurred sometime within the period of Miss Shedlock's first American tour. Letters passed between them in a faithful stream as long as Miss Shedlock lived, and hers was a long life. As was the custom with ACM, she bestowed names of her own contriving on certain of her cherished intimates, holding with W. H. Auden that "It is our right and duty, as it was Adam's, to give names to all things, and to any thing or creature which arouses our affection, we desire to give a proper name." [4] Because Miss Shedlock often appeared in recitals wearing a costume reminiscent of the French *Ma Mère l'Oye*, the peaked hat of the traditional fairy godmother on her silver hair, Anne spoke of her as the Fairy Godmother of Storytelling in America. Needless to say, the not infrequent use of the title annoyed those who could not stomach such play of fancy in the midst of articles of serious criticism and analysis. But Marie Shedlock was not without gifts of her own in this jest of accolade by name. "Pony" was the term of endearment by which she addressed Anne. How she happened on this choice is not known, but something of the stamina and steadfastness usually associated with the small and slender-boned beast, the pony, is somehow appropriate, and ponies too are of the breed of Pegasus.

Marie Shedlock returned to America in 1915, escaping the heartbreak of war in England, to undertake a second lecture tour, having added to her accomplishment her book *The Art of the Story Teller*, a classic in its field. That tour was conceived in the mind of ACM. She organized it with the help of a committee she herself chose, and gathered together funds for financing it so that the maximum amount of profit might accrue to Marie Shedlock. The multitudinous details of schedules in Boston, Philadelphia, and Pittsburgh, transportation, fees, the hiring of suitable halls, publicity, the supervision of program printing, the selling of tickets—all this she blithely accomplished with such help as she could muster from her office and staff in the New York Public Library.

For five years Anne sheltered, in one way or another, upheld, and promoted Marie Shedlock in the United States. Not until 1920 did Miss Shedlock return to England, too ill at the last to fulfill her scheduled final recital. Nothing daunted, ACM sold tickets for an imaginary recital and sent after her a "Fairy Ship" of messages from hundreds of people all over the world and with it a "small gift of gold."

Once more she was to inaugurate a great scheme in behalf of Marie Shedlock. It was ACM, working through Anne Morgan's Committee for Devastated France, who arranged in 1922 to have Miss Shedlock return to France to visit the libraries established by the committee. There the delighted villagers, children and adults alike, gathered in the barrack schools and libraries in huts set amid the wrecked and dismal aftermath of war, to hear "Fée Marraine" tell her stories in their own tongue.

From a scrap of paper on which ACM had written some largely illegible notes on Miss Shedlock, a few sentences emerge with clarity:

No one who has ever heard her will forget her, whether dressed in the traditional robes of a fairy godmother or in the lovely silver brocade chosen for her by Ellen Terry herself or in the everyday cloak and hat in which she walked the streets of American cities and towns and entered the *baraque* schools of war-stricken villages in France.

A List of Books Recommended for a Children's Library is hardly a title to stir the blood, but to hold in one's hand the tattered twenty-one-page pamphlet by that name, prepared for the Iowa Library Commission in 1902, is to be deeply moved, as is often true when one stumbles upon some token of a beginning destined for significant fulfillment. "With a Few Practical Suggestions as to the Selection and Purchase of Children's Books," the subtitle continues. "Compiled by Annie Carroll Moore, Children's Librarian, Pratt Free Institute Library, Brooklyn, New York, and instructor of the Iowa Summer School."

It was Alice Tyler, the noted head of Iowa's State Library Commission, who enticed Anne to the Midwest on a teaching assignment for three consecutive summers —1902 to 1905. The book list was the capstone of that venture.

How few the books worthy of mention in 1902 as being appropriate for the expenditure of funds in a public library. Twelve titles in the picture-book section by seven artists, but two of the seven were French: Boutet de Monvel and Vimar. This consideration of foreign picture books was revolutionary in 1902 and gives early promise of ACM's regard for the pictorial no matter what language the text might employ. The foreword to the list is full of suggestions for book selections in the library, with great emphasis put on the necessity for duplication of good titles rather than using titles which have only a modicum of worth. Interesting, too, is her observation that

> Children's literature as a whole has not yet been cast into sufficiently permanent form to make it seem possible to compile a brief general list which shall have more than timely interest or value; and therefore many of the books entered in this list should be replaced by better books on the same subjects as soon as better books are published. . . .
>
> When the necessity for duplication is clearly recognized in starting children's libraries, and the best books to meet the conditions are selected for duplication and a sufficient number of duplicates is provided to give every child the right book at the right time the problem of children's reading will be solved. This solution cannot be reached, however, until we have something approximating permanent literature for children, and that we shall *never* have if we base the selection of children's books on the ephemeral interests of children rather than on the fundamental interests of child nature.

The Iowa list contained no notes, with one exception, the *Heart of Oak Books* in six volumes. But in that one note the art of annotation of which ACM was master is clearly discerned. Brilliant in its brevity, describing scope and content of the books, it conveys at the same time the larger purpose of reading itself:

> A collection of traditional rhymes and stories for children, and of master-pieces of poetry and prose for use at home and in school, chosen with special reference to the cultivation of the imagination and the development of a taste for good reading.

" 'Choosing is creating'—an ancient Persian proverb," according to a scrap of paper on which ACM wrote the words, turning it loose in a melee of scribbled disorder, her sure-fire system for preserving aphorism and quotations she judged memorable. For Anne the choosing of titles for a list was an act of creation commanding the full powers of mind and spirit and revealing the tone, conviction, knowledge, and judgment of the compiler. Her own lists were vivid and rich in their variety. She knew everything about the books she chose and a great deal about the men and women who wrote them. The annotations, sure and incisive, reveal the separate and distinctive gifts each book proffers the seeking reader. As with well nigh every piece of work Anne accomplished, the prevailing mood governing it can be defined in one word—exhilaration. Take, for example, her "Seven Stories High," created originally as an accompaniment to an article on reading for Compton's Pictured Encyclopedia in 1932. Books for a child's own library was its theme. It appeared as a distinctive reprint year after year, the revisions being made by ACM throughout the years of its publication. In all probability it influenced more homes, schools, libraries, and bookshops than any other book list of its era, and more than one school of librarianship used it as a text of perfection. The annual appearance of her "Children's Books Suggested As Holiday Gifts" issued by the New York Public Library represented her wise and discerning choice of the year's output, and publishers, authors, and artists alike hoped beyond hope that the books for which they were responsible would find a place on the Christmas lists of her choosing (1918–1941).

In the matter of lists, as in many other professional concerns, Anne's mentor was Caroline M. Hewins, that redoubtable New Englander, librarian of the Hartford Public Library, who had fallen in love with libraries through diligent use of the institutions in the course of her work for a Mr. William Seavey, principal of a school, for whom she did research at the Boston Atheneum. She became the conscience of the American Library Association as far as work with children was concerned.

"What are you doing to encourage a love of reading in boys and girls?" she asked of twenty-five leading libraries in 1882 and, in the light of their own poor showing, stirred up action and reaction in many places. That same year, 1882, saw the publication of Miss Hewins' *List of Books for Boys and Girls*, published by the American Library Association, of which ACM wrote in *Roads to Childhood*:

> It was out of print before my time but I look upon the discovery of a stray copy of it as a milestone on the long path leading up to the appraisal of children's books.

ACM attended Miss Hewins' lectures as a student at Pratt when the reading of children was not uppermost in her mind. However, when she herself entered the world of children's books, she found in Caroline Hewins a sympathetic counselor and a continuing source of wisdom.

As in the case of many other people whom Anne encountered casually or in the pursuit of a common interest, enduring ties of friendship were the result. This was a recurring refrain in Anne's relationship with numerous people. The gift of her friendship was seldom superficially bestowed or sustained. Fortune and time served only to increase the measure of her devotion. So it was with Caroline Hewins. She spoke of ACM as "Little Anne"—"Dear Little Anne," the salutation of her letters —but ACM found no need for any other appellation than the name of Caroline Hewins. Miss Hewins formed the habit of appearing in New York for Children's Book

Week celebrations and for the Halloween storytelling. Often ACM called on her to perform what she defined as her only parlor accomplishment—namely, the recitation of Peter Piper picking his peck of peppers, from A to Z. Long years after the death of Miss Hewins, ACM, presenting the famous alphabet on some occasion recalling her memory, read it aloud. Marcia Brown, noted picture-book artist of the present day, was in the audience and was inspired to make her brilliantly absurd, robust drawings for the rhymes, resulting in a distinguished picture book which she dedicated to ACM.

The decade at Pratt gave Anne Carroll Moore time in which to search *Roads to Childhood*, many of which she herself had cleared in the wilderness, pioneer that she was. These roads have been traveled ever since by librarians and by others who aspire to serve, capture, and enthrall the minds and imaginations of children through reading.

In Howard Pyle's story "The Swan Maiden," when the three impossible tasks had been accomplished and the Swan Maiden rescued from wicked enchantment, the prince found himself in possession of three magical eggs harrowed from the nest of the crow. "Take the first egg," the Swan Maiden said to him, "and break it in your hand," and he broke the first egg in his hand and there was a minute castle. "Set it on the ground," she said, and he put it on the ground. Before their eyes it grew into a splendid palace—life-size in all proportion.

So it was with ACM. A decade of experience, thought, and imaginative experimentation encapsulated in her mind a golden embryo that needed only space in which to grow to its full meaning and magnificence. Time and space were soon forthcoming.

6

AT HOME AND ABROAD

The great pleasure of travel lies in discovering whatever one has the capacity to recognize and enjoy in its own setting.

ACM

IN THE year 1897 it was considered daring and somewhat hazardous for two young women to set up housekeeping on their own. Anne Moore and Mildred Collar accomplished it and had, as Anne described it years later, "the time of our lives."

Both young women were on the staff of the Pratt Institute Library, Anne in the Children's Library, Mildred Collar a teacher in the Library School. The apartment was on the top floor of a brownstone house, 335 Lafayette Street, within walking distance of the library. Their good friend and former classmate Carolyn Weeks lived down the block in a house twin to theirs. The two places lay in easy access of each other, a brief walk across the rooftops affording a comfortable route with entrance through the skylights, eliminating the stairs.

Anne must have been responsible for the cooking, an

art she pursued with passionate devotion whenever time and opportunity were favorable. Records of the venture are infrequent, but the impression remains of much gaiety and wide and warm hospitality. Echoes of parties float through the letters she wrote to her nieces during this time. She describes, in a letter to Rachel written on April 22, 1900, an Easter Monday party:

> I spent Monday morning making cake—nut cake baked in little heart and shamrock-shaped tins; these frosted with maple sugar to melt in your mouth. I went to the library at one—worked until five and then came home to make sandwiches—chopped walnuts with mayonnaise dressing and lettuce—"love drops" and fruit punch and to help deck the house. The dining room looked very pretty with asparagus fern strewn along the walls, a grate full of wood, pine cones and green boughs; Miss Weeks' brass candlesticks on the table under the china [The china consisted of a tea set of beautiful luster ware which had belonged to Anne's grandmother and which was kept on a shelf]; green candles there and on the mantel. The punch bowl was set on a patch of ferns with cousin Alice's violets scattered over them. Dishes of green "pillows" at the corner of the table and a few of the glasses in their green and white crimped cases, all ready to serve with. The punch was the best I ever made and I think the color was lovely—from plum preserve juice (my own recipe). I'll lend it you after we get the house cleaned.

In a letter to Virginia Bowman King, written in the 1930s, the memories of those days are vivid on the page. She speaks of Carolyn Weeks, saying, "She and I always had a May party in our apartment for library school students when we drowned their cares in a superlative fruit punch and in English poetry."

As recently as 1962 those parties came to light in the seventy-fifth anniversary issue of the *Pratt Alumnus*. In that number old graduates had been invited to contribute brief accounts of their recollections of days at Pratt. Mrs. Berth Trube Dean, graduate of the Library School, class of 1900, wrote:

> The most vivid impression was of two dynamic, radiant young women—apparently close friends—whose memory and friendship I have carried through life: Anne Carroll Moore and Mildred Collar. Miss Moore was head of the Children's Library which she had organized in a characteristically attractive room a few years previously. The class for children's librarians was a revelation, for it pioneered many new fields—including the physical features of children's rooms. But the appraisal and selection of the books themselves was the main thing; and this involved the appraisal of the author, editor, illustrator, translator and other points until then hidden. I can still feel the inspiration of Miss Moore's guidance. She had an imaginative quality, hard to catch in a practical way but so out-reaching . . . as to take one on wings. At the same time, for the more realistic-minded she could be baffling to frustration. She planned activities outside class to imbue us (I think) with the joy of youth. We had, for instance, a May Day party with a May Queen. Always something that had a touch of beauty. In the spring, also, she and Miss Collar took us out to the swamps of Long Island to gather wild azalea and hear the marsh birds sing.

It was Mildred Collar who conceived an idea and gave it voice—the year, 1901. "We need a change of scene," she declared and suggested a trip to England, Scotland, and Ireland. They counted their money. It amounted to three hundred dollars apiece. With this fortune in their pockets they set sail from New York on July 13, returning by the same ship nine weeks later. On the day before they sailed, July 12, Anne's birthday, they closed the apartment and went to Manhattan to stay the night at Everett House. A Mr. Upjohn (whose identity remains unknown) took them to dinner and afterward to the Victories Paradise Gardens on Forty-second Street, where they enjoyed a variety show that included, as Anne reported in the first entry of her traveler's journal, "A clever ventriloquist, musical dogs, a shocking Italian dancer and a very tame wire-walking."

On the day of sailing, "M. [Mildred] woke with a sick headache"—an entry that was to recur often in the journal. "M. was still feeling badly at ten o'clock so I called a hansom and we drove to the boat, stopping at Lord & Taylors to pick up a parcel."

Friends were dockside and streamed over the ship, including Aunt Carrie and the Blairs, the Scottish family whose son, as a small boy, was one of the children in the library whom Anne was to hold in her memory all her life. The voyage was not a markedly pleasant one. "M." recovered from her headache, but by three o'clock of the day they sailed the sea had turned rough and Anne endured her first attack of seasickness, a plague that was spasmodically to make her wretched throughout the voyage.

There were few congenial people aboard. Anne concerned herself with the children among them. She filled the pages of her journal with accounts of weather, the moods of the sea, the stars at night, and the shifting, silent clouds by day. But intermittently there appeared sharp vignettes of passengers observed, especially those who sat at the table with them.

Mr. Malkey and son are from Texas on a tour to the Continent and the Holy Land. Mr. M, a very warm-hearted and interesting man, with tales of the Ku Klux to tell. He isn't quite fifty but looks a good fifteen years older, has had nine children and amassed a considerable fortune and he says after this trip he shall feel that he can turn up his toes to the daisies and die with a clear conscience.

He hasn't shaved since he came on board and both he and the boy are so thinly clad, they look half frozen most of the time. They eat from the dish nearest at hand whether it is raisins or turnips, figs or baked beans. The boy is a lanky thing all arms and legs and often begins his meal with ice cream.

Eleven days at sea! The ship landed in Glasgow on July 24, and the real adventure began. No thought of making reservations had apparently entered the minds of the two travelers. They put their trust in a system of Temperance Hotels known to abound throughout the British Isles. As soon as they cleared customs they went by cab to Glasgow's Waverly Temperance Hotel. It was filled up, the city being *en fête* and crowded because of the Glasgow International Exhibition. One of the stewards on shipboard had taken the precaution of furnishing them with an address in case of emergency, so they went straightway to 24 St. Vincent Crescent and came upon a lovely, clean house with a big brass bell and brass plate on the door, the name Mrs. Croel inscribed thereon. Mrs. Croel appeared, "A fine old lady with high white cap, followed by a frolicsome kitten which leaped upon my neck three or four times before I could get away," Anne reports. But there were no rooms there. They were passed on to a Miss Granger nearby, where they found a room, with breakfast, for half a crown each. But such a room! Anne describes it:

A large room, furnished as a dining room—a huge sideboard (really a fine piece of furniture) taking up nearly one side of a great, square room—two big windows with green blinds inside, a mantel shelf on the other side and further along a very untidy-looking bed, a long dining table covered with red felt in the center of the room, a big sofa across one corner—some heavy chairs and pictures hung thick all over the walls: oil paintings, chromos, photographs of the royal family and Miss Granger's family intermingled with heads in various poses. . . .

We sat down in the general untidyness—the room had not been swept nor dusted and sheets and pillow slips were very dirty—feeling thankful to be settled anywhere for we were rocking from the motion of the steamer and confused with the strange sights as we had been driven through the city.

By tram, charabanc, coach, cab, and steamer they toured Scotland: Edinburgh, Callander, the Trossachs, Oban, Ayr (to see the cottage of Robert Burns. ACM did not like it—"too fixed up," she reported), enduring their fortunes in hostelry, fair and foul, with great good nature. Anne was the cannier of the two regarding matters of business and arrangement. It was she who inquired at hotels concerning rates, rejecting out of hand the more costly, and it was she who made initial inspection of rooms before Mildred disembarked from whatever conveyance accommodated them at the time. Always believing in the luck of the lone adventurer, Anne often wandered off on haphazard jaunts by herself, leaving Mildred to her own devices, which were likely to be founded on Baedeker. They were both splendid walkers. "Eight miles there and back" was as nothing to them, equipped as they were with short walking skirts and fortified with buns and Abernathy biscuits. The sharpness of their hunger is reflected in Anne's journal, which is peppered with accounts of culinary triumphs and disasters.

We took a tram to Princes Street and went to the Edinburgh Cafe where we had a most satisfying luncheon: one order of mutton cutlets, one of mushroom cutlet (there are two to each), one of salmon mayonnaise we might have dispensed with. I had a glass of delicious milk and a spice cake while M. had tea. . . .

Dinner was served at seven. Tomato soup, roast mutton, boiled potatoes, pear and raspberry jelly with whipped cream in the middle. Delicious. Crackers and cheese. . . .

Miss B. gave us tea downstairs. Bad marmalade, poor bread—made better by toasting at our suggestion—and the only two biscuits she had in the house. . . .

A gray morning on the water. Breakfast at 7:30. Ham and eggs wilted by the cooking. Paid twelve shillings for this decayed hospitality.

After Scotland came the Lake Country, London itself, and Ireland the last bit before the journey home. Anne kept a journal of the Irish visit in a small notebook especially bound in green moire silk, but aside from a spirited account of the horse show in Dublin, her joy on catching sight of the Limerick hills from the train, and a magnificent breakfast at Cork ("Porridge, boiled salmon, bacon and sausage, toast and marmalade—coffee pretty weak"), the record of Ireland is one of sights the usual tourist sees.

We hurried back to our car (from Blarney Castle) and were driven back to Cork by another road past St. Ann's of the Shadows but the bells didn't sound.

In spite of the Irish blood of the Moores coursing her veins, seldom in Ireland did the bells sound for Anne. It was England that proved to be her spirit's place. So it remained for her as long as she lived.

On August 2 they had started out from Keswick, England, by coach and four, the scarlet-coated driver causing Anne some uneasiness because his face was as red as his coat and his breath was heavy with the scent of whiskey.

The four horses pulled each a different way and the hill leading out of Keswick was tremendous. He raced the horses all the way up and we clung to the seats. He proved to be a fine driver and the ride was most beautiful. We stopped at the little old church at Wythburn, and went inside. We came down over a long hill into the vale of Grasmere and drove up before the Rothary Hotel about six thirty (in the evening).

The hotel, Anne discovered, was much too costly. She left M. sitting in front of its door while she set out to find lodgings. Someone had given her an address, but on inquiry Anne discovered that the house had been sold to an artist who had no interest in letting lodgings. The man in the shop where Anne had made inquiry assured her that any house in Grasmere would be safe for two young ladies to stay since every home was respectable. So she went, in the summer evening, from door to door, finding refuge at last in the Baisbrown's Book and Shoe Shop. Mrs. Baisbrown had two sleeping rooms, front and back, the back one having two beds: two shillings each overnight and fifteen shillings by the week, including attendance and light cooking. Anne took the back room and went to fetch Mildred.

By seven-thirty they were dining at the Moss Hotel, just around the corner from their lodgings, and found the meal good and well served. M. went early to bed, but the indefatigable Anne took a letter to the post office, walking through the churchyard of St. Oswald's en route. The choir boys were rehearsing. On the way back Anne went into the little stone church to have a look at it, choir practice being over. She talked to the organist, who lingered there alone. It was he who spoke of the rush-bearing service to be celebrated next evening. He urged her to come and to see the procession "so quaint and such an old custom," he said but did not explain.

Mildred was abed next morning, and Anne, making sure Mildred was to have toast and tea sent up to her, breakfasted well at the hotel and then started out on a walk. "I spoke to everyone I met by the way," she wrote in her journal, "and everything about the little village seemed wonderfully familiar."

Having purchased a penny volume of Wordsworth's poetry, she made straight for the churchyard, deserted at this hour of the day, and wandered there until she came upon the poet's grave. She mused there awhile, then meandered through the village, coming at last upon Dove Cottage.

> A nice old lady, Mrs. Dixon, took me in and showed me all the rooms. Very pretty, especially Wordsworth's study which opens out into the garden. Mrs. Dixon waited very patiently while I wandered about the garden and told me to pick a bit of white heather for good luck. She said she was having a hard time to get them gingerbread baked for the Rushbearing she had had so many visitors. When I asked what the Rushbearing really was she told me to sit down on the garden seat and she would tell me about it.

Anne records the tale as Mrs. Dixon told it:

> In ancient times there was no carpet to the church not even a stone floor and every year after the hay was gathered the farmers brought loads of rushes and strewed the church with them to take the place of a carpet. After the church floor was laid 'twas changed to a kind of procession. Every child in the parish has a flower piece, a cross or a wreath or what not and fetches it to the church wall about four o'clock in the afternoon—the band plays and the children march round the village with their "bearings" then they all go into the church and have service and afterwards they go to the school and each of 'em gets 2 penny worth o' gingerbread and a new sixpence. I've made the gingerbread for Rushbearing for 40 years.

All unknowing, the young ladies from Brooklyn had stumbled onto the observance of an ancient ceremony, scheduled to begin that very afternoon. Anne, having rested as she listened to Mrs. Dixon, started afresh up the hill to "The Wishing Gate" ("the second gate at the right after passing a farmhouse"). There, looking down on Grasmere Lake, she read Wordsworth's poem and made wishes of her own.

> Yea! even the Stranger from afar,
> Reclining on this moss-grown bar,
> Unknowing, and unknown,
> The infection of the ground partakes,
> Longing for his Beloved—who makes
> All happiness her own.

The realist Anne, having feasted Anne the romanticist on the haunts of the poet and his poetry, noted in her journal that that Wishing Gate was not mossy at all and was badly defaced with the carving of many initials. Moreover, the gingerbread she bought on her way home —Mrs. Dixon's gingerbread—"was the soft kind. Pretty heavy!"

By four o'clock the children had begun to gather near the old church wall, each with his bearing

> wrought with reeds, mosses, feathery grasses, bright-hued garden flowers and wild flowers. The old church wall bloomed from end to end.

Two hundred children marched in the procession, carrying such a variety of flower-bedecked banners, garlands, and symbolic floral pieces as to bedazzle the eye, but Anne in her journal noted and described dozens of them to the last flower and petal. After winding its way around the village, the procession marched through the doors of the church and the arches beyond, the children fanning out to place their bearings along the dim stone walls of the church interior. A brief service followed. There was the singing of the rush-bearing hymn and a short prayer. Then the children dashed to the school

yard for the distribution of pennies and gingerbread—
two squares to every child and each square bearing the
name of St. Oswald. The celebration continued through
Sunday and Monday with services in the church on the
Sabbath, and Maypole dancing, games, and contests on
Monday with the awarding of trophies and prizes.

Anne was captivated and enthralled by every part of
it. Homage to tradition was for her a law of life, and
heights of exhilaration the natural concomitant of celebration, ceremony, pageantry, and procession. In addition
there had been the children. By the end of the celebration, Anne knew scores of them by name and could
match child to parent, having conversed with many people at various stages of the proceedings. Small wonder
that Grasmere and the north of England were for her
beloved regions to which she returned on every trip to
England.

> There is I find a very definite connection between my
> childhood and girlhood in New England and my feeling
> so completely at home in the North of England as soon as
> I entered it in 1901—not as a tourist, but as one to whom
> it *belonged*—lock, stock and barrel

she wrote Bertha Miller in 1945, when they explored together the possibility of Anne's writing an autobiographi-
cal book for the Horn Book publications. She continued:

> I have always felt that way about England, and since it
> stems from literature and history rather than family, my
> childhood and youth may hold something of value to those
> who are searching for signs and values in this critical time!

Unhappily this plan came to naught. But England
loomed large in all that ACM thought, felt, and accomplished. As for the children at Pratt Free Library, shortly
after Anne's homecoming they were enjoying an exhibi-

tion of the rush-bearing ceremony and hearing from Mildred as well as Anne vivid accounts of the idyll of Grasmere.

In 1902 Anne's beloved brother Harry Vane Moore died at the age of forty-eight, leaving a young widow and two daughters. The affairs of the family were, for a time, in some disarray. Luther Moore, Anne's youngest brother, a brilliant young attorney at Saco, Maine, offered assistance at every possible point. As for Anne, she invited her sister-in-law and the two girls to make their home with her in the apartment on Lafayette Street in Brooklyn. It was a characteristically generous and highly impractical solution. However, more than once in her life, Anne flouted common sense with stunning audacity in behalf of a cause or a person important to her, and as often as not, like the seemingly foolish youngest son in all the folk and fairy tales, she brought off the affair successfully.

To the professional activity which increased for Anne as her reputation grew now was added the challenge of two young minds to be introduced to all the theater, art, books, and music that could be crowded upon them. Rachel was fourteen years old and Margaret two years younger. Anne longed to open doors to her brother's children and so she did, sacrificing reserves of strength and emotion in the process and impoverishing her pocketbook. As for the nieces, looking back on their years with Anne, their memories of the time were not altogether happy. Often they felt themselves dragged a long and tiresome way from Brooklyn to Manhattan, to operas and exhibitions that only partially held their interest. Even comforted as they were by chicken patties at Purcells and treated to other extravagant delicacies, tension and anxiety often accompanied the festivity. With

Auntie, there was the possibility of failure to respond with the degree of intensity she demanded and the subsequent endurance of her displeasure, implied though seldom spoken. They knew something of the frustration which the student at Pratt had acknowledged in her tribute to ACM. Hers was a brilliant sun, and the satellites orbiting around it rejoiced in its brilliance and governed themselves accordingly, but certain planets moving beyond that sun's circadian rhythms felt themselves deprived of an illumination which yet lay within their reach.

In the house in Brooklyn it was Anne who called the turn of events. The parties were Anne's parties. It was she who decided when the girls should appear in Kate Greenaway costumes. It was she who made up the guest list.

This was a fiercely loyal family. Anne's affection for her nieces, her great-nieces and nephews was both torment and delight to her, as it must have been for them. With the cruelty of youth, they often resented her insistence on a view of life uniquely her own, but their loyalty and love endured. As for Anne, her generosity toward them was unremitting, her faith in them unending, her love indisputable.

In her wisdom and with the years, Anne came to understand the truth of the matter. Writing to Bertha Miller, in the summer of 1939, she said:

> Perhaps the hardest thing we have to learn is that we may not judge others in terms of ourselves but rather in terms of their capacity and understanding.

THE NEW YORK PUBLIC LIBRARY

> *Without fee or questioning, the Public Library offers every living soul the certainty of knowledge, playgrounds for the mind and habitation for the spirit. As soon as a child can enjoy pictures in a book, the doors open.*
>
> ANON.

THE CONCEPT of a scholarly free reference library, its resources open to the public of New York City, first took form in the mind of a New England lawyer and schoolmaster. His name was Joseph Green Cogswell, professor of geology at Harvard and assistant librarian there from 1820 to 1823. He had been one of the group of brilliant students at Harvard that included George Bancroft, Edward Everett, and George Ticknor.[1] In the company of these men he traveled to Europe and studied at German universities, noting with special interest the resources of the great libraries he encountered there. At Weimar the young Americans repeatedly visited

Goethe, who was at that time a lonely, aging man. Much drawn to young Cogswell, Goethe made a commemorative gift of his collected works to the Harvard Library as tribute to his friend. In later years Cogswell with Bancroft founded a famous private school, Round Hill, at Northampton, Massachusetts. When ill health forced him into partial retirement, he accepted the invitation of a New York banker, Samuel Ward, three of whose sons had been students at Round Hill, to make his home with the Ward family, thus becoming part-time tutor and full-time friend-in-residence at the fashionable address of the Wards at Broadway and Bond Street.

Through his hosts Mr. Cogswell came to know John Jacob Astor, who by this time (1838) was seventy-five years old, somewhat unhappy in his retirement, and perplexed by the problem of deciding upon a suitable memorial to himself, one that would perpetuate his memory and at the same time afford some benefit to his adopted country, he having come to America from Germany and made a great fortune in the early days of the fur trade. He had toyed with the idea of building an actual monument to himself in Washington, D.C. Then he met Mr. Cogswell, who, in a letter to a friend, reported on these matters in January 1833:

> I have seen a great deal of Mr. Astor, having dined with him twice at his own house, and three times at his son's. He is not the mere accumulator of dollars, as I supposed him; he talks well on many subjects and shows a great interest in the arts and literature. I meet Halleck[2] there often, and some other pleasant visitors.

Six months later he wrote to George Ticknor:

> Early in January Mr. Astor consulted me about an appropriation of some three or four hundred thousand dollars, which he intended to leave for public purposes, and I

urged him to give it for a library, which I finally brought him to agree to do, and I have been at work ever since, settling all the points which have arisen in the progress of the affair. It is now so nearly arranged that he has promised me to sign the last paper to-day, and if so I shall see you in Boston early next week. Had I not foreseen that this object would never have been affected unless someone had been at the old gentleman's elbow, to push him on, I should have left New York long since. It is not made public at present, but I think it will be in a week or two. In the meanwhile say nothing about it.

Public announcement was made in Boston the following week and by circuitous routes finally reached the New York papers. That was in 1838. Had Mr. Cogswell foreseen the years of delay, the dilly-dallying on the part of Mr. Astor, who with increasing age found it difficult to hold to one plan above another for any length of time, he would have lost heart completely. Meanwhile, Mr. Cogswell purchased books, made buying trips to Europe, and somehow endured the frustrations of an impatient man. In 1842, four years after the initial announcement of the plan for a library, Washington Irving, having been appointed Minister to Spain, asked Mr. Cogswell to accompany him as Secretary of the Legation. When Cogswell's departure was almost an actuality, Mr. Astor, in fear of losing his companionship and his services, promised to complete plans for the library, guaranteed Cogswell the office of Librarianship and proffered financial support for his labors meanwhile and so held him in New York. Six years later, in 1848, the library was still a nebulous possibility. In March of that year Mr. Astor died, but the library was assured existence by the terms of his will. On January 10, 1854, sixteen years after the idea was first implanted in the mind of Mr. Astor, the Astor Library in Lafayette Place opened its doors to the public of New York City, the librarian himself standing inside the railing to give directions to the visitors. The details of the event were described in a letter to George Ticknor:

> The library has been open now about ten days, and harassing days they have been to me, one unbroken string of questions from morning till night, requiring constant and wearing repetition of the same answers. At nine a.m. I take my stand inside the railing and there I remain as a fixture until half-past four. They all look wistfully at the books, and ask, "can't we go into the alcoves and up to the second story," and, when I answer, "No," they break out into a railing accusation. But it's no use, I tell them, "You can't do it." I know not what I should have done if I had not hit upon this plan of a close corporation. It would have crazed me to have seen a crowd ranging lawlessly among the books, and throwing everything into confusion.

As for the reading of the young—boys fourteen years and older were allowed entry—Mr. Cogswell bewailed their choice of books in a further letter, his complaint falling strangely, indeed, on the ears of the librarian of today:

> . . . The readers average from one to two hundred daily, and they read excellent books, except the young fry, who employ all the hours they are out of school in reading the trashy, as Scott, Cooper, Dickens, *Punch* and the *Illustrated News*. Even this is better than spinning street yarns, and as long as they continue perfectly orderly and quiet, as they now are, I shall not object to their amusing themselves with poor books.

In the course of time the nucleus of the Astor Library drew within the radius of its influence two great additional resources of books and funds. First, the Lenox Library, established like the Astor as a memorial to the wealth and general distinction of a successful financier, one John Lenox, son of a Scottish merchant and importer. He found his chief pleasure in book collecting, among his enthusiasms the poet Milton, the Bible, and the acquisition of multiple editions of a favorite book of his, Bunyan's *Pilgrim's Progress.* "Original and peculiar" as a collector, so he was described by his purchasing agent, but fervent, knowledgeable, and widely read.

Samuel Jones Tilden, lifelong bachelor, once Governor of New York, whose disputed candidacy for the office of President in 1876 forms a curious chapter in American history, left nearly five million dollars to the city of New York, to be incorporated in a fund known as the Tilden Trust, "with capacity to establish and maintain a free library and reading room in the City of New York." The legacy was reduced to two and a half million after the legal squabbling of his relatives had subsided. By great good fortune and the perspicacity of distinguished boards of trustees, the three library foundations were bound together in a signed Agreement of Consolidation on May 23, 1895.

In December of that year, Dr. John Shaw Billings, noted Army surgeon of the Civil War, subsequently organizer of the Surgeons' General Library in Washington, which he brought to great distinction, was named director of the New York Public Library. On March 25 of the following year, 1896, the board of trustees of the New York Public Library, Astor, Lenox, and Tilden Foundation, addressed to the Mayor, Aldermen, and Commonalty of the City of New York, a document describing "the meager and unsatisfactory provision existing in the City of New York either for scholars and students in a reference library, or for home reading through a library of circulation," comparing the small expenditures supplied by New York to this cause of public education with the more ample means afforded like causes by lesser cities of the Eastern seaboard:

> . . . What is necessary for real public interest and lasting public benefit is a great central library of reference and exhibit, and in addition, the public must be provided with the means of procuring books for home reading within some reasonable distance of their residence.

It is to be noted that the site for such a library is mentioned for the first time officially in this document:

> No site within the control of the City could accomplish the ends in view as well as that of the Reservoir upon Fifth Avenue between Fortieth and Forty-Second Street.

A certain fire and eloquence informs this plea for public support, with its tables and statistics and other documentary evidence giving the history of the past as well as a plan for the future, culminating in this last paragraph:

> When we consider the extent to which an institution of the character proposed may fairly be expected to strengthen the police, diminish crime, raise public standards of morality, attract to our City men from every industry and every walk of life, add to the operative power of our people, and extend the influence of our Commonwealth, it can hardly be regarded otherwise than a privilege for the City to share in the work.

John Bigelow was president of the Board of Library Trustees at that time, having come into the picture as a trustee of the Tilden Trust. Accomplished professional writer and distinguished diplomat during the Civil War, he had served in France and was credited with preventing that country's recognition of the Confederacy. No doubt it was his rhetoric that spawned such extravagant declarations of faith in the accomplishment of libraries and librarianship. John Bigelow lived to be ninety-four years old, and it was into his hands that the Mayor of New York, on May 23, 1911, delivered the keys of the great Central Building at the celebration of its opening to the city. He died in December of that year.

For five years after the directorship of Dr. Billings, the scope of the library was limited to reference service. It was not forgotten, however, that the second Article of the Agreement of Consolidation of the three foundations read as follows:

> The said new corporation shall establish and maintain a free public library and reading room in the City of New York, with such branches as may be deemed advisable.

From this brief, formal statement was to come the drama and sheer humanity of the greatest public library system in the world, its diversified pattern of administration and its imaginative concept of public service destined to enliven and inform the life of three boroughs of the city—Richmond, the Bronx, and Manhattan—and to set an example to the world.

By the year 1900 the city brought pressure to bear upon Dr. Billings toward the fulfillment of the promise made at the time of consolidation, demanding a calendar of action and proposing to assume part of the financial burden. Consequently Dr. Billings, with a plan for unification of a library of circulation in mind, sent to fourteen of the existing subscription libraries in the city, privately financed or, in a few instances, receiving aid from the city, asking them to give full accounting of their financial status and holdings and putting to them, as it were, the familiar question from the Lobster Quadrille: "Will you, won't you, will you, won't you, won't you join the dance?" The cause of centralization was expedited by the gifts of Andrew Carnegie, who in a brief letter to Dr. Billings, dated March 1, 1901, offered to give the city sixty-five branch libraries. "Sixty-five libraries at one stroke probably breaks the record," he wrote, sounding like the valiant Little Tailor of Grimm's *Fairy Tales*, who killed seven at a blow, "but this is the day of big operations and New York is soon to be the biggest of the Cities."

Now and then, when Anne Carroll Moore was Director of Work with Children in the New York Public Library, at the monthly meeting of Children's Librarians, she began proceedings with roll call, not by names of staff members but by names of the branch libraries: Aguilar, Cathedral, Chatham Square, Epiphany, Harlem, Hudson Park, etc., through the complete litany. Her sympathy for the mystique of the names of things, the tone of her voice, and the rhythm of the syllables as she spoke them conveyed a sense of history though the subject was never formally presented in lecture or program. One came to know the founding personalities, the character of the neighborhoods, the multicolored life of New York branch libraries as ACM knew and cherished them: the Harlem branch, its origins going back to the time of Harlem as a township in its own right when monies accrued to the library from the sale of the land of Harlem Commons as early as 1820; Washington Heights, begun in 1868, supported by shares and subscriptions, where a boys' and girls' library made an early appearance, its subscription rate being five cents per week for those under sixteen; Aguilar Free Library Society, organized in 1886, to serve "those who were actually interested in Jewish communal affairs." So runs the tale away.

By national groups, by church affiliations, by parish

house and synagogue, by labor-union affiliation, by settlement house, by public schools, by Czech Sokol clubs meeting in gymnasiums, by German clubs and debating societies, by philanthropists and scholars—by such diverse shouts and murmurs were demands made for books and reading in New York during the mid-1800s.

One splendid system, the New York Free Circulating Library, originated at Grace Church in 1878, the setting a sewing class for young girls whose taste in reading was deemed to be deplorable. In an effort to improve matters, certain women of the church undertook to read aloud as the group learned to sew.

Two decades later, in 1899, the New York Free Circulating Library claimed eleven branches throughout the city, and by that time the use of the libraries by children was so marked that in several branches a separate room was set aside for them.

This well-organized system stood ready as the sound basis of operation for the New York Public Library when the year of consolidation among the City's circulating libraries came to pass. On the very day, March 3, 1901, that Andrew Carnegie wrote his letter to Dr. Billings, promising a clutch of branch libraries, Arthur E. Bostwick, formerly a chief librarian of the New York Free Circulating Library and of the Brooklyn Public Library, was appointed head of the newly organized Circulation Department of the New York Public Library.

The title of doctor, which his associates invariably used in speaking to or of Arthur Bostwick, was his due, since he held a Ph.D. from Yale (1883) in the physical sciences. Degrees of such magnitude were not common in the library profession of that time, and, no doubt, the staff of the New York Public Library spoke of their tandem directors in one proud breath as Dr. Billings and

Dr. Bostwick. Certainly Dr. Bostwick was not the pedant wearing his honors conspicuously. It was not he who insisted on the title.

New England by birth, he was very much a man of the world, welcomed and consulted in far places. His knowledge of science did not preclude an interest in literature. Before he became a librarian he had distinguished himself as editor and literary adviser on *The Forum*, Appleton's *Cyclopedia of American Biography*, and the *Literary Digest*. He was a genial man, gracious and comfortable in encounter, and Anne Carroll Moore was to find in him a decisive administrator, generous in sympathy and in understanding. The friendship between them was sustained throughout their lives. She dedicated the second of her "Roads to Childhood Books," *New Roads to Childhood*, "To Arthur Bostwick, whose zest for exploring new roads lights up every turn in the long road of an old friendship."

In 1905, after four years of creating a Department of Circulation in the New York Public Library, Dr. Bostwick held work with children as top priority for the library. On December 20 of that year, Dr. Bostwick wrote to Miss Annie Carroll Moore of the Pratt Free Institute Library asking her to call at his office the following week, as he wished to discuss with her the possibility of her coming to the New York Public Library to direct the work with children. The opportunity came at the time when life for Anne had come to a peak, presenting a natural point of division. A decade of accomplishment at Pratt lay behind her, but the growth and development of the Brooklyn Public Library, founded in 1903, was bound to overwhelm and absorb the service of Pratt Free Institute Library as a public library. Anne Carroll Moore might well have found herself at that period of time in a *cul-de-sac.*

As for her personal life, there was no longer need for her to maintain a home base for her nieces. Rachel, the older of the girls, had gone off to college at Bryn Mawr. Physically Anne was spent, her spirit much depleted. She was too ill to go to Manhattan. Consequently Dr. Bostwick wrote asking if he might call upon her at her home on Lafayette Street. When the day came, she was flat on her back, suffering what her cherished Dr. Butler diagnosed as emotional exhaustion. She received Dr. Bostwick in this unbecoming state of collapse, but the news Dr. Bostwick brought was exhilarating to the point of intoxication. He was tired, he said, of having to send hundreds of people inquiring about library work with children across the Brooklyn Bridge for their answers. Would she come to Manhattan and take over the untidy and more or less haphazardly organized work with children, giving it the direction she deemed best suited to the great metropolitan center?

Rivalries existed in this fair enterprise of library work with children. The public libraries of Pittsburgh and Cleveland were generally acknowledged to be leaders in this field, and their activities dominated the reports in professional journals. Anne was aware of this. In a letter to her niece reporting the great news, Anne revealed the scope of her ambition. "It's the one place I have ever felt that I might be induced to consider if I could have right of way, for taken in a big way it would knock the spots out of any other like position in the country."

Dr. Butler recommended a long period of rest before signing on. Mr. Bostwick suggested September 1, 1906, as a probable date for beginning. Anne closed up her share of the apartment, stuffed her unpaid bills, alarming in their plenitude as a result of her generosity to the family, into a shoe box, shoved it under the bed, and took off for England, on the *Minnehaha*, March 3, 1906. The mooing of cows accompanied her across the Atlantic, for she was sailing on a cattle boat, under Captain Robinson, in whom Anne discovered, of all things, a fellow devotee of Mrs. Gaskell's *Cranford*.

She had hoped for the full panoply of an English spring and summer when she set sail from Brooklyn, but London in March was cold, and after two weeks she abandoned it and went to Ventnor on the Isle of Wight. In the footsteps of Tennyson, she journeyed to Freshwater, seeking the house where he had lived and visiting the church he must have frequented. She sat in the pew she thought was Tennyson's and was confirmed in her choice by the sexton, "Though of course Miss," he confided to her, "him never come to church nor Lady Tennyson neither."

Her lively journal of these months from March until the middle of July recounts trips to Knutsford, where *Cranford* had its roots, and long walks with a Miss Hollins, who had known Mrs. Gaskell. She was there for May Day and found the celebration somewhat tarnished in its performance, with artificial flowers and gaudily colored feathers used in the procession, though the Morris dances were still beautiful in their authentic costume and tradition. The heath was populated by traveling caravans of carnival folk. Through her chance acquaintance with a churchly woman who visited the sick and the poor, Anne found herself concerned about a performer in one of the wagons, a young woman who shared a wagon with the show's "fat lady" and a snake charmer. The poor soul was dying, according to all reports, and lived on nothing but champagne. Then one day a man in one of the other wagons came to visit her.

He turned to Anne's friend and asked, "Is she going to die?" And the woman nodded her head in assent, whereupon the man turned to the patient in the bunk and shouted, "Don't be such a God damn fool as to die on the road" and stomped out. Anne records all this in her journal, initialing the profanity by way of polite abbreviation, and reports that immediately thereafter the woman showed signs of recovering.

Anne returned to Grasmere to revive old memories and went for the first time to Ambleside, which she loathed. Even though she had paid a week's lodging in advance, which the landlady refused to refund to her, she decided to abandon the place for Troutbeck, four miles distant, a village she had discovered on her own. There she found a countryside, a house, and a room full of comfort and inner consolation. She was to hold that place very dear forever after.

From March until the middle of July she wandered from lodging house to country inn, took residence in a women's club in London or visited friends held over in her affection from the first English journey with Mildred Collar in 1901. Long, solitary walks were her delight, as well as the other traveler's joy that was abundantly hers, the ability to become a part of the life of room, house, garden, country lane, or city street, wherever she found herself.

The precise and carefully kept journal of those months must often have given ACM pleasure in rereading. The honest love of good food was chronicled there and people, clear and sharply drawn, with glimpses of landscape and the English spring to "flash upon the inward eye."

> Gathered my first sprig of hawthorne and a shaft of yellow broome. . . . Saw daisies just peeping out in the fields. Primroses beside a little stream and blackthorn just

coming out in the hedgerows. The birds sang divinely and I began to feel happy. . . . The young lambs were a delight to see. Lots of primroses to left and right but not many trees nor were they far along in age. . . . We took the road past Buddle's and further on toward the lighthouse—nearly down to it having met some children who told us that primroses grew very thick down there. I got out and scouted through a hedge and over a rough pasture until I began to find such heaps and heaps I took off my hat and filled it and then I went on and scrambled over a very high stone wall and found myself beside a primrose-bordered stream with a bank of violets stretched blue above the yellow flowers. I never saw anything so beautiful and I sat down and filled myself full of it.

Not all the scenes are those of wood and stream. Anne spent Easter in London. On the Saturday before the day, she had risen betimes at her club and made her way to Covent Garden Market before anyone else was astir.

What fun it was to see the market wagons unloading and the donkey carts loading up. I dodged barrels, baskets, hampers of fruit and vegetables right and left being the only woman on the scene. Everybody was jolly and nice 'though very busy. I made my way through to the fruit and flower markets where I spent most of the time and before I left people were pouring in to buy Easter flowers. I had my hands full long before I could find a basket which I finally did at a shop outside the market. I lined it with maiden hair and filled it with forget-me-nots, most lovely white tulips with delicate green edges, lilies of the valley, yellow roses, a dozen bunches of violets and some feathery lavender flower. Then I took it on my arm and walked home trying in vain to get tea or coffee at an Egyptian restaurant that I passed.

On Easter Sunday she put on her gray silk and walked down through Trafalgar Square to Westminster Abbey, lingering outside to hear the chimes. After service, she walked through St. James's Park, "which was perfectly beautiful with all the flowers and the trees just bursting into every shade of green and yellow. I came out through the Cloisters of Westminster and walked past the Houses of Parliament before entering St. James's Park. Stopped long enough for a view at the upper edge."

On Easter Monday Anne was to catch the first view of a spot in London that she was to enjoy time and again: Hampstead Heath.

> Monday a perfect day. . . . I planned to go on Hampstead Heath joined by Miss Ogle. We start off a little past eleven by the new Tube and bus top. Everybody wears a holiday face. We have luncheon at a confectioners quite by ourselves and then walked to the Heath a mile or more. Punch and Judy shows were the first sights to be seen and I was delighted to see one again. Soon we came to the Coster boys and girls dancing in the road 4 in a line opposite 4, to the music of barrel organs. Such clothes, purple velvet, shirts trimmed with jet or fur, robin's egg blue cashmere waists black velvet capes and hats with blue, pink, yellow or green ostrich feathers nearly a yard long. . . .

The last page of the journal was full up before the journey was done. She wrote it in the lodging at Troutbeck.

> I believe it is the most beautiful day since I came to the Lakes—so clear yet with lovely clouds. I stopped to chat in the kitchen with Mr & Mrs Browne—saw my scone toasted and buttered and then had my tea at the long table in the hall and then I came up to sit in my little oak room in the gloaming. There is a young moon tonight, and Miss Clara brought my supper here between 8 and 9 and then I lighted three candles and by their light I am writing the last pages in the red book my dear girl gave me when I sailed away. What another girl I feel with this new strength and spirit and what a happy record is here contained!

Five months in England! For Anne, in the face of a strenuous new assignment, no better preparation could have been devised by doctor, sage, or philosopher. On September 1, 1906, she crossed the Brooklyn Bridge to Manhattan, refreshed, renewed in spirit, joyously determined, and destined to be numbered among the most distinguished of Knickerbockers.

8

THE FIRST DECADE

*I have never wished to formulate a scheme
of library service to children. My chief interest has been in discovering and putting to
work personalities who have something special to contribute—the more varied the contribution the better for the work—for it
should never become static.*

ACM

THE NEW YORK PUBLIC LIBRARY was a wilderness in
the library world of 1906." So ACM described it in a
letter of recollection. She knew a sinking of the heart
when she found herself stationed in her office, a bleak
room on the third floor of the Muhlenberg Branch Library at 209 West 23rd Street after the warmth and
color of Pratt. "Old friends came and wept to find me
without any visible environment, in an office space absent
of children or any signs that children ever existed," she
continued, "but I was having the time of my life."

Her assignment paralleled somewhat the work of Dr.
Bostwick, as head of the Circulation Department. For
her, too, the first imperative was to unite under a single
supervisory head all those who in any way had been

assigned to work with children. The category included
the branch librarians as well as the assistants scheduled to
staff the children's rooms. The latter more readily welcomed a clear directive and a consistent philosophy of
procedure than did the branch librarians, who found it
one thing to have surrendered authority to Dr. Bostwick,
a man of parts, as it were, and quite another to yield
autonomy and authority to a young woman, midway in
her thirties, whose area of supervision infringed on their
own. That was bitter medicine on the tongue.

"I had been resented, rejected by most of the Branch
Librarians who did not want to be supervised, who were
untrained for their work and had to be met on such terms
as I could devise," she wrote in retrospect.

One day Dr. Bostwick asked her, "How is it you and
Miss B. have come to an understanding?" (Miss B. was
famed for her recalcitrance.) "I would never have
thought it possible."

"It's very simple," ACM records herself as saying. "She
has no interest in and no knowledge of library organization. I talk with her about books and plays and Woodrow
Wilson and she lets me do anything I want to with work
with children in her branch."

Anne Moore was a gifted diplomat as well as a psy-
chologist whose knowledge of people was innate and
intuitive. She knew when to be conciliatory and when to
remain adamant. There was no wavering. Once she had
arrived at an opinion or fixed her goals of accomplishment, nothing could shake the strength of her belief in
her own infallibility. She had what the French call *la
grande confiance*. As well as admitting to no discouragement, she admitted to no mistakes; seldom did she apolo-
gize for any action. The closest she allowed herself to
come to an admission of regret was to say, "I did not

fully understand." A tenet of belief she proffered many a person was "Never deprecate yourself," and a show of humility was not a trait she counted among the beatitudes. She had upon her, however, that certain bloom which J. M. Barrie has defined in *What Every Woman Knows* as "charm." Few turned a deaf ear to her, and none could ignore her high originality.

During the first month of September, Anne went "on trek" to the thirty-six branch libraries of the city. By elevated railroad, subway, streetcar, and horse car (these did not entirely disappear from the streets of New York until 1907), trailing her long black skirts bound in horsehair braid as first defense against the dust and filth of city streets, slim in white tailored shirtwaist with narrow stiff collar, Anne went her daily journeys. City travel held no weariness for her. In all the more than thirty years of her life in the New York Public Library, she undertook such excursions with seemingly tireless energy, the burden lightened in the later years by an extravagance of taxis. In that first September she met the library personnel and listened to them, her eyes meanwhile alert to the character of every nook and cranny. She noted the space allotted to work with children, the appearance of the room (if there were a room), the initial impact of the place on the mind of a visitor, making notes in a small brown notebook remarkable for the range of topics marking its pages. Her immediate staff, the assistants who worked with children, were a heterogeneous lot seemingly blown together by a careless wind, whom she inherited from the past. She found them working to enforce discipline under the stigma of the sign SILENCE. Disparate though their methods were, they were united by one enormous concern—the theft of books from library shelves.

On these visits Anne sniffed out the quality of the book collections, noting the lack of judgment or any clear policy of selection, the remnants of Sunday-school libraries and cheap sensationalism showing through the skeletal beginnings of professional concern for the books children read.

One month after her arrival in Manhattan, she called her first meeting of assistants in charge of children's rooms—the place, the Tompkins Square branch; the date, October 1906. Her introductory speech is outlined in part in the brown notebook:

> It is not my purpose to present an historical sketch of library work with children, nor to make general statements as to its value. I have chosen instead to set out before you such aspects of the work as seem to me of the first importance in shaping work with children in the New York Public Library. First the selection of books. It does matter what books we put on the shelves of the Children's Room. Second, personal responsibility. Successful work in a public library is based upon demonstrated knowledge of children and of children's books. All problems connected with the work fall under these two heads.
>
> The first step to the knowledge of children is to have been a real child and to hold so vivid a recollection of the experience as to enable one to understand children and to meet them on their own ground. The next step is to have accomplished the difficult task of growing up so successfully that the experience becomes part of one's stock in trade. To the general intelligence, judgment, tact, enthusiasm and devotion required by other departments of library work, the work with children calls for the stronger sense of proportion, for clearer demands upon one's sympathies and disciplinary powers, at a time in the day when the initial power of most persons is depleted by the earlier work of the day.
>
> In the late afternoon there is a peculiar and a very exhausting nervous strain about the general government of

a children's library arising chiefly from the effort to do too many things at one time or from the attempt to turn off work too rapidly or from a failure to plan work with care or from the distinct physical limitation of the place in which the work is done. To escape this strain the sense of proportion of the children's librarian must be abnormally developed. . . . So far as I know limitation in space has never been recognized in public library service of children. What are some of the results of lack of system in children's work?

We have resorted to *devices* to secure what it is impossible to secure by any other means than by a definite recognition of the nature of the work and of its demands upon those who are to carry it on. A silence sign will never secure a quiet children's room. In my opinion it is a hindrance to that end. The best evaluative list of books or picture bulletin made will not take the place of a first-hand recommendation from a children's librarian who is capable of evaluating the *person* who is to make use of it.

No badge or button of club or league pledged to the care of books will take the place of a rock foundation of belief in the possibility of teaching children to take care of the books and that theft can be stopped, backed by as big a rock of determination to secure the desired end in every individual membership in the library.[1]

Nor do I believe that a glass partition which may prevent some loss of books from the children will take the place of the eternal vigilance which is the first requisite of every successful children's librarian. The question of loss of books from the shelves of the children's rooms of libraries is the burning question in the administration of them for the current year and the best energies of the administrative head of your children's rooms will be directed toward a full statement if not a solution to this problem. All special features in children's work, valuable though they may be, will be recommended most conservatively until the question of a library membership to which is attached greater personal responsibility on the part of the children themselves and of the assistants in charge of the work has been settled and until we have arrived at a more substantial agreement as to whether the selection of books is to be based upon discriminating knowledge or merely supplying the popular demand without reference to the development of taste and feeling for books.

Anne had the answers to the problems her assistants faced. She had solved them on a stage of smaller dimension at Pratt. But she issued no decrees from the heights of her authority, no directional policies announcing step-by-step procedures. Master of finesse, she chose instead to give them the illusion of independent thinking on their part, thus fully involving them in the procedures. She furnished clues which led them to foregone conclusions. "Library membership to which is attached greater responsibility on the part of the children themselves." This led straight to the self-registering scheme she had conceived at Pratt. In the matter of book selection, she issued no master list with directions for wholesale discarding of titles. Instead, she turned out their minds to romp in the wide fields of an enduring professional quandary: "whether the selection of books is to be based upon discriminating knowledge or merely supplying the popular demand without reference to the development of taste and feeling for books."

She insisted that books be read at a furious pace and with discerning judgment. The "P" slips of the period yield scattered records of questions to be answered and judgments proposed.

How far are children going to be influenced by the books they find in a public library?

The education of children begins at the open shelves.

Choose children's books for their vitality, and stand by until they find their market.

Try reading aloud.

Books about girls should be as interesting as girls are.

Look for fidelity to life and essential atmosphere.

Tenderness without sentimentality, humor without vulgarity.

Avoid the facetious, condescending, artificial.

Is the book conceived for children or grown-ups?

Age is no criterion of mental condition and capacity.

Book Selection—History.

Look for the dramatic. The story must be vividly told.

Facts in children's histories should agree with those established by more recent scholarship so far as possible. This need not exclude historical events which have been discovered to be legends which are true to human nature if not historical fact.

The incidental value of history is the conveying of facts.

Chief value to stimulate the imagination in the noble and heroic and to broaden the horizon by pictures of life under experiences foreign to their condition.

Historical interest for children lies in the event rather than in the conclusions drawn from it.

Avoid those histories which gain dramatic interest by appeal to prejudice. Especially true of American histories.

These were notes for subjects under discussion in the years 1907, 1908, and upward. Certain principles of administration are scribbled on note paper, as viable now as they were in 1910.

Fundamentals in successful administration.

See the end purpose clearly.

Have complete mastery of essential detail in order to feel free.

Have as full and varied a book stock as possible.

Keep your room attractive and alive: This is accomplished by your relations with children, their parents and other adults, and with the staff.

Keep alive to books on all sides. Know bookshops, reviews and reviewers. Cultivate an attitude of learning and a capacity for no end of surprise.

Ask yourself, "Am I doing this to please myself, the adult public or the children?"

Do not get Branch bound!

In support of this last item of advice, ACM scheduled the monthly staff meetings at different branch libraries throughout the city. The expedient and economical plan, after 1911, would have been to hold all monthly meetings at the Central Library. It was often suggested that this be done. But ACM pursued the greater wisdom of creating an informed staff, each member of which might know the work as a whole, the city as a unit in its diversity, and have the opportunity of observing every branch library in its own situation. Assistants were soon convinced that it was well worth the effort of arising early in the morning on the appointed days and traveling miles to and from the Bronx or Staten Island to see fresh neighborhoods and gather new strength from comrades in arms.

ACM feared once again the old threat of boredom, this time among the assistants. How often her sheer humanity broke through in unexpected places! In the first week of her retirement, when she held long conversations with her successor, she said of these monthly meetings, "Don't hold them in meeting to the last minute. They want to go to lunch with each other. Give them time."

By 1908—two years after her arrival in New York from her recuperative journey to England—ACM had gained professional status for the children's librarians within the organization, established a "Children's Librarian Grade" with fixed salary rate, defined the qualifications for acceptance in the grade, and had begun in earnest the building of a professional staff. Anna Cogswell Tyler, a graduate of Pratt Institute Library School, came in that year to give form and content to storytelling procedures and to develop a brilliant program of reading clubs that was unequaled in library history. Marcia Dalphin, also a Pratt graduate, who ultimately

brought to such a degree of perfection the art of relating
books and reading to a community—Rye, New York—
as to become a legend in her own time, came in 1907.
Julia Carter was another graduate brought across the
bridge from Brooklyn in that same year. She remembers
well those days and gives her own report of the training
period:

> I think of Anne Moore's teaching as having four parts
> and I call them "The Four Respects."
>
> The first respect was for the children. We were to
> think of and respect them as individuals and neither talk
> down to them nor call them pet names. We were to an-
> swer their requests for books, but were also to suggest
> other titles to them to give them a new and wider knowl-
> edge. Also, if the children wished for more adult titles,
> we were to consider requests and try to satisfy them.
>
> The second respect was for the books which were on
> our shelves. They were to be well-written, and none of
> them were to be rewritten in words of one syllable. If the
> books were factual, the authenticity of the author and his
> background was to be checked. If a story was imagina-
> tive, it was to be purely so and not have reality mixed up
> with fantasy. All books were to be sincerely and clearly
> written.
>
> The third respect was for our fellow workers. We were
> told again and again to remember that we were but a part
> of the whole. The branch work concerned all of us and
> all were to receive due credit and respect for their share
> in it. We were to know something of the other library
> departments, ask for and give cooperation. I well remem-
> ber Miss Moore's advice along this line. I had been given
> a difficult assignment and could not obtain from the
> branch staff the measure of support I needed in complet-
> ing the routine work of the children's room. I appealed to
> Miss Moore for help, asking her to use the authority of
> her position to bring pressure to bear on the branch staff.
> She replied, "I know the situation and I could give my
> order but that would not help. You must go back to the

branch and influence those people on your own so that
they will want to do as you wish themselves and not by
my order." After restless nights and many gray hairs I
managed it and the cooperation lasted.

The fourth respect was for the professional standing
of the Children's Librarian. They were not to be dictated
to by others against their better judgment. Miss Moore
felt that children's librarians were the best trained and
most informed staff members on the subject of children's
books and reading. The children were to be allowed free
use of books, and not just to use those that some authority
thought belonged to their age group or to their school
grade.

With this nucleus of professional help, Anne undertook to bring the other staff members to a point of
eligibility for the professional classification. Only one
among the twenty-seven was a college graduate; fourteen
had taught in high schools; two were formerly kindergarten teachers; four had previously had some experience
working in libraries. ACM set them to reading, she herself inciting them to fervor with lectures, her own and
those of invited speakers.

A certain amount of anxiety was entailed in working
under ACM. There was exhilaration, to be sure, for her
enthusiasm was contagious. The larger vision, the ultimate goal of the work was never sacrificed to petty tasks
and routine performances. She expected everyone to
function at the peak of his abilities; nor could she
tolerate complacency or listlessness in an assistant, and
she manifested her lack of sympathy with attacks of the
doldrums in several ways. One of her most effective
methods was a clearing of the throat, a kind of humming
under the breath that signaled irrevocable dismissal of
one's person as well as one's opinions and lack of interest
in whatever was being said.

She was unwittingly prone to expose such traits as
those which beset the mouse in Grimm's fairy tale "The
Cat and the Mouse Who Set Up Housekeeping. " You
may remember that after the two partners had gathered
enough fat to last through the winter, the question arose
as to a safe place in which to store it. "The mouse knew
she could never think of a place," runs the tale. In every
instance the mouse found herself predestined for in-
adequacy. So it was with many who felt themselves
intimidated in the presence of ACM. Tension and con-
straint were the result, and these led certain members of
the staff to frame their opinions in terms they deemed
pleasing to ACM. A very human trait, this! Sometimes
ACM was taken in by it, though none was quicker than
she to welcome the honest, outspoken ideas of a sincere
person.

Certain other workers under her direction felt themselves ignored. Year after year they pursued their work,
but nothing they did or described in their monthly "informal reports," those small essays that recorded the daily
life of the children's rooms, often with moving effect,
won them praise or recognition. One accomplished librarian, Priscilla Edie, confronted ACM with the fact.
"Is there anything wrong with my work?" she asked.
"You never remark upon it." To which ACM replied,
"If there were anything amiss, I would have told you."

Sometimes a shaft of wit was both probe and suture.
One young assistant was sent by the branch librarian to
ACM for reprimand because, impetuous girl, she had
been surprised in the embrace of the janitor (it was before the days of custodians), he compounding the crime
by his married status. The young woman's defense was
that she could not be responsible for the effect of her
considerable good looks upon the male psyche. "Ap-

parently you have had very little experience in handling men," said ACM, deflating the young woman's vanity and ending the interview.

Miss Moore was adept at recognizing the weakest attributes in character and temperament. She could thrust thorn to the quick on occasion. Nor did she spare those whom she most greatly cherished and on whom she depended in the largest measure. Scarcely anyone escaped, at one point or another, an encounter of great bitterness in a relationship with her. "But no one ever held it against her," said Anne Eaton when the matter was once under discussion. Some suffered at her hands and some were destroyed; but the gift of her friendship, the lasting lifelong strength of her support, the eagerness with which she brought people to a realization of latent abilities of which they themselves were unaware—these were incomparable, outweighing all else. Pages could be filled with the names of those whom she discovered in their chrysalis state, to whom she gave encouragement and in whose subsequent triumphs she rejoiced. She held no one in fealty to herself or to the New York Public Library. In the first years of her work she surrendered her chief assistant, Mary Douglas, to the St. Louis Public Library when Dr. Bostwick became a director of that institution. Visting librarians came for periods of work, and these too were carriers of ACM's spirit and philosophy. Her influence spread across the country: Siri Andrews in the Pacific Northwest; Lillian Smith of the Boys' and Girls' Library at Toronto; Jacqueline Overton in the distinctive Bacon Memorial Library at Westbury, Long Island; Marcia Dalphin in Rye, New York; Katherine Carnes in Atlanta, Georgia; Rosemary Livsey in California. During the First World War a flock of children's librarians was released to Anne

Morgan's American Committee for Devastated France, where libraries were a prime concern in the restoration of French village life: Jessie Carson, Alice Keats O'Connor, Marianne Greene chief among them.

The publishing field was to know the influence of Anne through members of her staff who became editors of children's books: Marian Fiery and Margaret McElderry. Writers developed among the group: Eleanor Estes, Helen Forbes, Eugenia Garson, Pura Belpré, Florence Adams, Mary Gould Davis, Anna Cogswell Tyler, Harriet Wright, Maria Cimino, Ruth Hill Viguers, Alexandra Sanford, Ruth Giles Lontoft, Shirley Barker, and Claire Huchet Bishop.

The year 1907 brought Anne her first encounter with someone peculiarly worthy of her friendship, Valfrid Palmgren Munch-Petersen, that vibrant scholar-librarian from Sweden, who came to the United States in August of that year, sent by her government to study the public-library movement. She was in the country for only six months, but it was time enough. She visited libraries on the Eastern seaboard, attended library conventions, counseled with leaders in the movement, interviewed Andrew Carnegie and the President of the United States, Theodore Roosevelt, who gave her ardent testimony as to his belief in public libraries.

Early in these months she came upon an aspect of library work of which she had not dreamed: library work with children. It was Anne Carroll Moore, in the second year of her appointment at the New York Public Library, who indoctrinated her. With Anne, Valfrid saw the children reading in an exuberance of pleasure, without hindrance or restriction, without commitment to age, school grade, or prescribed theories of education. With Anne, she watched the lines of black-stockinged

children waiting for the doors of libraries to open, the
story hours, the clustered heads bending over small tables piled with books, and all the solitary readers and
searchers of shelves, grazing like sheep in some paradisi-
acal pasture. When she returned to Sweden, Valfrid
Palmgren was determined that the children of Stockholm should have an equal chance with the children of
the New World. Public libraries got under way in Sweden in 1909. But not until 1911 did the first children's
library in Scandinavia, indeed in Europe, open its doors
on December 4, at 65 Drottninggatan, Stockholm. Anne
herself was a visitor to that library in 1912 when she
went as a delegate to the Library Association of the
United Kingdom in Liverpool and made a detour to
Stockholm. There she saw the image of the American
library carried across the sea by the devotion of her
great friend, Valfrid Palmgren.

Theirs was a friendship that endured for five decades.
They saw each other three times in that period, but
though space, wars, and turns of fate separated them,
they never lost touch. Valfrid Palmgren married a distinguished Dane, lived in Copenhagen, and became a
professor at the university there, reared a family, lost a
son in the Loyalist cause in Spain, and knew at first hand
life under the Nazi invasion. The friendship was inherited by the second generation. Finn Munch-Petersen,
Valfrid's son, represented his country at the United Nations in New York. Many were the feasts of food and
good talk ACM shared with him and his attractive wife.
It happened to Anne more than once in her lifetime,
this claiming of her friendship by succeeding generations: the grandsons of her classmates at Bradford; the
children and grandchildren of L. Leslie Brooke in England; the Petersons of Utah, who adopted her as a mem-

ber of the tribe to the third and fourth generations.

Ruth Sawyer Durand, writer and storyteller and among the staunchest of Anne's friends, first appeared on the scene in 1910, coming to Anne with a letter of introduction from Alice Tyler of the Iowa Library Commission. In a 1951 letter of recollection Anne wrote:

> I casually took her along with me to the Hudson Park Branch Library for a Christmas story hour. She told "The Voyage of the Wee Red Cap" for the first time before it had appeared in print. As you know, we have been the warmest and most understanding of friends ever since. We look for the same things in a storyteller, a diction free from the dictionary, a voice from the lower reaches rather than the higher brackets, and a *real re-creation* of the story for an audience of one or one hundred. Mrs. Durand knows infinitely more than I do about placement and development of the voice. I only know that the majority of storytellers I hear do not give me pleasure as a listener and I also know as a children's librarian that a well-modulated voice is the most effective means of control of any problem that can arise in a public library.

Anne gave to friendship a dimension of sensibility that few could equal. She wore it as a talisman like Hans in the old tale who carried the Golden Goose under his arm as he went to the palace to make the princess laugh. Whoever so much as touched a feather of it found himself held fast to the bird. And, in turn, the person touching him could not pull away. The result was a motley parade of men, women, and children, held together by the power of the great bird. Anne never doubted that her friends were held in such a manner to each other as well as to herself. She wove and interwove the fates and fortunes of her friends, issuing orders and commands in behalf of them all. "Write a letter, send a message, perhaps a visit would be helpful." And dates and addresses were included. "Command performances," Helen Masten called these directives, she as head of the Central Children's Room happily bearing the burden for fulfilling many of them. One young assistant embarking from New York for a week's sail down the coast to Texas was astonished to find herself the center of much attention at the time of the ship's departure. People she barely knew appeared in considerable numbers, showering her with gifts. Not until years later did she realize that the vacationing Miss Moore had suggested the bon voyage be celebrated in gala fashion. No system of notation, no birthday-book entries jogged Anne's memory in relation to the celebrations her friends enjoyed, the tragedies they might endure. Only in the multiple pages of her affection and concern were the data recorded.

Five years of innovative accomplishment in the New York Public Library lay behind ACM when the great bronze doors of the library at Forty-second Street and Fifth Avenue swung open to the world for the first time on May 23, 1911. The first day was celebrated with dedicatory ceremonies, followed by an open house for several thousand invited guests. The largest marble building ever built in the country, it had been metamorphosed from the waters of the old Croton Reservoir that had stood on that ground since 1842. A noble structure, it was "simple in design, Renaissance in style, based upon classic principles and modern in character," to quote one of the architects responsible for the accomplishment, Mr. Hastings of Carrère and Hastings.

That May day was warm for spring, and the cool marble spaciousness of the rotunda was doubly welcome to the six hundred guests seated there in that great arena.

None other than the President of the United States, William Howard Taft, was among the galaxy of speakers. Crowds on Fifth Avenue waited to catch a glimpse of him. The people lining Fortieth Street cheered the police-escorted cars that crowded into the entry there, but no one was aware of the President's actual arrival at the doors of the Forty-second Street entrance. He was escorted to an elevator, the building boasting two, their handsome bronze doors bearing an intricate design of the caduceus as a subtle tribute to Dr. Billings.

The procession formed in the trustees' room on the third floor, making an impressive entrance as they walked two by two down one of the grandiose stairways to the rotunda, Dr. Billings and his assistant, Edwin Anderson, leading the procession, which included an appropriate allotment of governors, mayors, park commissioners, architects, etc., the glory culminating at last in the presence of William Howard Taft and John Bigelow, president of the Board of Library Trustees, described in the press as "the oldest man in public service," he being ninety-four years old.

The only speaker who could be heard from the rear seats was President Taft. His perceptive understanding of the effort involved in the founding of this library was exceedingly human and refreshing.

It is to the librarians and trustees of these various foundations that I would convey my profound felicitations. Everyone who has had to deal with human nature knows the difficulty of securing from those who are independent in control of any organization, however large or small, a willingness to subordinate their own importance and their own freedom by a union of that which is in their custody with similar trust in the custody of others, even in order to render all the trust more effective in the accomplishment of their original purposes.

It was that aged, aged man, Mr. John Bigelow, whose speech must have struck home for ACM. He recounted his dealings with Mr. Tilden, who hesitated to make his contribution when he learned from the annual report of the Boston Public Library that 90 percent of the books taken from it during the year of its opening had been works of fiction. "He asked me," said Mr. Bigelow, "whether it was really worth his while to devote so much or indeed any money whatever to fostering an abnormal appetite for imaginative literature."

Mr. Bigelow answered the argument by quoting Mother Goose!

I said to him in substance that probably the first printed writing that ever made a lodgment in his mind was the reading, or hearing recited or sung, the melody of Mother Goose; that it never occurred to him that there was any incongruity in

Hi Diddle Diddle
The cat and the fiddle
The cow jumped over the moon
or
The dish ran away with the spoon . . .

The real luxury of a printed book consists in the degree its contents are capable of interesting us. To create a genuine taste for that luxury, therefore, everyone must begin by reading what interests him, and imaginative literature is far more captivating to all people in whom a genuine taste for printed literature has not yet been formed.

The following day, May 24, the corridors of the great temple were aflood with people, and books were circulated at the prescribed places. The Central Children's Room staff were horrified to discover that some few rows of books had been shelved without pockets and date slips in place, but otherwise all went well. ACM's report for the year of the great opening reads:

The opening of the new Central Children's Room on May 24th is the most significant feature of the year's work and marks an advanced step in the general development of work with children. . . . The fact that for the first time in the development of special work for children in The New York Public Library we now have in one builidng the offices of administration of this work, a children's room with such an equipment of books and furniture and people as makes it possible to give a very practical idea of the work the library is doing in the interests of the boys and girls of the city, and to direct visitors who wish to study special phases of the work to the points most favorable for observation and consultation with experienced workers in widely varied districts covered by the forty branch libraries. To the cumulative experience of the branch children's rooms the Central Children's Room owes much of its vitality.

It was a surprise to the greater number of adults to be admitted to the Children's Room in the central building on equal terms with the children in the use of the books and in the personal attention of the assistants, and they have availed themselves of their privileges in increasing numbers, but with unusual regard for the comfort and convenience of the children. . . . Visitors from European countries attracted by what appealed to them as "a new idea in education" and requesting detailed information concerning children's libraries and children's books have been a large segment of the public. Correspondents for foreign papers and magazines have written of the work in several languages and European visitors during the past three months speak of having read of these accounts and of noting children's libraries as among the most interesting things to be seen in America.

9

CHILDREN'S ROW:
THE CENTRAL
CHILDREN'S ROOM

As I came out of Wiseman's Street,
The air was thick with driving sleet;
Crossing over Proudman's Square,
Cold louring clouds obscured the air;
But as I turned towards Goodman's Lane,
The burning sun came out again;
And on the roof of Children's Row
In solemn glory shone the snow.
There did I lodge; there hope to die:
Envying no man—no, not I.

WALTER DE LA MARE

FROM THE BEGINNING when plans were under way for a central library building designed as a fitting structure for a reference collection of heroic magnitude, children's books were considered a necessity by trustees and director alike. The Central Children's Room was allotted spacious quarters, and its book collections and activities were fully financed by Reference Department funds from 1911 until the middle 1940s. Then, in the cause of economy, it was summarily relinquished to that segment of the library supported by city funds and its ultimate demise as part of the central building thereby assured.

An early plan designated the room on the main floor now assigned to periodicals as the appointed place. But the northeast corner of the building paralleling Forty-second Street on the ground level, with one secluded window looking out on Fifth Avenue beyond a stretch of shrubbery, offered easier access to children and gave them space set apart from the rest of the library. In actuality, the space measured about 3,390 square feet. It consisted of two rectangular rooms, their symmetry refreshingly broken by an arched alcove stretching between. Here tables and chairs built for the picture-book set were in perfect proportion and the inset of a wide three-sided window seat, with polished wood paneling at back and sides, offered a tempting area for sliding as well as an invitation to be seated. Here cherished old books of the past were housed in a glass-doored bookcase that stood against one wall. Above it hung fine old English prints, the "Cries of London," and the portrait of an eighteenth-century duchess. Framed small pictures from Randolph Caldecott's books hung on the wood paneling of the window seat. In the minds of certain of the staff they were associated with Lord Dunsany, the Irish playwright, because upon walking into the Children's Room one morning in the company of ACM and catching sight of those pictures, he shook his cane at them with all six feet of his vigor and shouted aloud, "My Lord! Caldecott! Why, I had them as a child." In the shelter of this many-cornered place, the smallest clientele found within hand's reach a choice of picture books for home borrowing.

The wider of the two rooms was given over to books

for use in the library, a perpetual and changing exhibition of the soaring significance of children's books. The shelves on the north wall held the picture books of the world freshly arranged each morning not in classified order, being only haphazardly shelved by national origin, but in such a way as to show covers and contents to good advantage, and laid flat every evening that their spines might know a period of respite. Each of the windows in this room harbored a small window seat. "What I loved about that room," a noted professor of English at the University of California at Los Angeles remarked in 1960 in a tribute of remembrance, "was the window seats. You could sit there all day and read and nobody on your back." The Fifth Avenue window was set in an alcove that stood one step above the floor level. In the course of time, this became a proscenium, framing a succession of celebrations and celebrities: musicians, puppeteers, and poets; artists, editors, publishers; actors, playwrights, and magicians; storytellers and ballad singers; novelists and essayists. From that alcove Kate Douglas Wiggin as speaker inaugurated the first Book Week meeting in the Children's Room in November 1919. The bright procession of the years is encapsulated in the names of those who celebrated Book Week, St. Nicholas Eve, story hours, or other occasions in that room, addressing audiences of adults for whom books and children were a vital and a joyous concern: Ethel Parton, Laura Benét, Stephen Vincent Benét, Marie Shedlock, Margery Bianco, Wanda Gág, Edgar and Ingri Parin d'Aulaire, Thomas Handforth, Anne Thaxter Eaton, William Pène DuBois, Nora Archibald Smith, Lizette Woodworth Reese, Boris Artzybasheff, Padraic Colum, Ludwig Bemelmans, Ruth Sawyer Durand, Dorothy P. Lathrop, Lynd Ward, Constance Lindsay Skinner, Anne Parrish, René D'Harnoncourt, Reginald Birch, Evelyn Scott, Theodore Seuss Geisel, Edward Ardizzone, Louise Seaman Bechtel, Frederic Melcher, Carl Sandburg, Elizabeth Janet Grey, James Daugherty, Paul Honoré, Isabel de Palencia, Monica Shannon, Pamela Travers.

As for the children, coming as they often did two by two, representatives from the branch libraries that stretched from the Bronx to the farthest reaches of Staten Island, what sights and sounds awaited them in that place: Susan Bloch, daughter of the composer, playing on ancient instruments, the lute and the viola da gamba, time and again as a gesture of gratitude for childhood days spent in the Children's Room; Kurt Wiese, drawing "The Five Chinese Brothers" before their very eyes; Walter de la Mare, reading from his play *Crossings* and his own choice of poems from *Peacock Pie;*

(Overheard in the Children's Room of the Harlem Library: "Was you down to the big library yesterday?"

"No, what was there?"

"*Walter* was there and he read some of his poems.")

Hendrik Willem van Loon, historian, in celebration of his book *The Songs We Sing,* playing his fiddle to the accompaniment of a small, garishly decorated piano borrowed from a neighboring night club for the occasion; Walter Wilkinson, the noted English puppeteer; Eleanor Farjeon, in New York for the opening of her play *The Two Bouquets,* written in collaboration with her brother, reciting Sussex rhymes to the children; Katharine Adams, in the heyday of her popularity as a writer for girls, speaking to an audience of them on the eve of her wedding day and her departure for Ireland, and the bridegroom himself, sitting in their midst.

The boys had their turn, three hundred strong of them, members of the boys' clubs in branch libraries, when they came to hear Corinne Roosevelt Robinson speak of her recollections of her brother, Colonel Theodore Roosevelt, in the days when he was a "rough rider"; John Mulholland, the magician, staging a costumed performance; James Stephens, the Irish poet, in full control of a different magic.

Louise Seaman Bechtel in her *Books in Search of Children* writes of this occasion:

> How well I remember a day in the twenties, in this room, when Miss Moore lit the candles and introduced that great Irishman, James Stephens. He was famous for his adult poetry and novels like *The Crock of Gold*. We [Macmillan] had just published his robustly retold *Irish Fairy Tales* and I hoped he would tell those stories. There were mostly children present who seemed awed at Stephens' gnome-like figure and that long, dour face of his. Then, in his beautiful Dublin-English voice, he began reciting his adult poetry. He said poems like:
>
> > Come with me, under my coat,
> > And we will drink our fill
> > Of the milk of the white goat,
> > Or wine if it be thy will. . . .
>
> Next to me sat a rough-looking boy of about twelve. At the end of each poem, he gave me a dig with his sharp elbow. Once he muttered, "I *never* heard *nothing* like this!" At the end, he seized my arm. "Gee!" he cried, "Gee, what a man! He sure does know his onions!"
>
> To see that boy touched by genius, surprised by greatness—I shall never forget it.

The "new" poetry of the twenties burst upon the heads of children when Louis Untermeyer gave them pieces from his anthology, *This Singing World*, the children listening long past the closing hour of the library to be finally turned out on the arrival of the wheeled steel cart of steaming suds and Tony with his mop come to wash the floor.

More beautiful than gold that floor of tile imported from the red quarry of Wales. No free-standing book stacks broke the full sweep of it. Light was reflected from it in warm effulgence. The walls of the room above the book shelves were painted in neutral colors, a fitting background for changing exhibitions. There was a time when N. C. Wyeth longed to paint a mural across the alcove of the Fifth Avenue window, having chosen the story of "Rip Van Winkle" as his subject. Miss Moore must have been tempted to accept so generous an offer, but she decided against it, knowing that a mural was more or less fixed for all time and must forever dominate or vitiate exhibitions of a different mood and character. The full series of N. C. Wyeth's illustrations for *Robin Hood* hung in the room for many a long year, having been given as a gift to the Children's Room. But styles changed in children's-book illustrations, and those changes were reflected through the decades marking the life of the room, for neither ACM nor the staff she assembled there were people who showed any tendency, as far as art was concerned, "to get stuck in a period," as one critic put it.

One of the advantages accruing to ACM by the fact that the Central Children's Room was supported by private rather than public funds was the freedom it gave her in choice of staff. She was not bound by the rules of the city which forbade the employment of anyone who was not a citizen, nor by the complexities of professional requirements as the New York Public Library System became more standardized in its employment policies. She was free to select assistants in accordance with her strongest propensities—namely, by intuition and by a response to traits of personality. As a result, a succession of young women of unusual gifts, aptitudes, manifold backgrounds, and varied educational experience headed up the Central Children's Room from its inception, or were members of its staff. Flora G. Cutler, the first head, was one of Alice Tyler's most brilliant students from the Library School in Iowa. She was given eight months' intensive experience and training under ACM before she was appointed to that position. Marit Blehr of Norway, daughter of a diplomat who was Prime Minister of Norway; Jessie Sibley, an early professional librarian; Leonore St. John Power, native New Yorker, with gifts of originality, invention, and a ready response to merriment and diversity; Helen Masten, who brought to librarianship innate good judgment, an easy understanding of children, and a rare concern for the public, child and adult alike; Maria Cimino, Italian in heritage, singer by avocation, storyteller *par excellence*, and an artist in her creation of exhibitions. For many years Nadia Rodzianko was an assistant in that room. Russian by birth and heritage, she was a legend in the minds of the public and staff alike, her beauty and compassion memorable attributes. Claire Huchet Bishop, French by birth though American by marriage, served intermittently on the staff of the Children's Room. She became a noted writer of children's books, her two stories "Pancakes Paris" and "Twenty and Ten" lasting contributions to contemporary accounts of children of the Second World War. Summer schedules were upheld by professional librarians from various parts of the country who welcomed a turn of duty in that room and looked upon it as something of a vacation. Katherine Carnes, librarian of the Wesleyan College at Macon, Georgia, having once been a member of the staff, came summer after summer. In a letter of reminiscence she writes:

> The time in the Central Children's Room set its mark on me for life. The emphasis on exhibits, flowers, colors

"As wise as a child three years old"

Anne at seven holding a basket. She was always to be fascinated by baskets, with their assurance of color and promise of surprise.

Luther Sanborn Moore

Sarah Hidden Barker Moore

*Almira Boardman Barker,
Anne's maternal grandmother, a
great lady who had been a
beauty in her day*

Alderwood. The front entrance to the great house.

The student at Bradford, 1892

Anne is second from the right, Flora Cutler beside her; at the far left is Marit Blehr, and next to her, Alice Tyler, of Iowa—all properly hatted and veiled for a picnic at Coney Island.

Portrait of Anne in the apple-green, corded silk wedding dress of her young aunt, Almira Barker.

The Supervisor of Children's Rooms in her first office of the
New York Public Library, 1906

The Superintendent of Work with Children of the New York Public Library in the golden era of the thirties

"*When I write my name in this book, I promise . . .*"

The academic procession at
Pratt Institute, 1955, when
Anne Carroll Moore was made
a Doctor of Letters

Anne Carroll Moore with
Anne Carroll Peterson, her
namesake, Washington, D.C.,
in the early 1950s

and light were all secondary to the emphasis on reading. How Miss Moore kept us on our toes about books! And not only books but the theatre and the multi-colored life of the city. Relentlessly she steered us toward the stars. Not one of us who followed her could ever be a mere drudge again.

Many a nonprofessional assistant found her talents developed and put to good use in the Central Children's Room. A name recurring in the reports is that of Katherine Seymour of Chazy, New York. Splendid woodsman she, a certain flavor of the out-of-doors permeating her storytelling, the vitality of her puppetry putting to shame the precious and finicky approach of some professionals in the field. Librarians from abroad asked to serve in the Children's Room for a space of time, welcoming the experience and the opportunity of association with Anne Carroll Moore: Mlle. Blanche Weber of the Institute of International Education in Geneva; Lydia Duproir of France; and Lillian Smith, the renowned head of the Boys' and Girls' Library of Toronto notable among them.

Every children's room in the city held "CH"—the designated abbreviation for the Central Children's Room in the Library Directory of Branches and Departments —in high regard, as a symbol of perfection and a source of refreshment. The majority of assistants spent some period of indoctrination there—days, weeks, or months— at the beginning of their assignments to the library system. All librarians in the system looked to CH with an air of expectancy as an arena where great and special events were celebrated, Book Week staff meetings, the Christmas staff meetings, St. Nicholas Eve celebrations, evening meetings of note and import.

In 1918 the American Book Sellers' Association, the

Booksellers' League of New York, the Women's National Book Association, and the New York Public Library contrived among them a significant series of meetings in CH. The chairman and originator of the project was Ben W. Huebsch, a prince among publishers who first launched into print Sherwood Anderson and other eagles in American literature and who founded with Albert J. Nock the distinguished liberal journal *The Freeman* (1920–1924), which has yet to be equaled in this land. His name is not often mentioned in relation to books for children, yet it was he who foresaw in 1918 the brilliance of the future for children's books and recognized the need for book publishers and booksellers to forswear ignorance of the subject and to inform themselves. It was he who asked ACM to prepare and deliver a series of lectures to a group of as distinguished book people as could be found in the city of New York—heads of publishing firms, editors, booksellers and librarians, writers, journalists, and artists. Tickets were available on request and each occasion drew a full house. Eight lectures in all were given, the first, "Children's Books; How a special literature for children originated, its growth and its expansion by subject." Then followed lectures on "Fairy Tales: their defenders and objectors"; "Histories: the readable and the reliable"; "Books about the War"; "Boys' books"; "Girls' stories"; "Illustrated Books, including picture books for little children"; and the final lecture of the series, the "Holiday Books of 1918." A watershed in the history of children's books in America was that year 1918, with Children's Book Week to be inaugurated the next year and Macmillan, the publisher, announcing its special and separate department, the first of its kind, for the publishing of children's books, under Louise Seaman Bechtel. The Central Children's

Room, meanwhile, after almost a decade of existence, stood ready to offer its resources and the proven validity of its founding philosophy.

With the passing of the years, the stacks and offices alike in the Central Building bulged with expanding collections, and some departments looked with covetous eyes upon the wide area of the Children's Room. Business librarians, from time to time, importuned the director of the library to surrender the space of the Children's Room to the greater need of business research. The claws of that argument were clipped somewhat by records showing the use of the room by publishers, writers, artists, interior decorators, stage designers, costume designers, textile and wallpaper designers, choreographers, and many others for whom the arts were a matter of business. Because children themselves did not use the room in comparable numbers to those served by the branch libraries situated in crowded residential neighborhoods, casual observers asked, "But where are the children?" Some library officials found it difficult to weigh the measurable count of bodies present and books circulated against such immeasurable assets as a philosophy of education given bone and sinew, proven by demonstration, the reach of its influence international in scope.

The children who were habitués of the room either came great distances, on book pilgrimage, or from the streets bounding Fifth Avenue, east and west, which were business districts not heavily populated by families. The children, being few in number, were well known to the staff, who watched their reading with interest born of intimacy. ACM knew many of the children also because she made it almost a daily habit to stop by CH as she entered or left the building, and the children who frequented the library became her friends, among them the fair-haired, beautiful Farren children, Constance, Mary, George, and Julian, their parents both in the theater. Miss Moore's book *Nicholas: A Manhattan Christmas Story* grew out of encounters with children there. One lonely child from Belgium, Aimée, spent nearly the whole of every day in the Central Children's Room, both parents struggling to make a living in the war years of 1918 and beyond and finding in the Children's Room a haven for their child.

On the southern wall of the Reference Room a bank of shelves was reserved for the display of books related to exhibitions. What diversity of interest was represented there through all the years and what a record of generosity on the part of "Cooperating Agencies," to use a term favored by sociologists. The seasonal subjects and those that became traditional thread the accounts of the annual reports: Spring, Heroes, Old Valentines; Feasts and Holidays, diversified by the celebration of such matters as Kites and Kite Flying; Toy Theaters, Pirates and Buccaneers; but unexpected excitement is discovered amid all the poetic, imaginative topics related to the humanities in such events as "an exhibition on aviation, lent by the Aero Club of America; a transportation exhibition, with small models of gasoline engines, ocean liners, electric and steam engines, lent by the New York Central Railroad and the New York Society of Model Engineers; a whaling exhibition for ship models lent by the Whaling Museum of New Bedford, Massachusetts; an exhibit of push-about boats in a miniature harbor, small motor boats, and sailing ship models made and lent by Mr. Paul Revere Stevens of Portland, Maine."

Long before the neighboring glass house of the United Nations ennobled the East River of New York, the Central Children's Room dramatized its allegiance to internationalism not only in its book collection, its staff, and its exhibitions, but also in its daily responses to the children and adults of the multi-nationed city.

On one occasion an exhibition stretched from April through October. That was the year 1933, when the Children's Room was *en fête* in the cause of internationalism. Children's books published in England, Ireland, France, Germany, Czechoslovakia, and the United States were successively represented, and each exhibit was accompanied by informative talks and discussion. The brilliance of the whole venture permeates the perfectly matter-of-fact account as Miss Moore states it in the annual report, which reads in part as follows:

> To the exhibition of French books selected and arranged by Mrs. Claire Huchet Bishop, additional distinction was given by the inclusion of paintings of circus subjects, drawings, and lithographs, by Edy Legrand, lent by the Sterner Galleries. The Vildrac Galleries in Paris also lent original drawings by this artist for *Les Lunettes de Lion*. Three talks about French children's books and their illustrators were given by Mrs. Bishop. Many teachers of French in public and private schools availed themselves of the opportunity to discuss their reading lists and add fresh titles to school collections.
>
> The twenty-second birthday of the children's room was celebrated during the French exhibition with a Guignol show given by the courtesy of the French Line. The theatre and the puppets were brought to the room from the *Île de France*. Two hundred children under ten years old, from the branch libraries and the Extension Division, were introduced to Guignol and spent a memorable afternoon. It mattered not at all that the play was in the French language, the pantomime being perfectly understood by children who knew not a word of French.
>
> Contemporary German books were selected and arranged by Ernest Eisele, who lent from his own collection a number of *Images d'Épinal*. These, with some drawings

by Wilhelm Busch from the Prints Collection, made interesting points of contrast with modern books. Mr. Eisele opened the exhibition with a discussion of "International Trends and German Children's Books of the Twentieth Century." Dr. Hellmut Lehmann-Haupt gave a lecture on "Modern Illustration and the Color Printing of Children's Books in Germany," illustrating his talk with a selection from the books shown in the exhibition. "German Books for American Children" were discussed by Anne Thaxter Eaton and May Massee.

The exhibition of Czech children's books, selected by Mrs. Jan Matulka from the Czechoslovak collection of the Webster Branch, was opened with a special program on July 12th. Dr. Jaroslav Novák, Consul General of Czechoslovakia, who was the guest of honor, spoke of the unconquerable love of books which had persisted in his country for centuries and of his own first impressions of the children's rooms in American libraries, with their free access to books and their natural ways of fostering new interests in reading.

The principal influence in Czech children's books and their illustration spring from folk lore and folk life. The vivid decorative sense applied to the making of even the books which are cheapest in price was well brought out in the selection. Paintings in oil and in water colors by Jan Matulka, representing the countryside associated with national folk legends, provided a colorful background. The importance attached to childhood as shown in the work of the artists Ales and Manes and the provision for a special literature for children made by the Czechoslovak Government of today gave entirely new impressions of the country of Comenius to many visitors from summer schools. . . .

The event that triggered this celebration was an exhibition held in the main exhibition room of the library, arranged by the Metropolitan Museum of Art and the New York Public Library, its subject: "Children's Books of Yesterday, an Exhibition from Many Countries." The catalogue was written by ACM and shows her at her bibliographic best.

The books have been chosen, not primarily for textual merit, but for their originality, their rarity and historical significance, for qualities of colorful illustration and ingenious design, for their power of invoking lively memories of childhood and youth. . . .

Pause for a moment before a quaint little book of spiritual instruction printed by Hugh Newman at The Grasshopper in the Poultry, London, 1696, and read these lines under the portrait frontispiece of the most redoubtable of parents:

> Learn little children,
> Born to live today;
> Art cannot make our glass of time to stay.
> Live much in little space of time, for why,
> You're not born to live, but born to dye.

Born to live is the most inspiriting testimony of the adjoining case to which Dr. Hoffman, wise parent and physician of the 1840's, contributes his *Struwwelpeter*. It was Dr. Hoffman who first uncurbed the comic spirit and mixed enough genuine fun with behavior problems to anticipate the comic strip by half a century. The famous picture book made by Dr. Hoffman for his three-year-old son is here shown, side by side, with that inimitable French book of manners, *La Civilité*, illustrated by Boutet de Monvel.

By such sharp contrasts, as well as by familiar trails of association, one is made aware of changing attitudes toward childhood in different centuries and of the changing form and perishable substance of children's books in many lands.

No demonstration in the world could have been more fortuitously staged than was Work with Children in the New York Public Library, with the office of its founding chief—Room 105, as it was known—on one floor and on the floor below the actuality of her inspiration

made visual in every facet of its character down to the
minutest subtlety of its concept. The Central Children's
Room became a show place of the city. The pages of its
guest books attest to the diversity of notables who lingered there awhile.

Two years after the opening of the Children's Room,
the International Exhibition of Modern Art in the 69th
Regiment Armory sent shock waves through the whole
of American culture and brought many visitors to the
city, eager to know at first hand the power of its insur-
gency. Among such visitors was a petite young woman
from Boston. She was secretary to the president of the
Women's Educational and Industrial Union, an organization that, in addition to selling jams and jellies in its
exchange, concerned itself with the wages of women in
industry and the betterment of their working conditions.
Her name was Bertha Mahony. A friend suggested to her
that after having known the heady experience of Du-
champ's "Nude Descending a Staircase" and other revolutionary pictures, she might find it reassuring to visit
the new library at Forty-second Street, especially the
Children's Room. She made the pilgrimage alone, and as
she sat in the Children's Room, watching children and
adults enjoying the place on terms of equality, it came
into her mind that a bookshop similarly dedicated to a
celebration of books, in a like atmosphere of freedom of
choice, would be a grand undertaking in the cause of
education for the Women's Industrial Union. By 1916
the bookshop was a reality in Boston, with Bertha Mahony in charge of it.

Anne Carroll Moore did not leave entirely to chance
the discovery of the Central Children's Room by men
and women whom she knew would recognize its quality.
When she read in the newspapers or heard from the

gossip of literary circles that some noted person was in the city, or expected, she wrote or telephoned them, inviting them to meet her in the Central Children's Room. By this means such notables as Ethel Sidgewick and May Sinclair had come at her invitation and remained to be caught in the net of her friendship. In 1920 E. V. Lucas, the noted English essayist, visited New York. Author of *Old Fashioned Tales* and *Forgotten Tales of Long Ago*, he had also written two books for children, *The Slow Coach* and *Anne's Terrible Good Nature*. ACM wrote a letter of invitation to him and had in reply the following:

May 26, 1920

Dear Miss Moore:

I wish I had seen you to congratulate you on the Room: but I am a diffident person and had no introductory document. So instead I walked about and admired, and then settled down in a chair and read for half an hour in a book which I had not seen for years and which I don't mind saying for all my diffidence I found amusing: *Anne's Terrible Good Nature.*

I shall tell some English librarians about your triumph. Believe me

Yours sincerely
E.V. Lucas

They never met face to face, but he like many another responded to her importunity and found the encounter memorable.

She captured Arthur Rackham on the very eve of his departure for England, he having been in New York to be lionized at certain exhibitions of his pictures. Anne, in company with a young artist, Joseph Paget-Fredericks, whose pictures were on display in the Children's Room, pursued him to the gallery—it was Scott and Fowles' of Fifth Avenue—on the chance of finding him there only.

to discover that he, meanwhile, in answer to her invitation, had gone to the library, a last-minute response to her invitation. ACM's account of the matter read:

> We fairly flew down Fifth Avenue and arrived breathless in the Children's Room to find Arthur Rackham, no other, tall, spare, matter-of-fact, looking at the drawings of the young artist with critical yet discerning eyes.[1]

No, he had never seen New York alight from the Brooklyn side, and he had nothing to do "but kick up his heels" between the moment of his encounter with Anne until the midnight sailing of his ship the *Olympic*. They dined at the grill in the Breevoort Hotel. Then Anne hailed a taxi and in this, her accustomed coach, she crossed and recrossed, with Arthur Rackham and the artist, the Brooklyn and Manhattan bridges until time to take him to the ship.

The most audacious of Anne's pursuits for the glory of the Children's Room had as its objective a king, a queen, and a young prince. In 1919 the officials of the city designated the New York Public Library as the most appropriate place in which to welcome in public reception the notables of the world who came to visit the United States at war's end. The Fifth Avenue entrance was uncluttered, the noble staircases on either side marble parentheses enclosing the rotunda that marked the entrance into the main exhibition room. There the king, Albert of Belgium, and Queen Elizabeth and the prince, Duke of Bravant, were to be honored.

It was unthinkable that a flesh-and-blood king, queen, and prince should enter the library and be deprived of so much as a glimpse of the Children's Room and in turn that children, steeped in the lore of kings, queens, and princes, should miss by a flight of stairs the sight of three such beings at one and the same time. Inquiry revealed that such, indeed, was to be the fact. Anne Carroll Moore approached all the chairmen of the Planning and Arrangement Committees, including the dignitaries of the Office of the Mayor, but the answer was the same. The schedule was too crowded; it would be late in the day when they reached the library. "There is no way, Miss Moore, by means of which the party can visit the Children's Room."

No way! When the hour arrived for the reception, ACM said to one of the assistants in the room, "Let's go upstairs and see." Crowds of people stood in orderly lines in the great room, a path cleared between for the royal procession. Anne and her companion pushed forward to the front of the crowd. It was apparent that the queen, walking to the king's left, would pass very close to them. When the moment came, Anne stepped forward and said to the queen, "Ask to see the Children's library. It isn't on the schedule."

Six o'clock was the hour of closing for the Children's Room. On this day, at 5:45 P.M., three policemen shouldered themselves through the door of the room and behind them came the king, the queen, and the young prince, followed by a flurry of equerries and ladies-in-waiting, one among them squealing with delight as she seated herself on a succession of the small chairs in the Picture Book Room. The queen, in her turn, cried out in happy recognition of the great French histories by Job that stood on the picture-book shelves. "I brought my children up on those books," she said. The heroic king in military uniform shook hands with the children and listened to what they had to say. The Duke of Bravant was the practical member of the family. "Who pays for all this?" he asked. ACM told them of Aimée, who had

only just returned to Belgium. Queen Elizabeth asked
for the child's address and said she would write her upon
her return. There is no way of knowing whether she
did or not, but among Anne's papers there is a far from
perfunctory note written by a lady-in-waiting at the request of the queen, thanking her for having had the wit
to have gotten the queen to the Children's Room on un-
scheduled time.

"When the curtain goes up, the scene must be there."
Anne had overheard Arthur Rackham speak these words
of advice to the artist in the Children's Room on that
day of pursuit and the bridges. In the first quarter of this
century, when curtains were rising on library work with
children all over America and in Europe as well, the
scene was there: the Central Children's Room, ordered,
inspired, and incomparable. Time is a cruel scene shifter,
working secretly and in silence, all the more easily when
none survives to keep the stage light burning. Anne knew
this. "As long as you are here," she said to her immediate
successor, "the room will be safe."

Now it no longer exists in the central building; but
beyond the curtain descending, the action and attitudes
engendered there persist on countless stages of the mind.
No child, be he Hindu, Dane, or Ghanaian, in school or
public libraries, wherever books are made available to
him—no child, lifting his eyes for a moment from the
pages of his book, but pays homage to CH though he
knows nothing of its existence. Such is the measure of
the drama once played against the scene of the Central
Children's Room.

10

THE SHADOW OF
THE TOWER

*Whatever disagreement there may be as
to the scope of the phrase "due process of
law," there can be no doubt that it embraces
the fundamental conception of a fair trial,
with opportunity to be heard. Mob law does
not become due process of law by securing
the assent of a terrorized jury. We are not
speaking of mere disorder, but of a case
where the processes of justice are actually
subverted.*

JUSTICE OLIVER WENDELL HOLMES

A LARGE PACKET of crumbling newspaper clippings
lay among the hoarded memorabilia of Anne Carroll
Moore. It gave account of the Leo Frank case, a *cause
célèbre* in its time that resulted in a wave of anti-Semitism
and demonstrated the heights of nobility and the depths
of depravity that human beings are capable of attaining
under stress. Like the Sacco-Vanzetti case of the twenties,
the controversy surrounding the trial and conviction of
the accused swept through the body politic, dividing the

country, arousing the consciences of men and women throughout the world, and leaving a bitter heritage of guilt that has increased with the years as continuing investigation and study substantiate the belief held by many that, in these cases, the cause of justice was subverted by prejudice, bigotry, and hysteria.

Even at a distance of fifty-five years, to read these yellowed columns of print is to be shadowed by the anguished terror of those whom the Furies pursue without pity. The shriek of Oedipus, the cry of Lear—"Horror! horror! horror"—ring in the memory, echoing as they do from the streets of Atlanta, Georgia, U.S.A. The image of Prometheus that Leo Frank invoked on his own behalf in an open letter to his enemy, Joseph Brown, ex-Governor of Georgia, proved tragically appropriate. "I remembered that when Prometheus was bound to the rock, it was the vulture, and not the eagle, that struck its beak into his vitals."

Confederate Memorial Day, like its counterpart, Decoration Day in the North, is dedicated to the memory of the soldier dead. The day is numinous in the South, commemorating as it does the loss of the Confederacy as well as the death of heroes.

On one Confederate Memorial Day, April 26, 1913, the curtain rose with epic irony upon the tragedy of Leo Frank. On that day a thirteen-year-old girl, Mary Phagan, was murdered, her mutilated body discovered in the basement of the pencil factory where she was employed. The superintendent and part owner of that factory was Leo Frank, a young man who had come to Atlanta from New York after some months of technical study in Europe, to establish and manage a pencil factory founded by his family. He had married an Atlanta girl and was held in highest esteem by the Jewish community of the city, serving on the board of managers of the Hebrew Orphans' Home and as president of B'nai B'rith. When he was accused of the murder he went to trial confident that in a matter of weeks his innocence would be a proven fact. The evidence against him was circumstantial and patently contrived. In the natural order of things it would have been proved beyond a doubt that he could not have committed this crime, but the times were not ordinary. A confluence of inimical events and circumstances, largely out of the past, compounded his doom. Old habits of thought obtained in the South as yet not bound to the North by ties of two great shared national wars. The War Between the States remained the ultimate tragedy in the minds of the Southerners. Atlanta was adjusting to a new industrialism, resented because it destroyed old patterns of life. The rural poor, black and white alike, flocked into the city in search of work. A rising crime rate overwhelmed the constabulary, which, in that fateful spring, was held accountable for a shameful record of unsolved and unpunished crimes. In this most recent case of murder, the least clue was seized upon with a fervor of hope for quick conviction and with careless regard for thorough investigation. At best, anybody from the North was considered an outsider. Leo Frank was regarded not only as an outsider but as a representative of the unwelcome industrial infiltration, and in addition he bore the ancient stigma of the Jew. Neither he nor his lawyers were prepared for the raging antagonism and bigotry of the populace that surfaced in the Atlanta of 1913. After a trial of four months he was found guilty and condemned to be hanged.

Not until the preparations for his first appeal were under way did the case of Leo Frank command the attention of the press in the North. Not until then did his lawyers ask him for the names of people who had known him in his youth. Among the first names he recalled was that of a librarian at Pratt Institute Library in Brooklyn. He wondered if she were still there. The lawyers found her in New York. By this means ACM came to the realization that the Leo Frank who sought her aid was the boy she had known and cherished since the day of her first encounter with him. He it was who had marked his departure with the gift of a plant to the Children's Library. He it was who had named his toy boats after the characters of the *Leather Stocking Tales*. His was the definition of heroism preserved in the reports of the Pratt Free Library:

> In ancient times a brave man only was a hero but now in modern times a hero has to be both brave and good morally and virtually.

Immediately Anne began a correspondence that lasted until the end. She undertook a campaign in his behalf. It never occurred to her that, as this world goes, she was a person without means in a position of limited influence. She inaugurated petitions. She wrote articles and letters describing the boyhood of Leo Frank as she had known it. One such letter was published in the New York *Times* in March 1914 and reprinted at least twice during the years that followed. The faculty of the Pratt High School where Leo Frank had gone as a boy were enlisted in the cause at Anne's request. Old letters of commendation written to Leo's father and mother by teachers and the superintendent of the school were resurrected from the file and sent with a petition signed by fourteen former teachers. These were to be presented to the Governor of the state and the Prison Commission at an appropriate time.

For all the tragedy of the situation, ACM could not forget that she was a librarian eager for testimonies to the influence of books on the character of man and boy. Late in 1914 she had apparently asked Frank to tell her what he had enjoyed as a boy. By this time the handwritten letters from Leo had given way to typewritten notes because his correspondence had become voluminous. On December 17 he wrote:

> . . . You must excuse me if I cannot comply with your wish and enumerate the books which appealed most to me when I was a young boy. When once more I am in New York I will be glad to do so and talk with you on this.

The trials went on. The first appeal for a new trial was denied by Judge Leonard Roan, who declared even as he handed down a decision against Frank that he was not certain of the man's guilt. For the second time, Leo Frank was given the death sentence. This time the date was set for April 17, 1914, his birthday. The State Supreme Court, in its turn, upheld Judge Roan's ruling, denying a new trial. When at last the case was debated before the Supreme Court of the nation, it too rejected the plan for a new trial, the decision based not on the question of Frank's guilt or innocence but on a technicality concerning the legality of the procedure in the original trial. For the fourth time Leo Frank was condemned to death, the date set for the hanging June 22, 1915.

The last refuge for Frank was a pardon or commutation of sentence by the Governor, John M. Slaton. Frank wanted to ask for a pardon, but in the face of mob violence which threatened to overwhelm the city, his lawyers thought the wiser plan a petition for commutation of sentence to life imprisonment. Meanwhile, Frank was held in the Tower, the Atlanta prison situated within sight of the capitol building. There he held strange court, for men and women of note came to see him by the dozens and wrote to him out of their deep sympathy and interest and concern: artists, stars of opera and stage, professors, senators, judges, journalists and reporters. More than one hundred thousand pleas for clemency flooded the Governor's office and the office of the Prison Commission.

At this point Anne went to the director of the New York Public Library, Edwin Anderson, and asked for a leave of absence. She intended to go to Atlanta to present in person petitions to the Governor and to visit Frank in prison. If the library were not willing to grant her the time, she declared herself ready to submit her resignation. Mr. Anderson was sympathetic to her cause, granted her a leave with the stipulation that the New York Public Library, as an institution, not be involved. Anne arrived in Atlanta on June 13. She spent eight days there, going to the home of the Franks immediately after settling in at a hotel. She had known Leo's mother in the Brooklyn days, but now she met his wife and father for the first time. Many relatives of the Franks had gathered in Atlanta to await the outcome of the hearing, which Governor Slaton held just four days before the end of his term. Anne talked with Frank's lawyers, who urged her to persist in seeking an audience with the Governor. She consulted with Rabbi David Marx and with many other Georgians of influence, Jew and Gentile alike, who were working in the cause of Leo Frank, and every evening was spent in the Tower in conversation with Leo and the men and women who gathered there.

On Thursday of that week she finally resigned herself to the fact that she could not reach the Governor. She took a trolley out to Lake Gatlin by way of comforting herself and there gathered boughs of Georgia pine to take with her to the Tower that evening. Her own words tell the story of that time:

For nearly two years I wanted a favorable opportunity to visit him in prison, fearing lest in the desire to give evidence of my friendship I might prove only one more source of trial and persecution. On April 29th, 1915 he had written: "Never fear that I will falter in this fight. I am fighting for name, honor and life, for loved relatives and friends. To me life without honor is unsufferable. I know I have builded right. My faith is undaunted; and while I do not at this moment know how, and while the future stretches dark before my mental vision, I feel intuitively that I will yet win the name, freedom, honor and life which are mine rightfully."

When the final hearing before the Governor began on June 12th, within ten days set for the execution, I went to Atlanta unannounced. I had never been inside a prison and as I wished to come into Mr. Frank's presence without announcement I went first to the home of his wife who accompanied me to the Tower of the prison in which he was confined. It was evening and I steeled my nerves for a trying ordeal. But as one door after another was opened for our admission and I observed the courtesy and respect of the attendants toward Mrs. Frank, I began to feel, what I afterward found to be true, that the sheriff was a man among his men whether jailors or prisoners.

Mr. Frank received me as I might have received him had he come unexpectedly into the library where we had first met and where all our previous encounters had taken place. We began where we left off for to each the other seemed unchanged.

Had I needed any visible sign of his innocence I should have found it at the first handclasp and look into his eyes. The years had developed the man from the boy but the heart and the smile of the boy remained with a deepened sense of the meaning of my visit. . . . The bars which had seemed so terrible as I pictured the restriction of the liberty of an innocent man became the sign of his safety and security as I remembered "the mass-meeting against Frank" I had seen in front of the Capitol, only a block away, that very Sunday afternoon. His presence radiated cheer and affection as he introduced a friend of his boyhood to friends he had made in Atlanta.

I went back to my hotel with an easier mind than I had known for two years. I remained in Atlanta eight days. I visited Mr. Frank every day and found him always cheerful, serene and hopeful, as ready to listen to others as to talk himself but with a fund of conversation as rich and inexhaustible as it was varied and interesting. . . .

Monday morning's paper, June 21, brought news of Governor Slaton's decree of commutation. In the face of public feeling, his was an act of enormous courage that cost him, as he knew it would, his political future. Slaton had been the fair-haired boy of Georgia politics, elected to office "on a tidal wave of popularity, enthusiasm unprecedented in Georgia's annals." By this one act he became the enemy of the mob who clamored for his death. For the first time in the history of the country, the militia was called out to protect the Governor of a state.

Frank's lawyers called Anne at her hotel Monday morning and advised her not to visit the capitol. Frank, meanwhile, at the Governor's instruction, had been smuggled out of the Tower and transferred to the prison farm at Milledgeville. Anne had spent the day with members of the Frank family, who, in the evening, drove her along the river. "Moonlight on the river," she wrote in her notepaper diary, "and the mob on Peachtree Road."

She saw Leo for the last time in the Tower Sunday evening, only hours before his transfer from the place. What he said to her then was to compensate beyond telling for all the talk about books he had been unable to give her previously. She rushed back to the hotel to scribble down on the inevitable piece of notepaper the gist of the matter, dated it, and slipped it carelessly among her records of the visit.

A librarian's work is very intangible. I have been thinking of this since you have been here and I want you to know before you go away how it seems in the life of one man, brought almost to the breaking point by the bitterest experience of life. What you did for me thro' the Library has gone to make up the *reserve force* I have relied upon to carry me thro' this. It is inexhaustible in itself but the renewal of it by your presence at this time has given me such a realization of your own faith in the ideal as inspires me anew.

The return to New York was almost joyous. Now there would be time for Leo Frank to prove his innocence. He wrote two letters to her from Milledgeville, the first on July 2:

Office of Warden
State Prison Farm
   Milledgeville,   July 2, 1915
      Georgia   Friday

My dear Miss Moore:
Your letter of 6/28 brought to me its message of cheer and inspiration. I was so glad to hear from one whose helpful friendship meant so much to me during those last trying hours in the "Tower." It was the voice and presence of the long ago, infusing spirit and exhorting manhood for the last final test—a test that tries the staunchest of mere human flesh. However, thank God, I passed successfully and with whole skin through the ordeal and I am now with ever increasing strength facing the new conditions.

I am gradually adjusting myself to "stripes" and the new environment. There is much to study of human nature here and I will make the most of it. I have gained in weight and my color is getting better daily. I have good appetite and

I sleep well. I have been given certain tasks in the Prison Building which do not over tax my strength. This too gives me enough exercise to keep me in trim.

The Warden and his staff are kindly and solicitous. I know I shall get on famously with them. This is the breathing spell in the present phase of my life to gain the strength and reserve for the spurt to freedom, vindication and that honor which is justly and rightfully mine.

Suffering, mental especially, is the "fining-pot" of experience, the leavening influence in Life. I should be better—more efficient because of this ordeal.

Won't you please send me the addresses of ——. I wish to write to them.

With every good wish, I am

Cordially,
Leo M. Frank

The second letter, dated July 17, 1915, follows:

Office of Warden
STATE PRISON FARM
  J. E. SMITH, Warden
  JOHN SAYE, Asst. Warden
Milledgeville, Georgia   July 17th, 1915

My dear Miss Moore:

I have your letters of July 5 & 13 & was certainly glad to hear from you. Was indeed grieved to hear that your sister-in-law passed away. I thank you for the book of views of N.Y. City as well as the other printed matter. I was waiting for the addresses you so kindly sent to me.

I am glad to report that I continue well, and am daily improving in health and strength. In my spare moments, I attend to my correspondence, read the papers & occasionally a magazine. Occasionally, too, I operate the Victrola whereby I can, thro' the ingenuity of modern science, bring Caruso, Alda, Farrar, et al. within the confines of the State Prison.

On last Wednesday, my dear Lucille visited me and remained in the vicinity. She will stay possibly until the beginning of next week. You know how comforting and pleasurable it is to me to have my wife near, & where the opportunity is given me each day of seeing her for an hour or two.

I still continue to get letters from friends all over the U.S.A. enclosing clippings in praise of Gov. Slaton's action. He will surely be a big national political figure some day in the future.

I hear frequently from my good friends in Atlanta & several have already visited me here. The officials here are kindness itself, for which, all things considered I am truly thankful.

I assure you I shall be glad to hear from you at any time the spirit moves you. We must keep in touch, one with the other.

With cordial regards & good wishes in which dear Lucille joins me, I am

Sincerely

LEO M. FRANK

Give my greetings to all inquiring friends.

In the night of that very day, July 17, one of the prisoners who worked in the kitchen in Milledgeville and thus had access to knives attacked Frank as he lay sleeping and all but slashed his throat from ear to ear. Two fellow prisoners, who were doctors, clamped the jugular vein and stopped the hemorrhage. "I am going to live," he said. "I must live. I must vindicate myself."

One month after this attempt on Frank's life, on August 16, twenty-five men broke into the prison, overpowered the guards and the warden, took Leo Frank to Marietta, the home of Mary Phagan, and there lynched him.

Anne was on vacation in New England when the terrible news reached her. She made straightway for Portland, Maine, and Cousin Alice. There she found succor, a welcoming room, a stretch of silence, and the summer sky and weather to heal her spirit.

Timeless and contemporary are the words she wrote:

Not until we become fully alive to the social, political and racial issues behind the tragedy can we realize that the father, husband, son or brother of any one of us might find himself in such a situation as Leo Frank faced in Georgia.

11

NICHOLAS

> *Every critic should try to create some-*
> *thing once in a lifetime, regardless of conse-*
> *quence. It's more difficult than praising or*
> *finding fault with the work of other people;*
> *it's more fun; it heightens appreciation of all*
> *that is admirable in any sincere attempt to*
> *tell something new and different in story or*
> *pictures; and it enlarges one's sympathies*
> *for things which do not "come off."*
>
> ACM

$\mathcal{I}$T WAS TOLD of Louis Couperous, the Dutch novelist whose series of novels, *Small Souls*, created a stir in the twenties, that his walking stick had become to him so much of a person as to oblige him, when spending a solitary evening at the theater, to purchase two seats, one for himself and one for his cane. The habit of endowing inanimate objects with life is as ancient as man himself. Anthropology bears witness to the fact that for primitive man every stone and tree, the very pots in which he cooked food, his weapons and his drums, all shared with him the common factor—life. Children never hesitate to bring alive in their imaginations toys, sticks, or teapots, according to their whim, nor to invent imaginary companions, according to their need. That such objects should speak with voices of their own follows the manner of their genesis.

The release of emotion through a surrogate person or object is an oft-told tale in literature and in life. Cyrano de Bergerac could speak the depth of his love for Roxanne only through the voice of another; in *Lili*, the musical play of our own time, based on the novel of Paul Gallico, *The Man Who Hated People*, the puppet declared his love while the puppeteer himself was locked speechless in his own person. The measure of the ventriloquist's appeal lies in the degree of wit, raillery, and impudence his dummy is permitted beyond the character and personality of the performer. The mystique of the inanimate embraces also the power of the symbolic. Hans Christian Andersen, that master magician of endowing the inanimate with life, understood the beneficence of symbols that accrue to themselves the past and the future, holding in their singularity essences and epiphanies. The amulet, the mascot, the lucky sixpence, and the rabbit's foot—these are symbols at the lowest level of meaning. At the highest level are the holy insignia of all religions, signifying in their design and patterns the long history of man's spiritual desiring.

There was an object in the life of Anne Moore. It began as a means whereby to catch the immediate attention of children. As Superintendent of Work with Children, she was expected to appear at the special events scheduled in the children's rooms, from Throgs Neck in the Bronx to the far reaches of Staten Island: Christmas story hours everywhere, Halloween at Harlem Branch, St. Patrick's Day at George Bruce, the Feast of Lights at Seward Park, H. C. Andersen's birthday at Hamilton

Fish, the Polish celebrations at Tompkins Square, the Czech story hour at Webster, puppet plays at Jackson Square, peep shows at Aguilar, the Cranford Reading Club at Fordham—bookish affairs and fetes created by an imaginative staff to bring drama into the quiet business of reading and to heighten the common day for thousands of children who trudged up and down the steep stairways of branch libraries to second floors, day after day, in search of pleasure and diversion.

The long journeys by subways, elevateds, buses or ferries, and taxi reduced by not one iota Anne's expectancy of pleasure in these events. She never ceased to be refreshed by the response of the children. Invariably she sat where she could watch their faces, straight on.

On each of these occasions, before the main event, as it were, the Superintendent of Work with Children was introduced to the audience and expected to speak to them. Now, it is no easy matter to address to good effect a group of children who, like John Gilpin, are "on pleasure bent." How many adults can accomplish it without condescension or without assuming that ghastly tone of exaggerated enthusiasm which is too often deemed appropriate to such an affair? For a storyteller, the initial approach is easy—"Once upon a time." But Anne was no storyteller in the accepted or professional sense. She knew instinctively what to say to children, but to be able to produce and hold aloft some object which aroused curiosity and held immediate attention was to capture the group quickly and entire. "I have brought someone with me," she would announce, opening up one of her copious handbags, or fumbling in some colorful subsidiary basket, bag, or carry-all hanging on her arm, to produce at last the figure of Nicholas.

For Anne, the wooden figure of Nicholas came to embody all children she had known or encountered in New York City, in Louisiana and Texas, in Boston and in Brooklyn, in Utah, Minnesota, California and the Pacific Northwest, in Canada, England, Scandinavia, and France. He symbolized the essence of childhood itself.

As the years passed, an accrual of memories and associations gathered about him. He acquired a symbolic patina, like the walnuts the Chinese fondle in their hands for a lifetime, and became a token of the richness of life which time and her own genius and incomparable capacity for friendship had bestowed upon her.

Nicholas came into being on the day before Christmas, 1920, when the staff of the Central Children's Room gathered up attractive trifles to send up to Room 105, ACM's office, by way of saying Merry Christmas to Miss Moore. Leonore Power was in charge of the room at that time, and in the course of her meanderings through the Gourmet Shop at Bloomingdale's she had come upon the sturdy wooden figure of a Dutch boy, designed as a toy, about eight inches high, his arms and legs articulated at shoulders and hips. His costume was of splendid stuff, first-rate homespun wool, blue trousers, a gray jacket, stitched about the edge with red yarn. He wore a minuscular gray woolen scarf about his neck, tied at a giddy angle, and a helmetlike wooden hat, permanently attached to his head by the woodcutter's skill. (Anne spoke of it as resembling the caps worn by the French *poilu*.) Miss Power bought him on the spur of the moment and set him atop the basket of delectables sent upstairs to the office.

Anne loved him at first sight. He could stand free of support since his feet were formed of wooden blocks, and his seemingly mittened hands were scooped out into small hollows, only the thumbs protruding. Anne discovered at once that the hands were capable of holding objects, small trinkets, birthday-cake candles, and many of the inconsequential trifles that are the delight of children. ". . . his hands were the kind of hands you want to shake or to fill full of things to give away" was Anne's own description of him.

He was immediately established as a tradition. Obviously Dutch, she called him Nicholas Knickerbocker after the patron saint of the Dutch, who had founded New York, and Washington Irving's well-loved Knickerbockers. The association with Christmas was natural since he had made his initial appearance on Christmas Eve. Moreover, he could easily be carried in her handbag, and it was there he took up more or less permanent residence.

Three points of extravagance marked Anne's wardrobe, no matter how tired or worn her workaday clothes might be: shoes, gloves, and handbags. The shoes were costly, setting off her narrow feet, her ankles, delicate-boned and slim, her legs tight-fleshed and shapely even in old age. The gloves were invariably of handsome soft leather. They were often lost, since she carried rather than wore them. The handbags were copious, conservatively elegant, of the finest leather, or they were of beautiful fabrics: wool, silk, and quilted stuffs.

As for the contents of her purses, no gathering of cosmetics was there. Who ever saw her powder her nose or reconstruct her hair, which was straight, fine in texture, and apt to be troublesome about the face, unless the need were absolute? She was one who dressed as appropriately as possible for the day's work, but, once assembled, never gave the matter a second thought. Her purse contained no career woman's notebook and pencil, no calendar or date book. There were eyeglasses—usually knocking about on their own without benefit of protective case—

a clutch of gloves, a dust of invisible hairpins, a changing collection of snapshots of children—nieces, nephews, and friends—and letters. When she opened her purse in one's presence, one knew something interesting was about to be shared.

The slender fingers—uncluttered by any ring, sensitive and thin at the tips, the nails astonishingly narrow from base to rim, with scant half moons visible—fluttered the current file, made their choice, and the listener would share for a moment a fragment of the wide and far-reaching world of ACM: a letter from her friend, the distinguished scholar and librarian Valfrid Munch-Petersen of Copenhagen; scraps of comments from Beatrix Potter or L. Leslie Brooke or Walter de la Mare, in England; news of Maria Cimino, on leave in the jungles of South America with her anthropologist husband, Will Lipkind; a letter from Marit Blehr in Norway; news of Leonore Power Mendelson, by then living in Yokohama, or of Mary Gould Davis, summering in Brittany, or Ruth Sawyer, on a folk-tale-gathering trip in Spain.

To have a letter of one's own produced from that file was a mark of distinction. If ACM read aloud from a letter one had written to her, friends made note of it and quickly reported it to the writer, recognizing it as accolade, indeed.

"I have brought someone with me," Anne would say, holding up Nicholas, who was seemingly alive in her hand. She recounted his adventures with such zest and conviction as to involve the audience in all she said. Nicholas was no imparter of knowledge. He was never used as nucleus for giving information. He gave rise to no such question as "How many of you know where Holland is?" The events he reported were apt to have happened to Anne herself: some encounter that had occurred on the way to a branch library, a ride over Brooklyn Bridge by moonlight, a book lately read, or an account of a personality recently come to town—all told with an eye for childlike drama and particularization such as might well have been encompassed by an alert boy from a far country on his first visit to New York. For Anne, like her description of Miss Harriet Friend in a book she was yet to write, "made little stories when she talked." Later, when Nicholas had become an established personality with two books of personal history behind him, he was to display manifold treasure, such marvels of the miniature as to bring forth from the children exclamations of wonder. At the end of her talk Anne might anchor in each of the wooden hands a small birthday-cake candle, light them, and invite the children to blow out their wishes upon them. The flickering uncertainty of candlelight never ceases to cast a spell upon children and adults alike, its wavering flame a reminder of man's first triumph over the dark, its brief light, burning close to the certainty of extinction, a confirmation of his courage. At any rate, children everywhere would blow across Anne's little lights, utterly convinced of the Dutch magic she and Nicholas had at their command.

Soon the children asked questions, as they often do after some experience has touched them to the quick and set them on the philosopher's quest for reality.

"Is he real?" they asked.

"Does he come alive at night?"

"He isn't real, is he?"

One day, in the Central Children's Room, when Anne was sitting in the Fifth Avenue window seat with Annie Astor of Ninth Avenue and her friend, Carlotta Lorenze of Third Avenue, the reality of Nicholas was the topic of conjecture and debate. It was the Italian child who had no whit of skepticism. "Why don't you write a book about Nicholas?" she said, sensing perhaps the indisputable proof of print. The suggestion tumbled about in Anne's mind and took root. She brought it to fruition in two books, *Nicholas: A Manhattan Christmas Story* (G. P. Putnam's & Sons, 1924) and *Nicholas and the Golden Goose* (G. P. Putnam's & Sons, 1932).

A bold and original design was called for to embrace the world of Nicholas as Anne felt it. She sought to distill the essence of New York in the twenties, to translate her own life, profession, and friendships into the state of awareness and wonder that children often attain in the best of their reading years, the middle years between eight and twelve. Searching for a schema, her mind turned, as it often did, to that small milestone among books for children, *Miss Muffet's Christmas Party*, a fantasy of well-known characters in children's books which was at the same time a penetrating piece of criticism of the literature of childhood. Its author was Dr. Samuel McCord Crothers, a noted clergyman, whose essays on literature combined clear-headed observation with charm, scholarship, and genuine love of reading.

The *dramatis personae* of Dr. Crothers' story was limited to characters in books and stories. Anne's cast of characters included the living and the dead, characters of fiction and fantasy as well as the supernatural beings of folklore: members of the staff of the New York Public Library, thinly disguised, doormen and mop-men, heroes of history, writers, artists, the very statuary lining the halls of the Central Building, children she knew, sometimes given fictitious names, sometimes appearing as themselves, pictures come to life from the walls of the Children's Room and the Prints Division. Scarcely a corner of the great Central Building but was transmogrified by the alchemy of her passionate response to the place and the reaches of its influence.

"It takes courage and determination to give a big party and mix EVERYBODY up with EVERYBODY and give EVERYBODY a good time," Mary Mapes Dodge is quoted as saying in the chapter "Brownie's Big Party," one of the most breathless episodes of *Nicholas*. What a document for the celebration of some golden anniversary of the library the reprinting of that chapter would be with a small *roman à clef* for people, books, and things, by way of clarification.

Anne Carroll Moore, the fantasist, like others before her and since, wrote out of the passionate enjoyment of an experience of life. It was the same force that begot *The Wind in the Willows*, by Kenneth Grahame, and W. W. Tarn's *Treasure of the Isle of Mist* and Robert Lawson's *Rabbit Hill*. Each of these books fixes for all time the gratitude of its author for certain gifts of life. For Kenneth Grahame, it was the pleasure he had in the English landscape, comradeship, and the felicities of English country life; for W. W. Tarn, the love of Scottish earth, which he knew as a geologist as well as a poet; for Robert Lawson, his delight in his own place and the character of the Connecticut countryside.

For Anne, there were countless beatitudes: the child she had been, children, books, friends, the New York Public Library, which she treasured, stone by stone, branch by branch, and the city and the life it encompassed—all these she prized. Bridges, taxis, flowers, food and wine, wind and weather, Maine, pageants and parades, circuses and balloons, ceremonies and celebrations, costumes, parties, surprises, small delights of sight and sound and taste: all these she cherished, and, being a woman "of courage and determination," she did not hesitate to bring together disparate parts. There is no plot, no prescribed conflict and resolution, no quest and consummation in her books, but character, personalities galore, atmosphere and sense of place, all crowned by a high mood of festival.

The hero is Nicholas, a very real boy in many respects: "I will stay on one condition," he says. "That I am free to come and go when I feel like it and not fussed over—" The heroine, his companion and confidante, is one Ann Caraway, "a lady of no particular age" who is reported to "make things happen, any time, not just at Christmas."

"To make things happen"—there is as brief and as accurate a self-portrait as one is likely to come upon in a lifetime. Ann Caraway is recognizably Anne herself, and many who loved her called her by that name after the appearance of the books. It came, fittingly enough, straight out of Walter de la Mare's *Peacock Pie*. Anne had brought home from England an early copy of the book. As was the custom with books she loved and revered, she had spread among the staff so happy a contagion of her own delight in it as to have created an awareness of it in many a mind. One night at dinner, at the Woman's City Club when it was housed in the beautiful mansion on Madison Avenue, one of Stanford White's architectural triumphs, ACM was discussing with a group of colleagues the problem of a name for herself in the book she was writing and someone said, out of the blue, "Old King Caraway supped on cake—" And there it was!

The writing of Nicholas was undertaken in a period of increased activity in her life. She began it in 1918, at the peak of her assignments of criticism for *The Bookman*, when the library was recovering from shortages of staff and all the dislocation caused by the war years. It absorbed her utterly, as any piece of writing out of one's deepest self is bound to do, and she fought for space and time in which to bring it off. For a while she took a room on one of the topmost floors of the Commodore Hotel, which gave her the necessary sense of remoteness, yet was within walking distance of her office. The view of the East River, to say nothing of the towers of the city at night, refreshed her eyes as well as her spirit. There she would write and then summon some friend at a late hour in the evening to read aloud what she had written and to order up from room service dishes of chocolate ice cream and raspberry ice served cheek by jowl.

A summer at the McDowell Colony gave her a breathing spell. Originally the two books had been planned as one, but Anne soon discovered that there was too much material for one volume, and since the story broke naturally into two halves, one centered in New York, the other in France and England, it was decided to publish *Nicholas: A Manhattan Christmas Story* as the first volume with a sequel to follow.

The choice of Jay Van Everen, a young Czech artist, as illustrator was the happiest ever, for in his strong black-and-white line pictures, reminiscent of woodcuts, he established a precise balance between the realism of the text and all that was implied in its fantasy. He too was a lover of the city, who caught the spirit of place in decorative excursions of his own. The book appeared in September 1924, its bright red cover, its fascinating end papers of Van Everen's Map of New York, its jolly square size—all distinctive and fitting. What joy she had in it, sending it *broadcast* to members of the family and to half a hundred friends the world over! Each such copy was no idle gift. She seldom inscribed any book she gave as a gift in a perfunctory way. No "All best wishes" or

"Merry Christmas" but always she wrote words that re-affirmed the relationship between donor and donee, and no recipient of books from her could ever again be satisfied with the clichés of friendship.

Brentano's Book Store, which in 1924 was at Twenty-seventh Street and Fifth Avenue, arranged in one of its windows a pyramid of copies of the book. Anne hailed a cab on a Sunday evening and drove down to see it. She asked the driver to wait until she had her fill of pleasure in the sight. There can hardly be a moment in the life of any author to equal that of seeing, for the first time, multiple copies of his book, displayed in the window of one of the country's greatest bookstores, on one of the world's richest and most fabled avenues. When she stepped back into the cab, she said to the driver, "I wrote that book." "Yeah?" he replied, casting half an eye on the display. Then he said, "My God, lady, did you write them all?"

Geoffrey Parsons, chief editorial writer of the New York *Herald Tribune*, reviewed *Nicholas: A Manhattan Christmas Story* for "The Three Owls," in a perceptive piece that conveys his understanding of Anne's intent and its fulfillment. It is given here in its entirety, for the sake of the book and for its revelation of the man, one of the noted journalists of his day, who did not disdain to write a piece about a book for children. The review appeared in the New York *Herald Tribune* of September 28, 1924. The plight of the great cities, it is interesting to note, concerned Geoffrey Parsons as long ago as the 1920s:

There is a man, a hard-working writer of politics and such truck, who every once in a while drives his car down a certain street, collects an assorted carload of strange children and takes them off for a party. He is a little man with a serious, wistful face and he is never more serious than

when he is driving off with his picnickers. That is probably why they like him—he is quite himself with them,
making no more effort than if they were grown-up.

"Why do you go off with those kids?" he was once
asked.

"To hear somebody tell me the truth," he answered.
"When I get confused and tangled they make it all clear
again."

There is the same touch in Miss Moore's "Nicholas."
Every grown-up knows what a cruel, jangling maze of
steel and speed is Manhattan Island. Once, years ago, one
loved it for its leisurely homeliness and its friendly cor-
ners. Now one works in it, is thrilled and appalled by it.
The city has been lost in the machine. It is the peculiar
and unexpected gift of Miss Moore's book that it recap-
tures the old magic of the town and makes New York
warm in one's heart, whether the heart happens to be
young or old.

Her method is the method of the carload of children.
She tells the truth about the city with the clear-seeing eye
of a child, relighting old beacons, discovering new magic
in every elevated train, behind each shop window. Would
you believe that New York could be made into a party, a
gorgeous, gigantic children's party, with candles and icing
and music and fairies? That is just what Miss Moore does.
As Mary Mapes Dodge says at the biggest party of all at
the library: "It takes courage and determination to give a
big party and mix everybody up with everybody and give
everybody a good time." Miss Moore and her Brownie
have both the courage and skill to live up to this incredibly
difficult formula. Everybody inside the pages and in front
of the pages does have a good time.

Miss Moore has a flair for parties above all else. She loves
them and she eats them as the mouth-watering repasts provided Nicholas testify. In a fairyland cabinet her portfolio
would unquestionably be that of Parties and Good Things.
Yet there is a mingling of old tales with these present excitements, of time both ruined and riveting, that shows an
unusual sensitiveness to the past. Here is a gallant effort
and Miss Moore has put all her heart into it. If it does not

come through as vividly as does the Manhattan of today, obliteration is the fact that intervenes. Fraunces' Tavern and St. Paul's help among the towers, but the difficulty is great. At any rate, Miss Moore never commits the fatal error of turning didactic. The parties of Washington and the Knickerbockers are either parties or they are nothing.

A rich handful of a book Miss Moore has written that will be equally precious to children who have cut their teeth on New York's skyline and to children afar to whom it is a longed-for fairyland, some day to rise above the horizon. Mr. Jay Van Everen has provided drawings in the manner of woodcuts as understandable as they are understanding of the event and for good measure one of the most engaging maps in and out of fairyland.

The ancient cities—London, Paris, Rome—these belong to the ages and the entire world, loved for their tradition and heritage. Walking the streets of these beloved places, one feels the past coexisting with the present. This is true to a shamelessly small degree in New York. The historic past is largely a lost consideration of American life in the twentieth century. It is thrown out the window, like the proverbial baby with the bath. Anne's desire was to instill in children an awareness of the traditions of New York, that they might be cherished as a universal experience, belonging to the world. She accomplished this to a degree. Much of the book remains timeless even in the face of mammoth changes wrought by the passing years.

By the nature of its theme and structure, the book could never have attained the immediate popularity of a *Pinocchio* or *Mary Poppins* or *Winnie the Pooh*, but for many children *Nicholas* remains a memorable reading experience. The high originality is there, palpable and enduring, and the pervading mood of delight replenishes the spirit and exists beyond the limits of time and place.

Nicholas and the Golden Goose, the second book, did not appear until 1932. It chronicled, as a matter of fact, the year 1921 in Anne's life. In that year she went to France to visit the libraries for children established there after the First World War by the American Committee for Devastated France. The committee had been largely the inspiration of Miss Anne Morgan, the daughter of Pierpont Morgan, the financier, a philanthropist in her own right and a great Francophile. She, with the help of Mrs. A. M. Dike and eight other American women, constituted the original committee. Having gotten the consent and blessing of the French government, they pledged themselves and their growing staff to render succor to the people who lived in the thirty smoldering villages behind the lines held by the Third French Army Corps, in the years when the war raged uncertainly back and forth across the country of the Aisne. Theirs was the first motor corps run by women. The tasks and their accomplishment of them were gigantic, including evacuation of the wounded, the setting up of dispensaries, the transportation of food and supplies, the organization of classes for children, and care of the old and sick. By 1919, when most of the immediate physical needs of the devastated region had been met, the committee enlarged the scope of its work to include solutions for pressing social problems and the restoration of the French way of life. Five categories for service were adopted: Public Health, Social Service, Agricultural Syndicates, Construction, and Libraries.

It was at this point, Libraries, that Anne Moore became involved. Miss Morgan leaned heavily on her for advice in this effort, because books for the children were among the first concern of the French themselves. Anne Carroll Moore could not go herself, but several of the most able and gifted children's librarians from the New York Public Library were enlisted in the cause. They were dispatched to France: Alice Keats O'Connor to Soissons, Jessie Carson as an organizing supervisor, Marianne Greene to Anizy-le-Château. The bowls of flowers on the tables, the large black book in which the French children wrote their names when joining the library, the brave displays of picture books opened up on shelves and window sills, the story hours, the reading aloud—all these bespoke the New York Public Library and Anne Carroll Moore. No official reports of the Committee for Devastated France equal the story as Anne tells it in this book.

The visit to France was followed by a sojourn in London, where the doors of artists, writers, and publishers were opened to Anne as an official representative of *The Bookman*, the chief American literary journal of its day. She was welcomed in her own right and bolstered by the knowledge that her solid accomplishment as a critic in its pages had been recognized beyond the borders of the United States.

These were the matters of fact in *Nicholas and the Golden Goose*. The matter of fantasy transpired in a series of letters Nicholas wrote home to the friends of the first book, together with certain adventures reported at first hand. The edged awareness of each of her encounters with people, places, sights, and sounds sustains a mood bordering on exaltation. That was, when one thinks of it, the dominant mood of her life.

With the publication of the books, the influence of Nicholas widened in the world. Children who had read about him made pilgrimages to the Central Library to see the window through which he had made his initial appearance in the first book. Artists, writers, and friends presented him with gifts, many of them exquisite miniatures. Louis Slobodkin, the sculptor-illustrator, gave him a tool chest, the awl and screwdriver, the hammer and saw made to exact scale and in good working order. The beautiful Nadia Rodzianko, whom Anne had discovered and enticed into becoming a member of the staff of the Central Children's Room, gave him a small golden Easter egg from the traditional collection she had brought with her from Russia in the dark days of her escape from the revolution of the Bolsheviks. A telescope, a small heart of purest crystal, a compass, a rabbit good-luck piece were among his treasures. People found pleasure in finding the exquisite and uncommon for Nicholas, as they did for Anne herself. Sometimes the gifts were judged as being quite unacceptable and found no space in the treasure chest. They simply disappeared, for Nicholas, like Anne, judged objects not from the point of view of their value or worth but sharply by the subtle light of taste and the quality of the imagination that had begotten them.

As far as Anne was concerned, Nicholas moved closer to the center of her private mythology, becoming, in her behalf, spokesman and spendthrift *extraordinaire*. Countless gifts were bestowed in his name, parties initiated at his request, extravagances of a hundred delights brought off by the lad. He acquired his own stationery, with the end piece for *Nicholas: A Manhattan Christmas Story* at its masthead, showing Nicholas writing a letter. Letters of gay and special import went out over his signature.

There can be no hedging the fact that for many of her friends and associates, Nicholas was somewhat *hors de combat*. Not everyone was willing to play the game for which Anne invariably called the tune, nor to enjoy the ceremonies of candlelight and other rituals of play she carried off to perfection. The congeries of her masculine friends, especially, were apt to balk at this bit of drama and were embarrassed by it. One or two of the brave among them told her their opinion and advised her to desist, and one good friend of long standing in California, "Cousin Oscar," said to her, "Anne, take that damn doll, lock it in your trunk and forget it." She roared with laughter and told the story on herself. But she remained importunate, using Nicholas in many ways for her own purposes. She judged people by their initial response to Nicholas and their acceptance or rejection of him, as one tests the temper of a friend by the quality of his humor or the depth of his feeling. He served to command a situation, to create a diversion, and to bolster and sustain her own opinions and convictions. "He served to keep her relationships where she wanted them," commented one astute librarian.

When he was lost in one of the hundreds of taxis in New York, certain people with whom she was associated sighed with relief. But the relief was short-lived. The children of the Psychiatric Institute at Presbyterian Hospital asked for him. Eleanor Nave, one of the children's librarians, who had a rare gift of reaching disturbed children through storytelling and puppet plays, had often asked ACM to visit these children to tell them the story of Nicholas. Mrs. Nave could not bear to have them deprived of his presence, and she contrived with the help of a very gifted wood carver to have the original Nicholas copied. The copy was presented to ACM as a gift from the children, appearing inside a box made as a replica of his own book. For a while Anne was troubled by him, and then little by little he merged into the personality of the first, and Nicholas the first and Nicholas the second became one.

The game went on into the mid-forties. When for a

second time Nicholas disappeared, Anne was utterly
stricken. "It has been one of the worst summers of my
life," she wrote to a friend in Ann Arbor, in a rare dis-
closure of suffering and unhappiness. Nothing was ever
quite the same again. That touchstone was irrevocable.

It was Walter de la Mare who, in the last analysis,
defined the role of Nicholas. In the 1940s, at the request
of ACM, he invited a friend of hers to tea. He too lived
among exquisite miniatures, which his *Memoirs of a
Midget* had brought to him from friends and admirers.
One could understand the sympathy that existed between
these two people, ACM and Walter de la Mare. Each
acknowledged childhood as a state of being like no other,
each knew the flashing insights of heightened imagination, each lived in a state of acute awareness of the mys-
tery surrounding all that exists, including the inanimate.
As the friend was about to depart, Walter de la Mare
said, "Give Anne Moore my deep and warmest regards."
Then, scanning the face of the visitor with those deep
eyes of his that were both kind and searching and recognizing that she was within the circle of belief, he said,
"And to her alter ego—Nicholas."

12

BEHIND THE LIBRARY LIONS

Why is it that they always think that all the whole thing amounts to is that for a few hours in the afternoon after school there is a mad rush of children, who come and read story books, and that for the rest of the time we all sit around and crochet?

The two biggest things about it are the spontaneity of their coming and going, and the training in discrimination and judgment which they get by choosing their own books. Even their unwise choices help. The sociological aspect of it always interests me —the way the children come together and love to be together, the way one comes because others come.

The community of interest is what, unconsciously, appeals to most of the children. It is the exceptional child who loves to get off into a corner and read alone, or come in when the other children are not here. And out of this develops a distinct educational value, a something which would be entirely lost if the comings and goings of the children were regulated or formalized in any way. A library, for children, should be quite separate from the formal part of his day, school and studying and set hours. The library is the only testing ground of the reality of the interest aroused at school.

> *It is nearly twenty years ago since chil-*
> *dren's rooms were started in libraries, and at*
> *first they were simply for circulation, until*
> *the need was felt of a place where children*
> *could read, a place that invited reading, and*
> *where the first early knowledge of literature*
> *and art, the first light of history, through*
> *folk-lore and saga, could be brought to*
> *them, for these are the things which make*
> *for personality and individuality, for the*
> *whole upbuilding of morals and spiritual*
> *life.*
>
> ACM

*T*HE GRANDEUR of the Central Building melted into a comfortable acceptance by those who daily trod its marble steps as public or entered by circuitous routes as habitués of the staff. They created in their time a folk-lore of the building. The sculptured six figures across the front attic, created by Paul Bartlett to represent History, Drama, Poetry, Religion, Romance, and Philosophy, be-came known as the Tilden girls, and the lions by Edward Potter, on either side of the first flight of stairs leading from the avenue to the esplanade, were the butt of many a joke and jibe. James Daugherty fixed their identity for all time in his incomparable picture book *Andy and the Lion* (Viking Press, 1938) by dedicating it to "Lord Lenox and Lady Astor," his inspiration outweighing the obvious fact that both of the beasts were male.

For Anne those lions were mastheads of courage and accomplishment. "Behind the Library Lions" was the salutation on many a communiqué of good report re-counting high deeds and accomplishments. The drudger-ies, the disappointments, the battles for funds were endured in private, except in official reports. She knew the discouragement of the perfectionist and bore it for the most part in secret, as was her habit.

A long view across the thirty years of her residence behind the lions reveals the magnitude of disasters that swept over ACM—wars and plagues (infantile paralysis in epidemic force), a great depression, budgets cut to the bone, with shelves in the children's rooms as empty of books as were Mother Hubbard's of food, shortages of staff as well as of coal. An *aperçuant* among the reports finds here sad documents of woe:

• The shortage of the supply of books and the worn-out conditions of the collections for circulation in busy branches have led to a thorough inspection of the available resources. The importance of large and continuous additions cannot be too strongly urged as the greatest need of 1914. A general building up of book collections is needed at branches where the circulation use has been declining for a considerable period of time and an increase of twenty-five percent of book stock is needed at each of the ten branches reporting the heaviest circulation use. [1913]
• Thousands of children have been led to expect certain definite things on receipt of their library card. Chief among these expectations is that of choosing a book to take home from well-filled circulation shelves. From the children's standpoint no other library privilege is comparable to this. The story hour, the library reading-room, the club, the book talk to a visiting class from school—each has its place, but the children are disappointed when these cannot be reenforced by books to take home. Everything except books is provided and made accessible in the children's rooms, even to the catalogue of books no longer supplied. [1922]
• Unless prompt and effective measures are taken to increase the existing supply of books by at least one-half, it seems inevitable that the circulation of books to children from several branch libraries must cease and the children's

rooms be used merely as reading rooms. . . . Why do the children keep on coming to a children's room with empty shelves? Unquestionably it is because they like to come and because they still have faith in the Library. This has been kept alive for years largely by the collection of books in the reading rooms, and by story hours.

There is a great and unnatural strain about the continuous administration of a large children's room with so few books.

Such conditions preclude any sound work, but they are sapping the vitality and initiative of the members of the Staff whose knowledge of books and varied experience of work should be free for the training of these younger assistants and students, as well as for proper library service to the children, their parents and teachers. [1923]

• Under existing conditions not only is it impossible to provide duplicates of recent books of fine quality, it is equally impossible to provide the children's classics in sufficient numbers to insure the reading of any one of them to a boy or girl within that span of life when the book is most desired and its influence most potent. [1924]

• A hundred thousand new volumes, at least, are needed to sustain a profitable book service to the homes during the next year. The situation is extremely critical because of the rapidly increasing impoverishment of book stock. It is so far-reaching in its implications as to create a vital need for a revised plan based upon the assignment of available funds according to condition of book stock rather than circulation statistics.

The use of books within the library, both for recreational reading and for reference, has greatly increased at all points. Children in family groups, where numbers have been doubled or trebled to save rent, and rooms are often without heat and adequate light, come day after day to read and to study the next day's lesson with the aid of library books.

"What we should do without the library I don't know," said the wife of a musician who had been for two years without employment. "We love music and books, as a family we love the home life, and these three things keep us

sane while making the rounds in search of employment."
The number of applications signed "not working at present" is a constant reminder of the silent part the library
plays in sustaining the mental life and spirit of those who
continue to turn to it for refreshment and courage to go
on. [1933]

These are among the matters ACM made public in her
reports. Behind the scenes battles were fought in the
cause of adequate salaries for the staff. Interdepartmental
skirmishes were frequent when fields of authority were
disputed between adult and children's departments in
branch libraries. Even within library walls the imperative
of excellence in books for children was sometimes under
attack because purchasing agents saw no reason why
cheap editions of standard titles could not be substituted
for costly books, if the text remained unchanged.

Anne was a fearless and a witty fighter. "Admitting to
no discouragement," she supported on every hand the
great humanistic design she had envisioned for children
in libraries. Consequently the staff, caught up in her exuberance, created and contrived ways of enticing children into an exuberance of reading.

Meanwhile the Lions Roared in Triumph!

• Twenty-two story clubs and reading circles are reported for older girls. Twelve of the number are organized
clubs conducted in the same manner as the boys' clubs. For
two years the girls of the Shakespeare Club read alternately
a Shakespearean play and a modern one. In this manner
they read *The Merchant of Venice* followed by *The Blue-
bird*; *As You Like It* followed by Percy Mackaye's *The
Scarecrow*; *The Taming of the Shrew* followed by *The
Piper*. They are now reading old English comedies beginning with *She Stoops to Conquer*. Pictures of the countries
in which the scenes of the play are laid and portraits of
the great actors and actresses who have played the leading

roles are used wherever obtainable. The growing appreciation and genuine enjoyment of dramatic literature are fine antidotes for vapid stories. [1912]

• The visit of Miss Marie Shedlock, the English storyteller, has been the event of greatest interest to the storytellers and children. Miss Shedlock first inspired the library story hour in America. On Hans Christian Andersen's birthday Miss Shedlock told his story, "The Steadfast Tin Soldier," and told something of his life to a group of children and their parents in the Central Children's Room. On Shakespeare's birthday she told "The Nightingale" to 270 delegates from the reading clubs assembled at the Central Building. This meeting took the form of a personal greeting from each club by a representative who carried back to the regular meeting of his or her club a full account of the joint meeting. [1915]

• Fortunately, the continuity of the story hour as an integral part of the work of the children's room is assured by the appointment of Mary Gould Davis to succeed Anna Cogswell Tyler. Miss Davis was one of the first of the children's librarians to make this effective connection between the story hour and the children's reading rooms. Her familiarity with all the conditions of work has given her a rare appreciation of the natural place of story-telling in enriching the reading tastes of boys and girls of different races, and a true understanding of what is involved in carrying on a story hour in almost bookless children's rooms. [1923]

• The outstanding event of the year, in which the children of the Extension Division, as well as the children of the Branch Libraries, participated, was the celebration of St. Nicholas Eve (December 5th) in the Central Children's Room. Few of the children had ever visited "the Fifth Avenue Library" before and merely walking up the steps was a great event. Once inside, it seemed the most natural place in the world to meet an English poet, whose birthday they had celebrated in their own libraries in April. No audience quite like it—quite so spontaneous and so varied in racial imagination—has ever assembled in the Library. As he read from "Crossings," his fairy play, and "Peacock

Pie," Walter de la Mare so identified himself with the children that he seemed at one with them, and each of them carried back to the children of the Branch Library from which he came the personal satisfaction of really knowing a living poet. [1924]

• The Fo'c's'le Club at the St. George Branch was inspired by a visit from Gordon Grant, and a loan exhibition of his pictures of ships. This club is keeping a log and imparting its enthusiasm for ships and sailors to a children's room which overlooks the harbor and the road out to sea. The introduction of marionettes at special story hours held at this branch is another enlivening influence of peculiar value in defining and sustaining the relationship of the Italian children living in the neighborhood, and has distinct possibilities in the further development of storytelling in other Staten Island communities.

The broadcasting of stories from Station WEAF was continued at stated intervals by different storytellers. There was an effective celebration of Hans Christian Andersen's birthday, and folk and hero tales of different countries were told. During August, the Supervisor of Work with Children gave a weekly talk on children's books, accompanied by reading from books mentioned. The response indicates that putting books "on the air" if the speaking voice meets the test has increasingly varied and interesting possibilities for libraries. There is, however, an art in the selection of material for transmission as well as the presentation of it. [1925]

• Holidays and anniversaries were generally observed with more than usual festivity.

On an evening in June the boys and girls of Hamilton Fish Park Branch held a colorful "Street Fair" on the roof of the library.

At the 115th Street Branch, Irving's *The Rose of the Alhambra* was presented as a puppet play and at Harlem Library story hours and plays in the Russian language were given.

At the Seward Park Branch, George MacDonald's story, "The Princess and the Goblin," was told with marked effect on the children's own reading.

Midsummer poetry hours at which the children read poems of their own selection were continued in the garden of the Woodstock Branch. On the anniversary of the opening of this branch a spirited dramatization of *Floating Island* was given in the children's room before a large audience of children.

The Poe Literary Club of the Melrose Branch had Percy Mackaye as a guest one evening in January and invited the members of the other library reading clubs to share a reading from his *Tall Tales of the Kentucky Mountains*. Mr. Mackaye proved his competence in handling boys as well as dialect. Asking to have most of the lights turned off, he put on his hat and sat down in a log cabin (figuratively), while the boys grouped close about him seemed to get the full flavor of the unaccustomed American speech along with the humor and drama of the stories.

The Eric Kelly Club of Polish boys was visited by Mr. Kelly, who gave a stirring talk about Poland accompanied by an exhibition of embroideries and objects of art. Parents and friends were invited to attend this opening meeting. [1931]

• At the opening of the annual holiday exhibition of children's books in November, Evelyn Scott, Reginald Birch, Louise Seaman and Bertha Mahony were guests of honor. Miss Scott's fine paper on *Writing for Children* was followed by brief speeches by Mr. Birch, whose black-and-white illustrations for the Gilbert and Sullivan operas were a feature of the exhibition, by Miss Mahony, and Louise Seaman, who paid tribute to the work of Helen Sewell, whose drawings for *A First Bible*, *Cinderella*, *Away Goes Sally*, and *Blue Bonnets for Lucinda* were represented in the exhibition.

The original manuscript for Lauren Ford's *A Little Book About God*, drawings by Ludwig Bemelmans for *Hansi*, by F. Luis Mora for *Tono Antonio*, and by Dorothy P. Lathrop for *The Lost Merry Go Round* were also included.

There has always been one basic belief back of the organization of school work in the Circulation Department, i.e., that the function of the public library in its relation to schools is not primarily to supplement the school curriculum, but to offer the schools an expert knowledge of the spontaneous reading interests of young people. During the past decade there has been a steadily increasing appreciation of this service.

The New York City schools have lately become reading-conscious because of extensive reading tests and surveys. Teachers were shocked to discover the low reading score and mediocre reading taste of many of their students. As a result, they are scrutinizing teaching methods and surveying community activities which influence reading such as the radio and the motion picture. Written book reports and credits for supplementary reading are shaking on their foundations. There is a definite drive for more books for young people in the school and public libraries. [1936]

• Early in the year the librarians in charge of children's rooms were authorized to spend one-half of the yearly appropriation for children's books immediately. Collapse of circulation was imminent at several points and staff, as well as the children, were disheartened by fruitless efforts to satisfy readers from bookless shelves.

Word spread like wildfire when the new books came, and children flocked to the branch libraries to reclaim their cards and renew their faith in the Library. Everywhere the book shelves were brightened and for a short time it became possible for boys and girls to find books they had long wanted to read. It was possible also for the librarians to reassert standards of cleanliness and care of books as city property. [1937]

• The year has been a challenging one both for older members of the staff who are able to contrast it with earlier years of unrestricted immigration and for the young college graduates fresh from psychology, sociology or history majors. The latter are seeing for the first time what a public library can mean to a stranger in a strange land and they are thrilled by its possibilities. Refugee children are frequently met at the boat by relatives or friends who have counted their library association as a major interest over a period of years.

No more heartening proof of the value of personalities

in libraries can be offered than the confidence of these self-appointed friends of the Library that a welcome is waiting in the children's rooms where they have been made to feel at home. "You can find a book in any language in the library." "Librarians can speak different languages." "You can learn English quick in a library." "You can listen to stories and look at pictures and sometimes see flowers growing there." "You can forget your troubles in a library." "You will find friends there."

These are a few of the many testimonies offered by those who have come to look upon the public library as belonging to them.

No wonder that for the first time since 1932 the circulation of books to children shows an upward curve, that there is storytelling in the play streets of the city and that significant festivals are celebrated on roof-tops on the lower East Side and in library gardens in The Bronx.

Poverty of book stock has been the cry from year to year. We must build up, restore, provide more generously in order to function. Yet suddenly we have tangible proof that we have functioned in terms of human need at a critical time. We still ask for more books, but no longer in the abstract. We need a great many books for our guests from Europe as well as for the children of New York. [1938]

There was a time when ACM considered resigning from the New York Public Library. She could not work in harmony with Benjamin Adams, the chief of the Circulation Division who followed Dr. Bostwick in that post in 1909. Two years after the opening of the Central Building, she wrote to Dr. Bostwick of her intent and had from him a letter so wise as to be universal in its application to professional affairs. It read in part as follows:

St. Louis. Apr. 4. 1913

Dear Miss Moore:

Your determination to resign, as expressed in your letter of March 30, takes me somewhat by surprise. I know you are not altogether satisfied with things, but I did not know that you had quite reached this point. You have told me nothing specific that seems to me to warrant it. If there has been nothing specific, I think you ought to see that there is some particular issue on which you can tender your resignation. I certainly shouldn't say, "If you don't let me do so-and-so I will resign"; but I should say specifically what I wanted to do and if refused I should resign, with the definite statement that this was the reason for resigning. All this could be done without rancor and leaving the best of feelings, I am sure.

Nobody will believe that you have resigned because you want time for lecturing and like the more independent life. Everyone will cast about for some specific reason and most will conclude that you resigned under some kind of pressure. You had better carry the war into Africa. . . .

That settled the matter. She carried the war "into Africa," with such good effect that several years later when Mr. Adams himself resigned, he wrote her a letter of gratitude, thanking her for her support and acknowledging that many of the reforms which he had brought about she had originated and brought to his attention. She put before him, in 1914, a plan for the reorganization of work with schools, recommending a position of supervisor of work with schools, to be maintained under the Division of Work with Children on the same level as the supervisor of storytelling and the supervisor of work with children in the Extension Division, then known as Traveling Libraries.

One of the most vital and successful libraries that had functioned as an independent institution, later joining the New York Public Library in its period of unification, was the Webster Library, serving an interesting locale made up mainly of Bohemian nationals. Under its librarian, Mr. Edward Gaillard, a vigorous program of

service to schools and teachers had been developed, con-
sisting of lending books to teachers and of setting up in
the library collections of special interest to them. When
in 1903 the library was absorbed in the New York Public
Library system, Mr. Gaillard became a member of the
Circulation Department, in charge of certain classroom
stations in schools and responsible for the selection of
books therein. This plan divided the authority of work
with children. ACM fought for a more logical organization.

> I would give the School Department what seems to be
> its logical place in the organization of the live work of the
> library, dividing it between the Children's Department
> and the Adult Department with the close cooperation be-
> tween the Children's Department and Adult Department
> relationship well-defined. It should be a definite division of
> the Children's Department and considered a regular fea-
> ture of its work constituting as it does a large part of the
> reference work of the Children's Room.

Here in this memorandum of 1914 she declares her
philosophy of work with schools.

> There is a great danger of turning a children's library
> into a school grade extra by the pushing of school work
> until library attendance ceases to be voluntary. On the day
> that everybody gets "sent" we lose the most valuable
> clause in our charter of liberty.

For Anne the words engraved on the heart's core, as
far as the children's libraries were concerned, were "individual, spontaneous and voluntary reading." Mabel
Williams, that sane and humorous woman whom ACM
met at a library convention in Massachusetts and plucked
out of a meeting for her own purposes, was responsible
for the clear evolution of the distinctive work with
schools which characterized the New York Public Li-

brary. It had begun as early as 1910 with the customary
class visits to the libraries, instruction in the use of in-
dexes, and the mysteries of the card catalogue. Under
Mabel Williams a declaration of independence from instruction as such within library walls became an actuality,
and from it emerged a proclamation of benefits that derived from exposure to books and spirited talk about them
by people who had read them and could excite interest
in others. Book talks as a distinct and separate genre, dif-
fering in purpose and invention from the accepted book
review in school, became the subjects of study, critical
appraisal, and analysis, recognized as arts in their own
right. In time the school authorities came to acknowledge that the class visit was an educational experience
larger in influence than reference work on a given assignment or adherence to the lesson plan for the day.

From Mabel Williams' vision, her eyes following
where ACM's had scanned the peaks, the distinctive work
with young people was to emerge with comparable space
and service in branch libraries for children in their
teens as was sustained on behalf of children in the elementary grades. And here also guns were fired in continuous salvos of salute honoring individual reading, spontaneously pursued: for knowledge—and pleasure; for
excitement—and pleasure; for information—and pleasure;
out of curiosity—and pleasure; for experience of life beyond one's own—and pleasure; for the triumph of art
over mediocrity—and pleasure.

All these running tides—work with schools, storytelling and reading clubs, the selection of books, the making
of exhibitions, celebrations, and routines—all these tides
washing the shores of children's lives in Manhattan, the
Bronx, and Staten Island flowed into one small sea at Fifth
Avenue and Forty-second Street, the office of Work with

Children, Room 105. If on judgment day an angel of the Lord thought it necessary, for some celestial reason, to bring together all souls, living and dead, who had known the influence of ACM, no blast of trumpets would be necessary. Let him but whisper "Room 105" and thousands would rise and assemble.

It was situated on a corridor of the south wing—a small room, with two great bronze-framed windows on the north wall, looking out on the court where the book trucks were loaded. A fountain had once graced that court, but traffic and cinders rendered it an anachronism, and its watery refreshment was abandoned. The windows opened inward, the degree of air admitted controlled by a great perforated bar and a bolt that supposedly fitted into the holes. The place knew only extremes of hot and cold in winter, and in summer the choice of methods lay between suffocation by heat or by soot and cinders. No plants would grow there. Countless pots of ivy and philodendron died as if by prearrangement, and ACM learned to discourage tributes of anything that was rooted and hopeful.

A table stood between the two windows, on it, leaning against the wall, a large, somber, dark-framed picture of children whose beautiful Slavic faces looked out in pensive, dreamlike trance. It was the original of an illustration that had appeared in *The Century Magazine*, designed to accompany a poem by Nora Archibald Smith, describing her emotions on watching streams of children coming from the story hour. The artist was W. T. Benda, noted in the world of theater and art as the creator of masks of extraordinary beauty. The telephone was on that table for the moment and such books as happened to be at the time foremost in the mind of Anne Carroll Moore. The office did not rate a second telephone until the year of her retirement in 1941. Every time the telephone summoned her it entailed a scramble from behind the entanglements of her desk, stationed at right angles to the westmost window and given a shadow of privacy by a heavy screen of leather with bright brass studding, a stumble around the chair where the interviewees sat, into the clear space before the table where ACM conducted her affairs in full view of people passing down the corridor and in full sound of an office staff adept at working at their separate tasks as if theirs was an ordinary office instead of the focal point of a disciplined, fascinating, and often joyous world in which one had to be prepared for "no end of surprises."

Bookshelves lined the east and west walls of the room. Rare editions of folk tales and certain basic reference books were comfortably available on the east, while on the western wall particular objects cherished by Anne were housed on shelves partially enclosed in glass: old children's books; the ceremonial doll of the Emperor of Japan and a crystal ball on its plinth, the gifts of Leonore Power, who lived in Japan; a sturdy wooden figure of a troll, from Marit Blehr's Norway, who at the flip of a finger could turn from troll to bear by means of an articulated head. Atop this bookcase stood a very beautiful wooden toy, a gull on wheels. When the wheels were rolled the wings of the gull moved in a verisimilitude of flight. This had been a gift from the children in Utah and was the creation of the art teacher at Logan. Anne cherished it for its unique beauty, as a gift from children, and as a reminder of the legend told among Mormons. In the first years of their settlement in Utah there came a time when their crops were all but destroyed by a plague of grasshoppers, blackening the sun. Suddenly a great flight of gulls winged in from the sea and devoured the pests. For this reason the gull is revered in Utah.

The new books pouring into Room 105 were shelved on the west wall, where they awaited the notice of ACM and assignment by her to members of the staff for review and appraisal. In the space to the left of those shelves stood a card catalogue filled with the rich accumulation of judgments, acceptances, and refusals of thirty-five years' study of books for children. Each review as it came in was read by ACM and either allowed to stand or given the imprint of a dissident opinion. On the other side of the door was a small cabinet for the coat and hat of one person and beyond that the great files that had accumulated in a golden richness through the years. A cluster of small desks like so many ducklings in a crowded nest stood in front of the east wall, and here was "the office" of the Supervisor of Storytelling, "the office" of the first assistant, a junior assistant, and "the office" of the Supervisor of Work with Schools until 1924, when Miss Williams moved to the luxury of an office of her own at the Fifty-eighth Street Branch of the library.

Into that room came trooping on a monthly schedule the children's librarians, each from her respective library. For them it was a time of private conference and discussion with ACM. Then off to the stacks of the library where the new books with typed reviews clipped to their covers awaited perusal and the verdict of acceptance or rejection by these librarians, each responsible to her own book budget and to the environment in which she functioned. ACM was proud of this staff that knew and respected the heritage of neighborhoods they served, addressing their book collections and their activities to the deep and holy origins of race and creed, and enlivening, at the same time, their participation in the contemporary scene.

The influence of Room 105 was to reach out literally across the world in the time of ACM. But the wider field of action never precluded her knowing at any given time the pace of life, the state of the book collection, the titles that were being discarded, the titles purchased, in the furthermost branch library or substation of the Extension Division. She knew at first hand, indefatigable as she was in her visits. She gathered news from her assistants in the office who went "on the road" in pursuit of their duties. She learned from the informal reports, from a hundred subtle clues she never quite defined, as well as from the splendid organization in the office covering these matters. She sensed where the dead spots were and was not above dramatizing their existence. One hapless librarian, returning from her lunch hour, found ACM, hatted and impressively suited, alone in the branch children's room pulling off the shelves books she deemed outmoded and slamming them down on the floor.

Any efficiency engineer studying the flow of traffic in Room 105 would have suffered a nervous breakdown. Small wonder that ACM found it necessary to remain there long after five o'clock to have the place to herself. She read then, to her heart's content, often far into the night, for dinner was a movable feast for her, to be picked up at the Oyster Bar at Grand Central on the way home or at some other restaurant where crowds of theatergoers were refreshing themselves after the performances. There were no regulations, in those days, governing permission to stay late at work, and Mr. O'Brien, the guard at the Fortieth Street entrance, was accustomed to seeing ACM, like a tired ghost, emerge from the doors of the library at odd hours of the night, as was the night watchman on his rounds with his police dogs.

The Central Children's Room did not shut its doors

on the daily public until six o'clock in the evening. If, between five and six, Anne came across some book she ached to share, she would call the Children's Room and summon certain members of the staff to "come up for a minute." In the excitement of discovery, Anne never considered whether the librarian had a dinner appointment or whether some hapless suitor, waiting inconspicuously in a window seat for the closing hour, was doomed to be abandoned without notice. It took more courage than most could muster to mention these facts to Anne in the face of her exhilaration. Each such encounter in the silence of Room 105 was considered to be worth any sacrifice and not one in a hundred would have escaped it. When Anne so much as turned the pages of a book, laying a finger on a chosen spot, it seemed a gesture of immense import. "Nothing like it has happened before," she might say. "Listen." Then she would read "Do you want a ticket to go away and come back or do you want a ticket to go away and never come back?" In this wise the moment, the voice, and Sandburg's *Rootabaga Stories* became forever fixed in one's recollection of events pleasurable and significant. She had the gift of illumination. The commonplace as well as the profound took on grace and sparkle in her companionship, and the quips and comments that she made clung to the memory. "What do you do with oddments of butter, Marie?" she asked the hostess whom she was helping to clear the table. Forever after the term rings in the mind whenever the problem confronts one. "Oddments of butter!" A certain group of intimates waited, one evening, on dinner for the arrival of the beautiful May Massee, that genius of an editor who, to compensate for her enormous endowments, had to sustain a tendency to be late to appointments. Anne sat there twirling between her fingers a

small carnation she had gotten hold of or brought with
her. When May at last came in the door, Anne reached
up and handed her the flower. "A pink for punctuality,"
she said. A children's editor of a most affluent publishing
house sent out invitations for a gala publisher's party.
When the affair came off, it was dismal. On every hand
there were signs of an impoverished economy. It was
apparent that the children's department was a deprived
area as far as the publisher was concerned. The slight of
unnecessary austerity chilled the bones of all guests, and
the program only compounded their misery. On the way
home someone said, "It was exactly like a Sunday-school
social." "That's to be expected," said Anne, "whenever
anything is announced as 'a gala.'"

Instigator of many a fete and celebration, Anne
scorned organized and contrived mirth. The programs
she furthered in the library seemed to rise in the headwaters of spontaneity though they occurred on schedule.
The annual celebration of certain birthdays—those of
Kate Greenaway, Randolph Caldecott, H. C. Andersen,
Walter de la Mare, L. Leslie Brooke, Marie Shedlock—
gave each librarian an opportunity to frame in space and
time the books and pictures of those designated fete-
worthy, endowed certain writers and artists with new
life in the contemporary world, and created for the children an authentic sense of happening, a cause for joy.
Children rise to expectancy like fish to worm, and the
simplest gesture of preparation is bait enough to lure and
hold them. They are as wise as that citizen of Santa Fe,
New Mexico, who when plagued by the recurring question of a tourist, "When does the fiesta begin?" at last
answered her, "What does it matter, Madam? The fiesta
is in the heart."

Even before the existence of the lions, ACM conceived

the plan of celebrating Christmas in such manner as to involve children of all creeds. "Everybody's Christmas," she termed it. Room 105 sent to each branch children's room a packet of books, made up of ten or twelve chosen titles, mostly from the output of the year. Each book was wrapped as a Christmas package, to be opened on Christmas Eve in the presence of the children. Often the children took a hand in the unwrapping, turn by turn. Nothing equals the pleasure of opening a package, even if one is involved in the task only vicariously, even though the contents of the package is certain to be a book! But what book? Time for guessing what the book might say, for exchange of opinions, for confessions of enjoyment of books similar in nature, for questions and comments— time for talk—was allotted for these important matters. The books were there in the reading rooms to be used during all the twelve days of Christmas. Like all drama begotten of feeling and artfully staged, there was no evidence of studied preparation. The Christmas packages were, to the children, a comforting event in a place where there were books and something was always happening.

One day in the fall of 1918 a newly appointed co-editor of *Publishers' Weekly* came through the door of Room 105, bringing with him a handsome, white-haired man, Franklin K. Mathiews of the Boy Scouts of America. The editor was Frederic Melcher, New Englander, who as a bookseller in Indianapolis had endeared himself to a great segment of the Midwest. He knew books. The Hoosiers loved him for that and for his lack of Bostonian superiority. He was also the secretary of the American Booksellers' Association, and it was in that capacity that Mr. Mathiews had sought his aid. As an officer of the Boy Scouts of America, Mr. Mathiews had been horrified at the kinds of books the boys were reading. What could be done about it? He could hardly have found a more sympathetic conspirator than this New Englander. When Frederic Melcher was born into this world, he must have entered reading. He was a genuine lover of books, with such vivid memories of his own boyhood reading as to make him especially susceptible to the plight of those children who were never to know the pleasure of books of genuine spirit. Mr. Melcher thought something could be accomplished by a sustained campaign, nationwide in scope, with a Children's Book Week to be celebrated in schools, libraries, and bookshops across the country. He envisioned, too, a plan to encourage authors of children's books and to entice others into the field. After preliminary talks they had come to Room 105, a location that had gained some repute as a hatching ground. The Three M's—Moore, Mathiews, Melcher! Three musketeers who were troubadours as well and made things hum. Theirs is an oft-told tale, one to be cherished by book people as a living tradition. Children's Book Week gave way to Book Week, fixing on the calendars of the years an opportunity for declaring a celebration in praise of books and reading. The Caldecott and Newbery medals which Frederic Melcher gave to the American Library Association to be awarded annually were the prototypes for the plethora of awards that followed.

The first celebration of Children's Book Week in the New York Public Library was held in the Central Children's Room in 1919, with Kate Douglas Wiggin the speaker of the day. ACM, for this reason, found pleasure in describing Kate Douglas Wiggin as the godmother of Book Week and Frederic Melcher as godfather.

When the war came, the First World War, Anne welcomed America's entry into the arena, thinking of

England and all that country held for her. She could not but rejoice in the panoply and panache in which the city was bedecked. New York never looked more beautiful from Washington Square to Central Park. The splendid buildings gleamed in marble and Indiana limestone, the chocolate architecture of the nineties all but gone, with remnants of great private mansions standing solidly among the stone façades of skyscrapers that towered toward the stars. The clocklike symmetry of glass and steel had not yet been announced. Flagpoles lined both sides of Fifth Avenue with flags of the nations dancing and shimmering in a clean wind. The city seemed eternally *en fête*, and midway up the avenue the old Tyrolean building of Max Schling, the florist, spilled flowers from window boxes in great profusion.

Children in libraries asked for books on aviation of which there were none. A list of adult books on the war was gotten together recommending titles to be purchased for the children's rooms. Maps and geographies were in great demand as children sought to know where their brothers and fathers were "dug in." Anne met the time as she had met the lesser tragedy of the Spanish-American War, by stressing the ideals of sacrifice and courage. Mabel Williams, with the help of the office staff, created a reading list on the topic of heroism that stands for all time a distinguished accomplishment among library publications. A club of Jewish boys at Hamilton Fish Park Library named their club "The Hero Club" and took as their pledge the final quotation from the heroism list. "I am a citizen of America and heir to all her greatness and renown."

As for the library lions, they were never again to see such sights—parades day after day, with Woodrow Wilson, the President of the United States, in tails and a top hat, marching at the head of one of them. Bands played on the esplanade; opera singers performed at the tops of their lungs; stars of the theater hawked war bonds hour after hour; ambulances, wooden ships, airplanes were on display; soldiers, sailors, and marines in splendid drill formation; and the immortal Mary Pickford, Charlie Chaplin, and Douglas Fairbanks appeared as a trio. Heroes of all nations, wearing their medals, shouted for victory, the only amplifier being a megaphone. It was as though there were a three-ring circus in the space between the lions, the gaiety gone awry, like an episode experienced in a nightmare.

The rotunda of the library served as a fitting background for special ceremonies. Cardinal Mercier trailed his crimson robes down the steps of the foyer. The French Society of New York borrowed the library to tender a reception for Marshal Joffre and M. Viviani. That day was memorialized in the library unofficially by another event: a child was born on that day in the library, the daughter of Mr. Fedler, the building's maintenance engineer, who lived with his family in the apartment allotted him, a perquisite of his position. They named her Viviani Joffre.

When the war ended, how quickly hope and exhilaration trod upon its heels! All the fiddles began to play! There would certainly never be another war! A renaissance of the arts surged through the country—in the theater, in the writing of novels, in pert and gallant little magazines sprung like crocuses heralding the spring.

Children were involved. Within the next few years, the publishing of their books became the concern of major publishing houses. Louise Seaman at Macmillan, May Massee at Doubleday, Alice Dalgliesh at Scribner's —these three young women were pioneers as heads of departments, the sole concern of which was responsible publishing of books for children.

George H. Doran, publisher, feeling the time propitious, announced in early 1918 the publication of a new literary monthly, *The Bookman*, with Eugene Saxton[1] as one of its editors, to be followed by young, red-headed John Farrar, whose literary bent came via the New York Public Library, his mother having been a staunch and gracious librarian in the Extension Division for a considerable period of time. It was Eugene Saxton who sought out ACM, asking her to assume responsibility for the space in the forthcoming magazine allotted to books for children.

The years of ACM's contribution to *The Bookman* are generally designated as the era that inaugurated in America the reviewing of books for children on a sustained and continuous basis. There has been some hairsplitting among the Ph.D.s as to the validity of the assumption that no reviews of books for children preceded hers. As if it mattered. The truth of the matter is that these essays collected in *My Roads to Childhood* far outreach the term "review." Every critic worth his salt is read not alone for his appraisal of titles, or his critical analysis of a writer's work, but for his account of the tilt of the world as he feels it, the temper of his experience in relation to the common fate of man, revealed in art and literature. *My Roads to Childhood* remains no mere collection of reviews of books, many of which are out of print. Its pages are informed with passion, spirit, and intellectual force, based on a breadth of experience of life and a perceptive reading on many subjects, transcending boundaries of narrow specialization. The portrait of a great personality is here revealed as well as a philosophy of criticism.

The Bookman was sustained from 1918 until 1924, its bright blue cover, its double column of clear print reflecting much of the excitement of the period. "It was courageous of Eugene Saxton to pick me," Anne wrote to Bertha Mahony Miller in retrospect, "for I was no longer young but already middle-aged."

A letter from him in 1922, when he had left *The Bookman* for Harper and Brothers, reflects his pride in that choice:

> I am glad you remember that we started the children's reviews and essays. As I tell J.[ohn] F.[arrar] I grow jealous every now and then when someone points to the great editor apropos of some feature that antedated his coming. I'm not jealous. I couldn't possibly have done what he has accomplished with the magazine and no one knows that better than myself.

When the revised edition of *My Roads* appeared in 1939, ACM sent Mr. Saxton a copy at Christmas time and had from him gracious acknowledgment:

> Dear Miss Moore
> It was very nice of you to remember me in your distribution of Christmas copies of the new edition of *My Roads*. The memories of the very beginnings of those papers go back to the old days when you made your first appearance in *The Bookman* and that seems a long time ago. One of the nicest things about the length of the period is the fact that the book is vital and attractive today. That is sufficiently a rarity in publishing experience to make it noteworthy. I am sure many thousands of young readers have found a new and delightful road into your enchanting country through the pages of this book.

At the time of Anne's retirement, he wrote in part:

> I am glad to know you are to have more time for writing. The personal record will cover a period of New York

literary history when more has been done for the reading of the younger generation—and largely by you—than at any other time. . . .

On July 2, 1943, Anne wrote to Bertha Mahony Miller:

Dear Bertha:

Eugene Saxton's death was such a shock to me I could not pull the Three Owls piece together until yesterday. While we did not often meet in his Harper years I always felt I could rely on his friendship and his sound editorial judgment. There was always a lovely card from him at Christmas time. It did me good to hear Mr. Huebsch say, as we came out from the service at The Little Church Around the Corner, "I feel that half my life has gone." We were all back in 1918 that morning. Stanley and Ted Rinehart asked to take me wherever I wanted to go which was behind the library lions. Later I bought a copy of *Western Star* [by Stephen Vincent Benét] [2] at Scribners and gave the rest of the day to it—a living book—and as I wrote John Farrar, his only consolation for the loss of so dear a friend was the privilege of publishing it.

More than once in her lifetime she was to forge from grief and the ache of remembrance a ritual of reading and to seek solace behind the library lions.

A FLIGHT OF OWLS

For next to the pure joy of creating a thing one's self is the discovery of something created by another. The instant recognition and detachment of a piece of original work from a mass of ready-made writing and the presentation of one's findings and conviction constitute the reviewer's main chance. His function is to declare the book's quality and give it a place in association with other books. To the degree that the review stimulates the desire of the reader to read the book to confirm or to differ with the critic will it be contributory to thought, discussion, criticism, fresh creative work. And this, as I see it, is the true objective for the reviewer of children's books no less than for the reviewer in the general field.

For many more years than any of us like to recall children's books, if read at all when written about, were read for ulterior ends. They were considered en masse rather than individually, both in the educational field and in the publishing field. They were tagged for moralistic trends, for a physical age limit, for collateral reading, for anything and everything save appraisal of them as books in relation to books in general.

ACM

ITH THE APPEARANCE of *The Bookman* essays, in the magazine and as separate volumes, such an oncoming tide of people rafted into Room 105 as to create an outward flow of shaping waters that edged on beaches far beyond the margins of the library. Editors, artists, and publishers and their kind might well be expected to find their way into Room 105, but many others came to check all points of the compass with ACM: trustees of libraries in search of librarians attune to children and their books; architects asking for aid in planning children's rooms at the drafting-board level; representatives of foreign governments seeking advice in the selection of books in the English language to serve as interpreters of American life.

One Dutch "navigator"-historian, Hendrik Willem van Loon, came first in gratitude because he found his *Short History of Discovery* acclaimed in *The Bookman* when other reviews and the bookshops themselves gave it little room because it looked strange. His *Story of Mankind* he brought to Room 105 and to the Central Children's Room literally chapter by chapter, as he wrote it, the manuscript, rolled like wallpaper, bulging the pockets of his ample overcoat. In the dedication of *The Songs We Sing*, music arranged by Grace Castagnetta, he crowned his regard for ACM:

This book is dedicated
to
Annie Carroll Moore

in cheerful recognition
of all the many miracles
she has performed
within the delightful realm of
the world of books
where the readers sit in little
chairs
and rest their elbows on diminutive tables
when following the adventures of Ferdinand.
For if that room is now filled
with much more sunshine, gaiety,
beauty and common sense
than ever before,
it is mainly through the efforts of
Annie Carroll Moore
who opened wide the windows
and said
"A little less stuffiness right here
would surely do none of us
any harm."

James Daugherty, muralist turned illustrator and author, in a confrontation with ACM confessed to a love for Washington Irving and a desire to give the Knickerbockers pictorial reality. The result was a splendid collaboration between two Irving buffs, *The Bold Dragoon and Other Ghostly Tales* and *Knickerbocker's History of New York*, appearing in editions edited by ACM and illustrated in full spirit by James Daugherty.

Ann Morgan, the instigator of the Women's Committee for Devastated France after the First World War, leaned on Miss Moore for aid and thirstily absorbed her philosophy of librarianship, and the young clergyman, John Brett Langstaff, who during a period in England conceived the idea of transforming a shabby building where Charles Dickens had once lived into the David Copperfield Library for the tattered children of the Borough of St. Pancras, asked Miss Moore to serve on his board of counselors. When the day of presentation came, on November 1, 1922, Anne was present, in the mansion house of the Lord Mayor, among the gathering of notables: the Burgomaster of Leyden, bringing with him a gift of Dutch children's books as a tribute to Dickens; the French Ambassador with a gift from his country; John Galsworthy as speaker of the day; and that girl from Limerick, Maine, Anne Carroll Moore. As was the habit with Anne, she saw and heard the proceedings with eye for pomp and decor. In a letter to her great-niece Margaret Warren, Rachel's child, she gave account of it:

> I've written Mother about speaking at the Mansion House which is the official residence of the Lord Mayor. I had to say, just as Mr. Galsworthy did, "My Lord Mayor, My Lady Mayoress, etc." Wasn't it fortunate there was a gold collar on my black satin dress since the Lord Mayor wore his great jewel and the Burgomaster of Leyden his silver chain and the Mayor of St. Pancras a big gold chain? I was the only lady who spoke and I expected to feel scared to death standing up in the Egyptian Room of the Mansion House but it was really quite nice, for everyone was interested in David Copperfield's Library— and that was what it was all about.

When Mrs. Robert Bacon of Westbury, Long Island, fixed on the idea of a children's library as the perfect memorial to her husband, Robert Bacon, formerly this country's Ambassador to France, her footsteps and those of the architect led to 105. ACM promised Mrs. Bacon that she would hold that library under concern as though it were in truth a branch of the New York Public Library. The initial collection of books was a duplicate of one chosen by the children's department of the New York Public Library for English-speaking children of

Rio de Janeiro at the request of Edwin Morgan, Ambassador to Brazil. To this nucleus Mrs. Bacon added many rare illustrated books in the French language as well as in English. "It is, as far as I know, the best and most varied selection of books yet made for a children's library," ACM was to write of it. "Not merely a gift to children of Westbury but a unique contribution to the educational institutions of the whole country." Once again ACM relinquished one of the staunchest and most gifted of librarians, Jacqueline Overton, to head up the library at Westbury.

For two consecutive years—1921 and 1922—the outgoing tides of influence swept Anne to the shores of England and France. There she acquired such wealth of friendships and experience as to refresh her for a lifetime. Of the visit to devastated France, in 1921, Nicholas has made excellent account in the book *Nicholas and the Golden Goose*. In 1922 Anne returned to France to hear her cherished friend, Marie Shedlock, tell stories to the French children in the libraries established by the American committee. Such an event had been conceived in a private dream of ACM and was brought to fulfillment by her persuasive powers. She was a gifted dreamer, brilliant in the practical execution and funding of her dreams.

Only by indirection and in certain letters to her family is there the smallest hint of the depths of feeling Anne must have known when she saw the children in war-torn villages of France enjoying libraries staffed by young women she had trained whose vision derived from her own. The skills with which they adapted the tenets of library work with children to the French psyche and the French need were her skills and hers was the great design formed out of the clay of Pratt and the multiracial city of New York. It is well that she had invented Nicholas to stand as emissary between her and the world, to serve as a voice by means of which she could control the expression of her private ecstasy and her inner pride.

When she went to England from France in 1921 she took with her splendid photographs of the libraries and the children in them. It was of these matters she spoke immediately to the editors and publishers who welcomed her as the major critic of children's books in America without peer in England. Nicholas and his French companions were given space in the London *Times* right beside the court calendar as "most newsworthy story of the day." "How on earth did he get into the *Times?*" asked the astounded Walter de la Mare, in a letter of October 1921.

Three enduring friendships grew and flowered out of that first visit Anne made to England in the role of writer and critic rather than as librarian. The cast of characters was L. Leslie Brooke, Beatrix Potter, and Walter de la Mare. Marie Shedlock introduced her to L. Leslie Brooke, whose pictures of famous trios are definitive, "The Three Bears" and "The Three Little Pigs," and whose "Johnny Crow" with his garden and his garden parties is probably destined to endure as long as laughter itself. In a long letter to Rachel, her niece, written from Grasmere, on June 23, 1921, Anne recalls the first two encounters and announces the possibility of a third:

> I had an enchanting afternoon with a family tea round the dining room table at Leslie Brooke's, Miss Shedlock and Miss Glover, who is an old friend of the Brookes, meeting me there. Mr. B. is quite deaf but adorable and his wife, a daughter of Stafford Brooke, one of the most gracious hostesses I have ever met. You would have loved both the home and the studio, everything was so *real*. Mr.

Brooke and I literally fell into one another's arms and he
wants to give me for myself one of his originals. They
were immensely pleased with Nicholas, who sat on the
easel in the studio. Their eldest son was missing and finally
reported lost in the War and one sees the tragedy in their
eyes but in no other way.

Last Sunday afternoon I had tea and late supper at
Walter de la Mare's. His daughter, "Jinny," a girl of
seventeen, met me at Crystal Palace Station and after looking me over and proposing a taxi, finally consented to take
me on the top of a tram. We found rather an interesting
actor singing verses from *Peacock Pie* which has been set
to music by another guest of the afternoon—a very good
voice— Mrs. de la Mare had been called to Oxford by the
illness of the eldest son, and a daughter just past twenty
received me with her father who is very good-looking and
likeable. There is a boy of fifteen—a very lovely family
altogether. . . .

As for Beatrix Potter, she was reportedly a hard nut to
crack, and Mr. Warne, when he delivered to Anne his
letter of introduction, hastened to say, "I can only wish
you luck." Now it happened that at this time *The Tale
of Peter Rabbit* and *The Tale of Benjamin Bunny* were
rolling from the presses in French translation, *Pierre
Lapin* and *Jeannot Lapin*. Anne bought fifty copies of
each and sent them to the children of the library at Soissons. Having mentioned this fact when she posted from
Grasmere her letter of introduction to Beatrix Potter,
and having promised to show her pictures of the French
children and their grandmothers, Anne was immediately
invited to luncheon at Castle Cottage in Sawrey, near
Ambleside, and given full instructions as to the best route
of traveling. ACM tells the story of that visit twice over,
one in *Nicholas: A Manhattan Christmas Story* and secondly in a remarkable book to which she was to contribute an appreciation some thirty years later. It shall

not be spoiled by telling it here. The fact remains that the two indomitable characters recognized in each other like traits of determination, discernment, and forthright expression of opinion, and their friendship and devotion to each other held until the end of Beatrix Potter's life in 1945. Anne not only had luncheon but stayed for tea and dinner and all night, visiting Hill Top Farm, the first of Beatrix Potter's holdings in the region and the scene of many of her books. Such a state of affairs was characteristic of Anne. She was often an instantaneous visitor, repeatedly coming to a sudden decision to stay when she had previously declared a visit impossible. The aura of a house determined the shift in the winds of her decision. If a pine tree grew in certain proportion to the window through which one saw it, or if the room invited a session at the writing desk, she grew content and happy and announced, "I think I'll stay for a while." She was a visitor easily pleased once she had come to stay. The only inconvenience she could not tolerate was a Murphy bed, that hidden peril that springs from the walls at the touch of a button.

Of the three rare spirits, L. Leslie Brooke was the most merry and most puckish, yet his critical judgments were bold and original. The first letter from Leslie Brooke was written from The Four Winds, Elmhurst, Surrey, on August 4, 1921. After reference to the fact that Anne had chosen for herself one of his original drawings at Warne's, the publisher, the letter continues:

> Did Nicholas become a Wordsworthian at Grasmere? He would have kicked, at first, at the absence of childish fun. While such things as
> "And three times to the boy, I said
> 'Why? William, tell me why?' "
> would have offended all the cries of child study. But per-

haps if he approached him in the spirit of Lamb's Daddy Wordsworth they may have come to terms.

I do not know at all when you return to America, we hope you will not forget us altogether. Johnny Crow must give you a caw of reminder now and then. (Quite so—as you say—caws and effect) With our very kind remembrances, yours sincerely, L. Leslie Brooke.

In 1927 Leslie Brooke writes to her from Oxford:

And I join with you in your admiration of de la Mare as poet and editor. Though if the Atlantic were not between us I should be prepared—greatly daring—to maintain the position that the introductory story of this book[1] is in the wrong key. I have no doubt that it is sound allegory for those who can read allegory—and I am quite sure that it is most characteristic of one of the chief and most charming qualities in its author—a sense of mental remoteness and atmosphere charged with strangeness. But it seems to me that it is just this conscious and abnormal atmosphere that is the wrong approach to so catholic a collection of English verse—the boy is a self-conscious little boy and the original collector was a self-conscious and consequently lonely man and neither of them embodied the essential spirit of the main English character. It's like putting a Rossetti frame on Millais' "Boyhood of Raleigh."

Anne wrote him apparently asking for an expression of opinion as to the elements that make for greatness in a picture book. In a letter of September 2, 1928, he quotes W. H. Hunt as saying, "Draw firm and be jolly," and he reports himself as looking forward to receiving *Millions of Cats* because "I do not find that cats come easily myself." The letter continues:

You know as well as I do what elements are essential to picture books which are to have a perennial interest. . . . I am not going to be beguiled into platitudes. But to see how instinctive the inspiration of the very best type of picture book is, it is worth looking at the first draft by

Caldecott of his *House That Jack Built*. Warne published it some years ago, but it is little known. It is just a series of scribbles but implicit in each scrawl can clearly be found the very dog, cat, rat, etc., that has become classic. Of course Caldecott is an extreme instance of instinctive drawing and though I have seen a sheet covered with "tries" after a special effect of expression in a face—I do not think he had the patient building up that so many have to do before they achieve the appearance of facility. I imagine his plan was rather to tear it up and begin again.

In 1929 Anne had sent him a copy of *Knickerbocker's History of New York* inscribed by both herself and James Daugherty. His hearty response to James Daugherty's illustrations reflects his own spirits and exuberance:

He has got into the contemporary skin of his author in a wonderful way or adapts himself to the same taste in humor and draws all with a line and with a sense of style that are distinctly not essentially of today. I don't know how long it is since I have found such fullblooded gusto. . . . I am especially struck how the work gathers weight as it goes on. I don't see how more force and tension could be put into drawings. [He then cites the pages.] His line looks as though it had come boiling onto the paper—and that is enough for any man's good name.

Rachel Field's *Hitty*, illustrated by Dorothy Lathrop, he dubbed "The Hittiad," and in a letter from Hurstcote, Cumnar, Oxford, January 15, 1930, he gives a fascinating glimpse of how one artist reads the concept of another:

As to the illustrations, there is first of all the craftiness in the choice of them. They are all most carefully confined to Hitty's immediate world, and in that way give a decorative unity to the book which would have been lost had the artist allowed herself to be led aside even once into the human element of the stories and introduced a new standard of proportion and measurement and life. I should never have had her courage and should have come a most prodigious cropper.

Beatrix Potter's letters from 1921 until 1945 are rich documents of her life as Mrs. Heelis, sheepherder, deep in content with her house and the countryside she loved as a child, her farmer-lawyer husband, and her privacy. But there was the agony of the Second World War soon to come. In a letter of 1938 she wrote:

> To think that in one's old age one must hear the sound again. . . . It's different to the last war—seems less to do individually, partly, of course, because we have grown old. This is a war of young people in uniform—and more and more a war of mechanics and chemistry. Last war we were drying foxglove leaves for the druggist; now no demand; so much is synthetic in production. . . . It was a lovely green April, plenty of grass for the sheep, and a good lambing time in spite of the privations of frost and snow. A spring of flowers. The hawthorne hedges on the big thorn bushes of the fell side have been like drifts and patches of snow and the bluebells a sheet of blue. It is unbelievable that such a lovely peaceful land should be in shadow. . . .

Her responses to Anne's own books are no polite acknowledgments but documented evidence of her pleasure in them. The gift of *Nicholas: A Manhattan Christmas Story* was acknowledged in this wise:

January, 1925

Castle Cottage
Sawrey
Ambleside

Dear Ann Caraway and Nicholas,
    What a delightful book you have made! It was a great surprise when I opened the parcel. I am sure American children will love it and ask for *more*. Do let us hear about Nicholas in France. Ann Caraway need not fear the task;

she can write a book that has wisdom, pathos and fun. Tears and laughter.

My favorite parts are about the Knickerbockers, and General Washington; and I think it is wonderful how cleverly Ann Caraway has worked in two real live—very gentlemanly—young fellows as companions to Nicholas. "Ben" being a small boy is easier.

I had no idea that New York is so "Christmasy"—a real old-fashioned Christmas.

We have had a wet one here, wild, windy and much floods; and influenza in the village; but so far my husband and I have escaped it.

I have no book to send in return; there should have been a painting book for children to colour, but the engravers made a muddle of it.

With congratulations and very kind regards,

yrs. sincerely,
Beatrix Heelis

In December of that same year she sent her Christmas greeting via the Bookshop for Boys and Girls in Boston. The letter with its almost Biblical concern for the sheep is so full of her snap and ginger, one cannot resist quoting it:

December 12, '25

Sawrey
nr. Ambleside

Dear Miss Carroll Moore,
I do not know the home address of Nicholas: Peter and Flopsy want to wish him a very Merry Christmas and they hope that the Bookshop will be so kind as to pass the message on. We will read his book again on Christmas Eve and think of his merry doings across the Atlantic.

Here—there has already been some old-fashioned weather, 4 weeks hard frost, with skating & hard snow. But it thawed suddenly last Monday, and although the frost had been enjoyable & lovely to look at—I was not sorry to see green grass again. I wonder how the sheep live in countries like U.S.A. and Canada? Ours scrape and dig with feet & heads to get at the rough grass on the hillsides; but frozen snow soon means anxiety to the shepherd and hunger for the sheep. They are next now to eat hay; and there are too many to feed, many hundred in a flock.

There have been two letters recently from Miss Bertha Mahony of the Boston Bookshop, forwarded through Messrs. Warne, and also copies of the "Horn Book." The letter which asks for particulars about "Beatrix Potter" is very perplexing. I have a most intense dislike to advertisement (and I have got on quite well enough without it). And I object to being supposed to be the wife of Sidney Webb, a member of the last socialist government. He married a Miss Beatrice Potter, no relation. There were photographs of him in the newspaper, and it said his wife had written children's books. There has often been confusion between us. I thought it would be best to write this for Mr. Warne, to forward through the New York branch of F. W. Co., to whom Miss Mahony had applied. "Beatrix Potter is Mrs. William Heelis, she lives in the north of England, her home is amongst the mountains & lakes that she has drawn in her picture books. Her husband is a lawyer. They have no family. Mrs. Heelis is in her 60th year. She leads a very busy contented life, living always in the country and managing a large sheep farm on her own land."

I don't think anybody requires to know more about me. In the second letter Miss Mahony asks how I came to write the books. I used to write picture letters to a little invalid boy years and years ago, the eldest child of a friend. Peter was written to him in a letter. He is now a hardworked clergyman in a London parish and I believe he has the letter yet. About 1900 there began to be a fashion for little picture books, and I thought Peter might be worthwhile publishing. But I could not find anyone else who thought so. It was refused by many publishers, and I got a small number printed for myself, with pen & ink illustrations like the scribbles on the original letter. That is the history of Peter Rabbit. I have never been able to understand what is the attraction of the book, but it continues to sell.

The Horn Book is pleasantly written. I wish all such books of gossip—British as well as American—were in equally good taste.

But I *don't* want to be exploited! And I am very grateful to Nicholas for his reticence. . . . Has Nicholas been abroad again?

With kind regards from us both,

yrs. sincerely,
Beatrix Heelis

Throughout the years of their friendship, Anne sent visitors to Sawrey and always they were received with utmost cordiality. "We had a call from Mary Haugh and her husband a week ago," she wrote in 1937 of Mary Haugh Zipprich, one of the best storytellers on the staff of the New York Public Library, with an Irish edge to her tongue and a look of beauty on her face. Beatrix talked to her about storytelling. "I was trying to ask her," Mrs. Heelis wrote, "whether the art of live speech, that speaking storytelling is not the real thing? I expect P[eter] R[abbit] comes nearer to word storytelling than the later books which she probably has to cut and put in her own words." All this was preamble to a lively account in the same letter:

Mrs. Fausler of the New York Metropolitan Museum has been to Messrs. Warne's office, wanting to borrow the Peter Rabbit originals—they are willing to lend them and I have no objection. I don't think the P. R. drawings "represent a very high watermark in the history of book illustration," to quote Mrs. Fausler!! In fact I think them bad, the rabbit on the cover I have always thought a horrid monstrosity—all out of drawing—but undoubtedly it was that first book—P. R. "which hit a mark" of some sort. The much better-executed illustrations of following books of the series did not make the same hit. . . .

The letter returns to the topic of Mary Haugh:

I was very interested to hear her praise *Sister Ann* [a sly remark on B. P.'s part, this, ACM having told her only a month previously that she thought *Sister Ann* not worthy of publication as a book].

I did so much enjoy your visit. You are over my head intellectually, but you appreciate old-fashioned simple memories and pleasures. I am glad you and Nicholas had a pleasant passage back to New York. My love to you both,

Beatrix Heelis

No small part of the inheritance Anne bequeathed the generations was her record of friendships. She had a genius for the gift. The devotion of these three innovators in poetry and art to ACM and her work attuned children on both sides of the Atlantic to an appreciation of those who served them with the highest art in drama and rhyme, poetry and picture. Anne alerted the American public to the distinctive genius of each of these three, beginning at Pratt in 1903, when Beatrix Potter's *Tailor of Gloucester* appeared in a packet of books from England. She recognized that the little red books of one B. Potter were more than toy books and stocking stuffers. Beatrix Potter always resented the tendency of the English to consider her books little more than the toys among which they were displayed. Johnny Crow's pre-emptive position as a folk hero among the picture-book set was due in great measure to Anne's promotion of the sturdiness of his characterization, the humor of his predicaments, and the agility of the line that placed him on the pages of his books. In the music of Walter de la Mare, Anne heard reverberations of the threat and the wonder that is natural to the mysticism of childhood. Her scheme of celebrating in all the branches of the New York Public Library the birthdays of Leslie Brooke and Walter de la Mare was sometimes questioned by newcomers to the staff who did not at first recognize the cleverness of the idea. Not only did these gentle fetes heighten the common day, but they set a-rattling in the memories of children the names of *Johnny Crow* and *Peacock Pie*, Leslie Brooke and Walter de la Mare, and made them as familiar as the rhymes of Mother Goose.

The letters of Walter de la Mare reveal a mind that mused on visions peculiarly its own and saw, through a half-open doorway, as Henry Beston put it, the haunted possibilities of the undiscovered and the unknown. He was reticent, contained, remote, and surprised that anyone was listening. The measure of his accomplishment seemed never to affect his modesty, and that so great a man should know timidity added to his charm.

"I have only once met Arthur Rackham," he wrote ACM in answer to her letter describing her encounter with the artist, "but I am sure Childs was the right eating house—a good old word which is now almost as obsolete as 'tavern.' It is one of the few restaurants in New York that I have the courage to enter alone (what a confession)."

In a later letter, written on May 6, 1940, in which he addresses her as Anne and signs himself "Yours ever, W. J."—nearly twenty years after the beginning of their friendship—he writes: "I know we share certain theories and convictions about children and childhood and if at any time mine seem to differ with yours, then that will be at my peril."

On each of the April birthdays a cable went to Walter de la Mare, with birthday wishes from the children of New York, the first when he was fifty-one in 1924. Each brought from him a letter rejoicing in the fact that he was thus remembered. Among letters of the latter years one is given here in its entirety:

April 25, 1952   4, South End House,
                                          Montpelier Row,
                                          Twickenham.

Dear Ann,[2]

You were a Dear to remember I'm all but Eighty: so
you see how quickly now I'm catching up, but never,
never, NEVER shall I manage to squeeze into what's called
Time so much as you are doing. As a matter of fact I'm
still so attached to my inkpot that I begrudge leaving off
for meals. And you know how meals are spent in England
just now—BANQUETS. However I manage to keep going,
though it is rather reminiscent of my memories of a railway now defunct that used to be called The London
Smashum & Turnover Railway.

You will know what a real joy it was to see Pamela
Bianco the other day. She looked younger than when she
was twelve, I think; though perhaps my fading inward eye
may account for the memory of her being twelve. Any-
how she has the same marvellous grey eyes—or grey-blue,
or blue-grey, or blue: we had a little argument about it.
And she brought me a lovely picture, which fits into my
little parlour with perfection. How I wish you could come
and see it. Also, how I wish I could come and see *you*. But,
alas, it doesn't seem likely now.

How well I recall that Santa Claus feast with you behind the Lions—in the candle-light; some of the pansy
faces even.

                                          With my love,
                                          yours ever
                                          W. J.

It was Anne's custom to use narrow strips of paper,
seemingly torn from the backs of old envelopes, as mark-
ers in books she read. These gave her ready access for
quick referral. Then slightly marked in pencil, a wavery
line indicated the choice she had made from the page.
She seldom removed the papers. They stood yellowing
on her bookshelves, tattered pennons marking the pleasure spots of her reading through the years. In her copy

of *Come Hither*, that wide and luminous anthology of Walter de la Mare's, the flag stands at page 738, in the section called "About and Roundabout," where erudition and delight are chock-a-block, under the guise of notes. The thin pencil line marks the passage. It is Walter de la Mare's own comment: "Words are but a *means* of conveying poetry from one imagination to another. So may a smile make lovely a plain face; or sunbeams weave a rainbow in the air. Even words themselves may be needless; for two human spirits may hold converse together (of which only the rarest poetry in words or music, paint or stone could *tell*) without one syllable of speech between them." One may surmise that such was the understanding between these two friends, for whom childhood was chief among the bonds they shared.

Three years before *The Bookman* came to an end, day broke for another literary magazine, this one published by the New York *Herald Tribune* as a weekly supplement to the paper, its title *Books*, under the editorship of Stuart Sherman, previously a professor of English at the University of Illinois, who had become critic-at-large. His assistant editor was Irita Van Doren, a vital, vigorous, and charming woman of letters in her own right, who as the wife of Carl Van Doren increased the fame and prestige of that first family of American letters.

The year was 1924. How favorably stood the stars then on Anne's behalf! Her own book for children, *Nicholas: A Manhattan Christmas Story*, was promised for September publication. Six years of contribution to *The Bookman* lay behind her. In that time she had honed to a cutting edge the skills of the reviewer and had so intermingled them with knowledge and intuitive perception as to raise to an apogee of art the criticism of books for children. Interest in the publication of children's books surfaced like a great wave, and authors and artists of enormous gifts rode high on the swing of it, the result a spate of glory in the blackness of the terror-ridden twentieth century. The editors of *Books* knew the time had come to recognize the Lilliputian renaissance in full panoply. They cast their eyes across Fortieth Street and Sixth Avenue to the New York Public Library.

In a letter to the nieces written from Cousin Alice's in Portland and dated September 1924, Anne wrote:

> Did I tell you that I was asked some weeks ago if I would edit a page of criticism of children's books for a new review called *Books* Stuart Sherman is going to edit for the *Herald Tribune*? While I was considering the matter I went down to Westbury, Long Island, to take charge of the Children's Library Mrs. Robert Bacon has given to the town in memory of her husband. . . . When I found Miss Overton needed a vacation, I took part of mine down there. . . . I got the best rest I've had outside of England and I needed it just then.

In that placid and beautiful place Anne drew up her articles of confederation with the *Herald Tribune* and sent them to the editors. The title came first. Five iron owls roosted on the weathervane of the Westbury Library, swinging with the wind. Anne chose three—one to represent the writer, one the artist, and the third, with ruffled feathers, the critic. The page would be called "The Three Owls." No advertising was to appear on the page. Anne was to be responsible for a lead article every week, for the selection of books to be reviewed as well as for the matching of reviewer's talents and interest to the titles under consideration. The date of a book's publication was not to preclude discussion of books of former years. Anne was to have control of the illustrations chosen for the page and to be free from the burden of responsibility for makeup. When there was no immediate reply to this document, Anne decided that the editors could not comply with her demands, so she returned to New York and planned to take off for Portland for the rest of her vacation, but at the last minute she was summoned for a luncheon conference with Irita Van Doren and informed that after a series of conferences all stipulations had been met. "It promises some very good fun," Anne commented in the letter, "if I can continue to regard it as an adventure."

The fun and adventure of "feeding the owls," as she called it, was sustained by Anne from 1924 until 1930. It was no diminution of zest and spirit that grounded the owls, but the Great Depression and the realization on the part of *Books* that a department of books for children could not be further sustained on so splendid and lavish a scale. Anne was invited to continue as a contributing member of the staff, but she decided to cut clear, taking the three owls with her until such time as they found a new roost among the rafters of *The Horn Book*, from which shelter they circled the scene in briefer flight in the form of "The Three Owls' Notebook" from 1936 until the day of her life's end.

The accomplishment of "The Three Owls" under the aegis of the *Herald Tribune*'s *Books* has never been equaled, nor is it likely to be. Vitality infused the pages, born of the diversity in interests, knowledge, and abilities of those who wrote in answer to Anne's request: lawyers, doctors, musicians, poets, engineers, professional magicians, novelists, critics of other great newspapers—Harry Hansen, of the Chicago *Daily News*, Llewellyn Jones of Chicago's *Evening Post*—editors, heads of bookshops, Geoffrey Parsons, May Lamberton Becker, and Will

Cuppy of the *Herald Tribune* staff, John Farrar, editor and publisher, authors and artists of children's books by the score. Chart geographically the background of the contributors. What distances the owls encompassed in flight to return with freighted wings—England, Scotland, France, in the person of Esther Averill, of the Domino Press in Paris, with writers, librarians, and acquaintances at focal points in Boston, Fort Worth, Cleveland, Baltimore, Seattle, Los Angeles, Washington, D.C., Salem, North Carolina, Logan, Utah, and Santa Fe, New Mexico. All the divergence of interest, the points of view, were made adhesive by a "continuity in the manner of presentation." The group review was abolished as a matter of principle, those catchpenny listings of titles on related subjects with their sentence-long notations, their hurried and harassed summaries. The sense of time and space was not the least of the charisma of these pages. All directions in which a book might lead were imaginatively explored and all accompanying associations disclosed and laid before the reader, inviting contemplation. Here, for example, is a piece by ACM on a book by Marian Hurd McNeely, illustrated by William Siegel, its title *The Jumping-Off Place*. Now this was not a great book but a good piece of writing. With what care Anne considers the title and the author! How far its reach, how genuinely critical, how it sticks in the memory!

In an earlier story, *Rusty Ruston*, Mrs. McNeely planted a garden in Kansas and made it the background for the story of a seventeen-year-old girl earning her way to college. A living and likable girl was Rusty and her flower garden was very real. The story suffered, however, from too much sprightliness and exaggeration of character. One felt too conscious of the author doing it as one read. In short it seemed a made-up vocational story on an essentially sound base of good ideas.

In *The Jumping-Off Place* Mrs. McNeely has done a more significant and a more permanent piece of work. She has transplanted a family of children, headed by a girl of seventeen and a boy of fifteen, to a homestead in South Dakota to which their uncle had staked a claim. The uncle's death does not deprive them of his counsel, for he has left a notebook of instruction and comment relating to the new life and a sense of his lovable, reliable presence in their midst.

There is more genuine atmosphere and character in this story than we have found in any recent book for girls. The neighboring homesteaders are well characterized and one feels throughout the poignancy of life, death, and unending struggle to conquer the land.

If Mrs. McNeely can write like this she should abandon the practice of introducing irrelevant "light touches" which get in the way of her story. There are a few even in *The Jumping-Off Place* which recall the reader sharply from moments of genuine emotion to the commonplace. But the story itself rings true to prairie and to children. They live there in actuality rather than by hearsay and even one born and bred in the mountains or by the sea comes to feel the call of the prairie and is grateful to Mrs. McNeely for writing a story which will give to New England girls, for example, something truer and more intimately related to their own home life than they are accustomed to find in Western stories. Nor do we stop with New England. This is a book for children of other countries—a true picture of American life.

One feels that girls who have read and liked it will go on of their own accord to *My Antonia* and *The Song of the Lark* of Willa Cather.

Mr. Siegel's pictorial designs for the book are in striking contrast to Beatrice Stevens's for *Betty Leicester* in that they do give an impression of the prairie, while Miss Stevens conveys not a hint of what Maine is like but rather the dress and ways of the '90s, and this we think is unfortunate, since it is by the quality of Maine in the book and the simplicity and naturalness of Betty Leicester herself that the book survives rather than by the story of what happens. After forty years one would have chosen a more effective format for a new edition, but *Betty Leicester* is doubtless good for many years to come and we may yet welcome her in a pictorial setting more like the Maine of Sarah Orne Jewett's stories, on which we fed with delight as they came from the presses, to which we still turn with a deeper realization that she has given back "the very life" of the Maine we carry about with us.

All the drama, changing excitements, the whirligigs and divertisement that emanated from those pages of critical studies were in truth held within the bounds of two major disciplines: the discipline of literature and of form. Anne never confused literature with sociology, pedagogy, psychiatry, and child study, worthy subjects in their own right that are too often emboldened to tromp through books for children, indecent in their weak disguises, to an extent that would not be tolerated in books for the adult. When it came to criticism, Anne held with T. S. Eliot. "We can therefore ask, about any writing which is offered to us as literary criticism, is it aimed toward understanding and enjoyment? If it is not, it may still be a legitimate and useful activity; but it is to be judged as a contribution to psychology, or sociology, or logic, or pedagogy, or some other pursuit—and is to be judged by specialists, not by men of letters."

Early in Anne's career when she was preparing lectures for Iowa and in the first days of Pratt, the word "ought" in relation to the selection of books for children occurs twice but it never appears again. She was not one to prescribe books by rote: grade, age, reading readiness, or "pots of message." When Agnes Hansen, the director of the library school at Pratt, asked ACM what could be done to prepare children for the threat of communism, fascism and all, Anne replied, "You can only give them what you've found to be the highspots of life, and festivity rates very high. That's what you remember when it comes to a vote." "After every war," Anne wrote, "people want to wipe the decks clean and tell children what they ought to think. Little will come of it."

Deeply read in the heritage of English letters, Anne considered books for children within the sweep of her own experience of literature, for literature was her passion. She knew that children felt the pull and tug of it and might be caught for a lifetime in its enduring joy. "The more we know about literature," writes Northrop Frye, "the better the chance that intensity of response and the greatness of the stimulus to it will coincide." In the cause of that transfiguring coincidence Anne Carroll Moore used her strengths and powers to the utmost.

As for form, it was a word writ large in the lexicon of her judgment. For her it included style, direction, freshness of encounter, as well as balance and proportion. A lack of form in personality, in the appearance of a place or of print on a page, the manner in which one brought off one's work, the lack of form was for her ultimate damnation. When the first issue of "The Three Owls" appeared, the headpiece proved to be less than appropriate, and other accidents marred the first issue. Then Anne asked Boris Artzybasheff, the artist-designer, lost to children's books when *Time* magazine gave him the long assignment of making portraits for their covers, to draw three owls for her. He stayed up all night to bring to completion in time for the second issue the magnificent drawing of three owls, wings curved, heads curved, boughs beneath them curved, great tropical trees curved above them, the drawing that later became the end papers for *The Three Owls*, Books Two and Three. Under the signature of this strong embracing, curved design, the forms of picture-making and the writing of books for children were explored in a golden time.

Meanwhile *The Horn Book* of Boston had emerged as the major journal of criticism of books for children. It had begun as a small publicity sheet issued in behalf of the Bookshop for Boys and Girls, which in 1916 became a project of the Women's Educational and Industrial Union. Bertha Mahony was in charge of it, she being the young secretary in the organization who had envisioned a bookshop with a mission: to sell the best children's books available in a setting that invited exploration by the children as well as by adults. By 1924 the four-page leaflet had become a magazine, published four times a year, Bertha Mahony the editor and her assistant editor Elinor Whitney. As the magazine evolved, outdistancing its New England boundaries, it offered critical appraisal of a high order and, as a lagniappe, varied and fascinating articles concerning artists, editors, writers—all the tangential interests of those concerned with the making of books for children.

At the beginning ACM had been skeptical of the Bookshop, but when she saw Miss Mahony in action she knew her to be a woman of uncommon gifts and sensibility. Anne's great-nieces and -nephews, a lively tribe of Bostonians, hold the memories of their visits to the Bookshop with "Auntie" as among the most vivid and blithe of their childhood recollections. On October 1, 1936, *The Horn Book* editors, in friendly agreement with their parent organization, took over the ownership and publishing of the magazine on their own, an act of great daring and courage in the annals of publishing. The Bookshop was surrendered to the Old Corner Bookstore of Boston. It was then that ACM offered "The Three Owls Notebook" to Miss Mahony and Miss Whitney as a gift and as affirmation of her faith in their venture. The

pages headed by three diminutive owls soon proved to
be a powerful attraction, and it was not long before they
flew home to *The Horn Book* with pieces of eight in
their beaks.

With the appearance of "The Three Owls," ACM's
influence on *The Horn Book* increased beyond the range
of her own articles. Bertha Mahony Miller came to depend on her for editorial suggestions as well as criticisms.
Anne laid to with customary incisiveness. She was largely
responsible for the appearance of special issues dedicated
to such people as Marie Shedlock and L. Leslie Brooke,
Helen Sewell, Elizabeth MacKinstry, etc. If certain titles
were never reviewed, it was because ACM had dropped
a word of suggestion. The issue of January–February
1937 elicited thorough and typical analysis from her:

The Woodstock
January 20th 1937

Dear B E M.

The Horn Book has just come and its pictorial aspect is
fine—excellent make-up. I liked the Editor's own part immensely—"Definition of a Poet" leaves me cold and I
wonder how it may leave other readers. Does it tell anybody anything they really want to know? What one wants
from a poet is a good *poem* or so at least it seems to me.

"Mountain Woman" is excellent. I hope I can send
you a copy of the poetry of New Mexico I had for Christmas from a former assistant now teaching in a Mission
School there. There are lovely things in it which would
bear reprinting if she is willing and you like them. *The
Junior Bible*, with due respect to Edgar Goodspeed &
Macmillan, left us longing for a King James version. And
so C. C.'s article seems to me a total loss—merely a piece
of writing which the Nuns and Brothers, Heaven bless
them, would also consider superfluous. The New Children's Bookshop is an interesting commentary from New
Russia. The *real leading article* of the number is Esther
Averill's. She tells things one wants to know and *knows*

far more than she tells. [ACM then discusses an auto-biographical article by Mabel Leigh Hunt.] *It is so incredibly naïf and personal and commonplace.* For goodness sake, B.E.M. and Elinor Whitney, call out your ancestors if necessary to *edit* such an article as that, for you invite more of the same when you fail to do so. Setting a premium on mediocrity is the last thing you want to do. That article makes me fairly *cringe*. Do be careful when editors recommend as I've no doubt Helen Fish did— Which brings me to the Mukerji article which I consider *very important.*

May [Massee] should not attempt it and I've already heard rumors of her passing it on—Entre Nous—very wisely and tactfully. I think it should be done preferably by a man rather than by a woman, who really knows the East—even if you have to *wait.* And I believe in waiting for such a piece. I probably understand the Oriental mind least of any writer of contemporary criticism and kept Mukerji's respect because I *said so little.* I was profoundly moved by the manner of his leaving the world and I am sure many others share my feeling. Don't be in any hurry to estimate his contribution to an enduring literature for children. It is *assured.* Curiously enough I met Mukerji for the first time in the Bookshop for Boys & Girls in Boston. "I wish you wouldn't *preach* so much," said I. "How can I help it since I was educated for the priesthood?" was Mukerji's reply—I think we understood one another there and then but I of all his friends feel least competent to tell what was in his heart when he left this world so suddenly last summer. I wish I might come to Ashburnham before I sail on March 19th. If I can possibly arrange it I will let you know. I cannot as yet set any date. The Annual Report is consuming all my time and thought. With my love to you and William.

As always
Anne Carroll Moore

The two women, Bertha Mahony Miller and Anne Carroll Moore, for all their common heritage of Irish blood and New England tradition, approached argument and debate by opposite directions: Anne, direct, hard-hitting, and straightforward; Bertha, less revealing of her opinions in discussions and full of surprises because one seldom knew from preliminary discussions what final line of action she might pursue. Sessions between the two must have often been stormy, but nothing could shake the measure of affection they shared, based as it was on the respect each bore for the other's intellectual capacity, and many were the days of camaraderie in Boston and New York they celebrated. The role of critic was the most enduring of all Anne's assignments and accomplishments. "The Three Owls" winged out from *The Horn Book* for the last time in the December issue of 1960, and from that flight they did not return.

The critic of books for children is seldom held worthy of recognition by his peers. Men and women of letters admit to their circle, in terms of equality, critics of the dance, theater, films—the whole spectrum of "The Seven Lively Arts"—but books for children run the risk of being strained through the sieve of "stock responses" belonging to pedagogy, science, ethics, and sociology before their legitimacy as literature is considered.

When, for example, *The Three Owls, Second Book* appeared in 1928, the person on the *Saturday Review of Literature* responsible for assigning books to appropriate authorities or critics sent the book to a member of the Child Study Association. The result: a diatribe, in part, against the book because it did not give "proper recognition to the notable progress made by psychologists in determining the influence exerted by the interest, emotions and mental grasp of early childhood in shaping pre-school literature." It was as though a fishmonger had been asked for his appraisal of Eleanor Clark's *The Oysters of Locmariaquer*.

Even that perceptive, sympathetic, and widely cherished writer E. B. White—even he fell victim to the disease of expecting the children's critic to be concerned with dogma rather than with the living stuff of literature, albeit he did so in retrospect. Twenty years after the fact he attributed to ACM attitudes she could never have assumed and ascribed to her words she did not speak.

Well nigh the whole world of letters rejoiced when, in 1945, it was rumored that E. B. White had written a book for children, its title *Stuart Little*. When it appeared it was heralded with trumpets of acclaim and is now considered a classic. Two voices of dissent were heard at the time of publication, one made public, the other stated privately. Malcolm Cowley's criticism appeared as a review in the New York *Times*, October 28, 1945. He praised the book but with certain reservations concerning the fragmented structure of the tale. The second dissident was ACM. At this time she had only the *Horn Book* owls as mouthpiece. So deep was her regard for E. B. White that she could not bring herself to comment on the book in that space. "I was never so disappointed in a book in my life," she wrote Bertha Mahony Miller, "and I choose not to mention it." But out of her deep concern she wrote a letter to Mr. White.

In 1966, as special celebration of its twenty years of abundant life, NBC presented *Stuart Little* on television, with Johnny Carson as off-stage narrator and all the characters played by human actors except Stuart, who, being more mouse than man, was obliged to be represented by an articulated toy.

The New York *Times* of Sunday, March 6, 1966, observed the event with the publication of the history of the book, written by Mr. White himself, a photograph of Johnny Carson and a headline, "The Librarian Said It Was Bad for Children." The article read in part:

A few weeks later, back home in Maine, a letter arrived for me from Anne Carroll Moore, children's librarian emeritus of the New York Public Library. Her letter was long, friendly, urgent, and thoroughly surprising. She said she had read proofs of my forthcoming book called *Stuart Little* and she strongly advised me to withdraw it. She said, as I recall the letter, that the book was non-affirmative, inconclusive, unfit for children, and would harm its author if published. These were strong words, and I was grateful to Miss Moore for having taken the trouble to write them. I thought the matter over, however, and decided that as long as the book satisfied me, I wasn't going to let an expert talk me out of it. It is unnerving to be told you're bad for children; but I detected in Miss Moore's letter an assumption that there are rules governing the writing of juvenile literature—rules as inflexible as the rules for lawn tennis.

Now ACM never mastered the typewriter. She had no recourse to carbon copies, therefore, unless she had employed a typist. When she desired to have a record of certain letters she deemed important, she copied them in her own hand and then carelessly shuffled them among her papers. The letter to E. B. White was one such. There are certain discrepancies between the document and Mr. White's recollection of it.

35 Fifth Avenue
June 20, 1945

Dear Mr. White

Ten days have gone by since I delivered the galleys of *Stuart Little* to Miss Nordstrom. I've written you countless letters in my mind and have destroyed several attempts to put on paper my personal reaction.

I was delighted to be given the opportunity to read E.B.W.'s story in advance of publication and I took up the galleys with anticipation—I laid them down in perplexity and genuine concern. Had the manuscript been sent to me by a publisher for a professional opinion I would have had to say that it seemed to me a double risk—for publisher and author. Illustrations may help but they cannot supply what seems to be lacking—a completely realized fantasy. After the first chapter I feel the story getting more and more out of hand, the invention becoming labored and Stuart himself staggering out of scale.

By the time I came to the school chapter the two worlds were all mixed up. He might readily pass from one to the other but to keep him alive in both at once proved too much for me to take.

Realizing that E.B.W. had once said in a letter that he could not write on his children's story unless his temperature was up, I thought perhaps the trouble is with me—temperature too low or too high applied to the reading. I put the galleys aside for several days and read them for a second time with certain children at various age levels in mind. Children are more unpredictable than adults and I hold no such belief in the infallibility of their acceptance as do many. It has taken a long time for certain books to win a sure place and it has required the permanent market of libraries and schools to reinforce the publisher's faith in their authors. I fear *Stuart Little* will be very difficult to place in libraries and schools over the country.

The prestige of Mr. White's name will undoubtedly assure an initial sale. It is precisely that element which gives me genuine concern and leads me to write as I have before publication of a book which I feel may become an embarrassment rather than the source of continuing pleasure and rewarding return any book from his pen should command.

Published anonymously it might not matter greatly. Children's books as you well know often pass with the sales of a season. Published under the name of E. B. White at this time it matters a great deal to children's books that the book should have inherent qualities which seem to be left out of this one.

I wish it were possible to talk with you both instead of writing one of the most difficult letters I have ever attempted. Since the book is in press you may wonder why I make the attempt and I can only say because I can't seem to help saying something.

How far beyond the effect upon a child for good or ill are the opinions expressed here. ACM's chief concern was that so true a writer as E. B. White should not appear before children in less than the full regalia of his greatest capabilities. Mr. White was not responsible for the tawdry headline of the article in the New York *Times* announcing the Johnny Carson show, but the sight of it angered those who knew with what passionate devotion ACM had served the highest gifts of writers and artists as well as the potential reach of children as readers.

14

FROM A BALCONY

> *Somehow the poetry at the heart of life*
> *only strikes clear when one finds it in the*
> *everyday living of a member of one's own*
> *family—a New England family at that.*
>
> ACM

THE ROADS of Anne Carroll Moore took her to England and to France, but it was a flight of owls that winged her westward across the Wasatch Mountains to Utah. There she was destined to enliven a region, to set upon it an enduring pattern of taste and sensibility, and to endear herself literally to the generations.

In Salt Lake City, for example, a group of women, one of whom had encountered ACM in 1927, read children's books together for twenty-three years or more, becoming themselves authoritative critics of books their children and their grandchildren read. Mrs. De Fonda Collier, the catalyst of the group, reported in 1961 that it was she who had suggested to the women that they study literature for children. "What's in it?" someone asked. "Well, more than you think," she replied. It had begun in the summer session at Logan, Utah, 1927. "I had a full schedule of required courses in education which did not include literature for children," she recalls, "but I had a free period at ten o'clock. On that first morning I wandered down the hall past the open door of a large, well-filled classroom. There was Anne Carroll Moore. The second day and every day during her stay I was on the front row."

The college at Logan was at that time a state agricultural college, the president of which was Dr. Elmer George Peterson, who in the 1920s was troubled by the fact that the students had little opportunity to encounter the humanities. The head of the English Department, Dr. N. A. Pedersen, held a like concern. It was he whose attention had been caught by a section in the *Herald Tribune Books* called "The Three Owls." "There was such liveliness there," he said as he remembered the time, "such pace, to say nothing of the acumen. I wished there were someone at Logan like that who could incite students to read. When I discovered that Dr. and Mrs. Peterson were scheduled to go to New York, I suggested that they go to the New York Public Library and see who that Miss Moore might turn out to be."

The Petersons[1] appeared in the Central Children's Room on December 5, 1926. Propitious day! St. Nicholas Eve, as Anne numbered it on her private calendar. They had expected to find Miss Moore somewhere in that room. She was summoned from her office. In the interim, before her arrival, Dr. Peterson walked about the room and finally burst out with the words, "Oh, Utah could use a place like this."

She went to Utah for the first time in June 1927. She was told that a room in the college library would be assigned to her as a base of operations. From that center she would be expected to speak to students, faculty, and the general public. Outside of that, hers was a free hand. It was an assignment that well fitted her heart's delight. She commandeered copies of essential titles from the publishers, sending out before her great boxes of books which became in time the basis for the Anne Carroll Moore Library, with a plaque outside the door so naming it, its subsequent support coming from the college library.

By the time Anne arrived in Logan, she had already fallen captive to the landscape as she observed it from the train windows.

> There is an Old World spell upon the Wasatch Mountains. I felt it strongly on my first visit to Utah. Crossing the mountains from Ogden to Logan I was reminded now of the land of the Frost Giants in the Waldres of Norway and now of the English Lake Country, so beautiful and so friendly seemed the treeless fells with their soft covering of pungent sagebrush, the green fields and the quiet valleys. The long rows of Lombardy poplars separating the farm lands are a gracious reminder of the Holy Land of which these pioneers were always dreaming as they planted the desert.

The room allotted to her was spacious enough to accommodate five great windows that looked out upon the Wasatch Mountains, and it held welcoming bookshelves along its walls. Anne set about immediately to make it a living and an enticing place. An initial reception was scheduled to be held there. Some of the ladies of the community came to help with the preparations and brought as offering the standard jardinieres of ferns to be set about the room on wrought-iron stands. At the sight of the dreary house-bound pots Anne grew indignant. "Don't be so Bostonian!" she exclaimed. "Bring in things that grow in your gardens and in the countryside." She had seen the farm gardens filled with roses and peonies, and these she hankered for as decorations. A letter to Rachel Moore Warren written after the fact, in July of that year, tells the story:

> I spoke twenty-eight times in ten days including a ward meeting or Mormon Sunday School. I took by request the Mappe of Fairyland and about fifty choice books from my clinic. A specialist in children's health had already changed the physical diet of Utah, and they were no less ready to absorb new kinds of books. It made the usual run of women's clubs of Eastern parent-teacher associations a pallid kind of thing by comparison. When I told how I prized my twenty-five-year-old autographed copy of *Miss Muffet's Christmas Party*, seventy copies were ordered by telegraph in the hope that Dr. Crothers might write in them also. They stole a march on me by sending for *Nicholas* in bulk and I spent the last morning autographing. There was something deeply touching in the response to poetry and romance and pictures.

In August of that year Anne sailed for Europe to attend the international library meeting in Edinburgh, but it was Utah that left the lasting imprint on her spirit and made the year memorable.

In 1931 she returned to Utah to find Martha Peterson, the youngest member of the family, a child of eight. Between them they staged a reading party in the library which Martha remembers as a chief glory of her childhood. She as hostess was charged with the task of putting before each of her eight guests a book she deemed appropriate for her and enjoyable. What possibility for discussion, agreement and debate and flights of enthusiasm this small scheme engendered! It was all capped with actual refreshments that had been carefully chosen to be consumed easily while reading without soiling the pages of the books.

There are no more welcoming people on God's green

earth than the Mormons, and Anne was from the first taken into the community as a beloved person. She was invited to return in June 1938 for the celebration of the school's fiftieth anniversary. A birthday letter to her great-niece, Margaret Warren Brown, written with the sprawl of haste, engenders breathlessness even as it is read thirty-four years after the fact.

Dear Margaret,

Happy birthday from the snow-capped Wasatch Mountains, with golden wishes gathered from the 50th anniversary celebration of this land-grant college. It's a marvellous place.

It has been a wonderful week, all told. The weather glorious, cool part of the day as Maine in early October. I arrived in time for the singing of Haydn's Creation on June 3rd. Was met at Ogden by a delegation of children from the Pingree School with bouquets of roses—Nicholas had to appear in the station—the Forty-Niner was ten minutes ahead of schedule so Mr. Peterson and Martha found me surrounded by children. Then came the 50 mile drive over the mountains—Martha is now 15 but essentially the same as at 4, 8 and 12 my previous visits. She is as tall as I am but utterly without self-consciousness and so companionable.

No time to tell you of the events at which I marched in the procession with nearly a hundred delegates from universities and learned societies. President Sproul of the University of California gave the commencement address. The governor of Utah was there and also spoke. Monday night, Drinkwater's *Lincoln* was played extremely well. . . . There have been banquets, luncheons, and all manner of doings. My clinics came off with a bang and I have given three parties in the library for children.

There follows news of the family and the customary greeting of love and affection, signed Auntie.

As for the Peterson family, Anne became an auxiliary

member of it. The girls, growing up, paraded their prospective husbands before Anne for her approval, and Chase, one of the sons, graduating from Harvard with many honors, insisted that Anne be there to share with the family all the pomp attending bestowal of hoods and capes. Chase later became Dean of Students at Harvard.

When Martha was married and the mother of a baby girl, she named the child Anne Carroll, telling ACM she had saved the name for this event all her life. Anne felt that this child, more than any other, gave her a hold upon the generations yet to come.

Anne never knew of another namesake—a small Chinese child, Anne Carroll Reicher, whose mother as a student at Pratt fell under the spell of ACM. When she and her husband adopted a Chinese orphan, to add to the family of their own children, Mrs. Reicher knew what name she wished to honor.

The decade of the thirties is remembered by most Americans as the time of the Great Depression, and ACM met manifold administrative problems in the course of affairs at the library, but her own life attained in those years—especially from 1932 to 1938—succeeding periods of rewards for labor of the past. The twenty-fifth anniversary of her coming to the New York Public Library ushered in that special period, and the observance of the day was so attuned to Anne's taste and desire as to seem a dream made actual. The genius of Mary Gould Davis, the Supervisor of Story Telling, was largely responsible for the affair, and she involved all the diligence and talent of the staff to bring about the big party. The scene was the Central Children's Room. On an evening in September 1931 Anne was asked to appear there. She came with Storer Lunt to find the place brilliant with candlelight and flowers, and men and women of the literary world, old friends and out-of-town guests waiting to greet her. She was escorted to the center of the room, and there she was seated in a high, curved rocking chair that had belonged to Washington Irving. Frederic Melcher was master of ceremonies. He announced The Procession of Branches. Winding through the length of the Children's Room they came, the children's librarians, each dressed in the costume representative of the national character of the neighborhoods they served—Italian, Chinese, Czech, German, Serbian—the beautiful Mrs. Rodzianko appearing as she had on the day she was presented to the court of the Czar. Their faces were radiant in the light of the sparklers they carried.

Dr. John Finley, the editor of the New York *Times*, was among the guests. He was so moved by the sight that he rushed out to summon photographers from his paper. Speaking in the mode of the day and from the habit of his masculinity, he said to Miss Davis, "Why aren't these young women married?" To which she replied, "Most of them are."

Everything about the evening conspired to create a heightened festivity. It appeared to be unrehearsed and spontaneous, though Ruth Sawyer Durand told a story, and *The Tinder Box* was given as a puppet play, as was another written for the occasion, *Rootabaga Processional*.

A great portfolio of original drawings made for Anne by artists of the time was put into her hands, and at one point Mr. Melcher poured from a large cornucopia a shower of letters, telegrams, messages from everywhere, into her lap.

"The surprise party was quite the loveliest silver anniversary anyone ever had," Anne wrote in a letter to Jean Pond. "It was so spontaneous and so festive. No speeches but done with a lovely feeling for everything and everybody. Of course I couldn't sleep a wink that night, so I read all the hundreds of telegrams and messages stretching from Maine to California, from Japan to England and France and Italy. As for the portfolio with all the artists' originals, you must come and see for yourself."

Anne was never to forget that evening, and it shone with heightened meaning in the face of what was for her the fiasco of the fiftieth anniversary of the establishment of work with children in the New York Public Library. In 1956 the library published, in Miss Moore's honor, a *Festschrift*, its title *Reading Without Boundaries*. Old friends of Anne's and experienced members of the staff had been asked to write on assigned aspects of work with children. ACM accepted the publication with guarded politeness for a time, but in short order she came to resent it, feeling that the library administration which authorized publication without her knowledge, advice, or consent had exploited her accomplishment for its own pragmatic purposes, with little feeling for or support of the actuality of the past. The campaign she waged against the publication was one of the most bitter and vitriolic of her lifetime. It was cruel treatment of those who in good faith had brought the publication into being, but for Anne Carroll Moore the integrity of an opinion or a principle she held to be true was more important than any other consideration. She was accustomed to sacrificing everything and everybody if in her opinion the cause justified it. If it were cruel, so be it.

A king and a queen were crowned midway of the thirties—George the Sixth of England and his Scottish Queen Elizabeth. What ceremony and panoply a coronation promised! It was ACM for England once again! The year was 1937. The grand-niece had accomplished library school. Anne left the dark room of the Woodstock Hotel and sailed for England on the *Europa*, the date March 14. Three months in England—with a small trip to France besides—stretched before her. She landed on the twenty-fourth at Southampton, sent her baggage on to London, and went to Stonehenge to see it at day's end under a lowering sky.

Old friends awaited her in London: the Brookes family, giving parties and teas in quick succession; the de la Mares; Eleanor Farjeon a hostess for tea and an afternoon; Kathleen Lines escorting Anne to church in the Inner Temple; dinner with Helen Waddell at a Serbian restaurant in Soho.

Old haunts in the Lake Country were revisited, and Beatrix Potter made her a welcome guest once more. Villages within range of London were observed in all their manifestation of decor deemed suitable for the coronation.

The event itself was something of a shambles as far as Anne was concerned, for though good money had been paid out in advance for a seat, there was none forthcoming. Anne wandered from place to place during the procession and pieced out what she had not seen by viewing the whole thing in a cinema. But the city itself was a great sight for all to see, with the old buildings brilliantly lighted every night.

Anne went to the Coronation Ball on her own. The bagpipes played, all the old dances were in swing—merrie old England to the life—and Anne ached to dance in the reels. She met a company of actors there who asked her to have supper with them. They proved to be a charming lot, and Anne blessed her stars for giving her the courage to go places by herself.

When Anne Moore returned to New York in June, the American Library Association met there in annual convention. She was a center of attention, for in addition to all she had to tell she wore, at appropriate times, her coronation cape—a rich black velvet all-enveloping wrap that reached to her ankles. Royal it was too, with its crimson satin lining and an antique silver clasp at the throat. It was made to her order at Liberty's in London and, like the apple-green corded silk of Aunt Allie, it served as ceremonial for the spirit.

The Balcony awaited Anne. Before she sailed for England she had taken a lease on an apartment at the Beverly Hotel, 125 East 50th Street, on the sixteenth floor. A previous stay at the old Panhellenic Building on Mitchell Place had endeared the neighborhood to her, for from a certain height one could see the East River, and that was a source of refreshment. The Beverly had the view. It was an ideal dwelling for a career woman at the top of her success. A large room formed the living area, with a foldaway kitchen attached. French windows opened onto a balcony that could hold six or eight people comfortably crowded. The river shone beyond. Moreover, the facilities of a big hotel lay below floors and could be commandeered in case of large parties.

Second only to Alderwood in Anne's affection, the Balcony came to fulfill a long need. It enabled Anne to spread her hospitality lavishly. Her letters of this ample time are filled with accounts of suppers, teas, dinners, the menus lovingly itemized. The Balcony meant that she could receive in her own place the guests that came to the Children's Room for Book Week. It gave her too the homely satisfaction of being domestic. On St. Nicholas Day, 1938, she wrote to one of the nieces:

> I go to Wilmington on Monday the 26th. So Christmas day, Sunday, the Balcony will hold open house for the family. I'm asking Madeline and her husband—the Bedells

and such Warren-Browns and Willys as may be able to respond. The more the merrier, says Nicholas. Storer unfortunately will be in Wilmington on that day and on Monday.

We had a lovely St. Nicholas Eve in the Children's Room. Mrs. Durand came unexpectedly to tell a story heralded by a box of the loveliest red roses. Miss Massee sent red roses also and the room fairly glowed with their color and fragrance. I had invited the staff for supper at The Balcony and Mrs. Durand came too. Sunday I achieved a really excellent dish of creamed chicken and rice, cranberry sauce and superlative fudge for dessert. Incidentally, I cleaned my silver, sitting in the sunshine of the front window. I had a lovely day remembering lovely things in the lives of my father and mother— Looking back from the world of today there is calm and a sense of permanence. "It is a great thing to live at all and more to live well," wrote my father in the 1890's and it still holds in the 1930's.

As for the Balcony proper, it boasted a set of window boxes. These gave an illusion of country gardens, for Dudley and Storer Lunt kept them filled with privet or boughs fetched from the country, and at Christmas time Storer shopped the tree market for pines the appropriate size, pointed firs against the sky.

One winter's morning Anne rose to close the windows against a blow of wind and saw her Christmas trees topped with snow. She told the young artist, Bob McCloskey, about it and in due time he made a lithograph of the scene, cold, blue and mysterious, that she might keep it always in her mind.

During the years of the Balcony, honors began to accrue unto Anne. The University of Maine conferred upon her a Doctor of Letters in 1940. Anne went in person to receive it, grateful for the fact that in the citation mention was made of her father's service as a trustee of the college when it was the State Agricultural School. Anne had previously held honorary degrees in some disdain. Apparently she had written Dorothy Canfield Fisher of her feeling. Her letter elicited from Mrs. Fisher a memorable rebuttal:

> Let me tell you something in connection with your degree from the University of Maine, which was said to me years ago when I was about to receive an honorary degree. I had said something evidently like what you are feeling about honorary degrees to a friend, a scientist, who answered very seriously that he thought that attitude of half-scorn was entirely wrong, and that every American who had any opportunity to share in an honor granted to other ability than the ability for material success, should leap to take advantage of the opportunity.
>
> It made quite an impression on my mind, and I pass it on to you to think about as you walk across the platform to have the hood dropped round your neck.

The following year, in 1941, the Women's National Book Association bestowed upon Anne the first Constance Lindsay Skinner Medal, an award she cherished because of her friendship for Constance Skinner and because it honored those who celebrated books and reading.

In spite of wars, depressions, and recessions, those years of the thirties—from 1932 to 1938—were distinguished by a renaissance of arts as far as illustration and book design were concerned. Anne Carroll Moore took cognizance of these matters by setting apart in the annual Christmas lists the first few pages wherein she named and described such books in some detail. Among those artists so honored was Dorothy Lathrop. In a letter to Anne, written in 1944, some years after the demise of the Balcony, Dorothy Lathrop makes clear the reason for the special aura that still surrounds the Balcony days.

The time seems very long ago when Rachel [Field] and Elizabeth MacKinstry and Jo and I came to your parties on the Balcony, every one of us so filled with enthusiasm for our work—each one of us looking forward. But not one of us could match your joy of living or keep pace with your adventuring.

I never think of you without seeing bright balloons tugging at their strings, or countless lights shining over a mysteriously humming city, or without a lift of anticipation for adventures just around the corner—around every corner.

15

RUE AND
REMEMBRANCE

*Growing old is quite a responsibility . . .
and so many people make such a mess of it.*
ACM

$\mathcal{A}$NNE'S RETIREMENT DATE from the New York Public Library was set at October 1, 1941. A flick of the
calendar on September 30, and there was an end to thirty-
five years of being the center of a universe, the boundaries
of which she herself had extended beyond the expectations of any librarian in a comparable position. Hers was
the authoritative voice in the world of children's books.
With the growth of her influence through *The Bookman*,
the *Herald Tribune Books*, and *The Horn Book*, to say
nothing of the book-selection policies of the New York
Public Library, her voice remained in command. When
she retired at seventy, she faced no diminution of her
power, her zest for books and the children who read
them; she knew no waning of her zeal for the discovery
and acclamation of those genuine, original men and

women among the artists and authors who unfurled to the world their separate banners of singularity.

The University of California at Berkeley acknowledged her retirement by inviting her to teach, in the spring semester of 1942, at the Graduate School of Librarianship, with freedom to treat the subject of libraries for children in any way she chose. Sidney B. Mitchell, the director, asked for no commitment of outline or syllabus, which pleased Anne immensely.

Beyond that appointment there were no definite plans for her future, but publishers were quick in their attempts to sign her up. Her autobiography was sought by more than one editor, and she was actually committed to two titles, *Reading Boys Like* and *Reading Girls Like*, as well as a long-postponed biography of Mary Wright Plummer for the American Library Association's series of biographies of noted librarians.

Anne was convinced of her ability to retire. The letters in which she spoke of her plans for the future exuded from their pages the accustomed exhilaration with which she gave account of events in her life. Whatever had happened or was to happen was recorded with an edge of triumphant expectation and a conviction of her own speciality as a person on whom circumstances bestowed distinctive tokens of recognition. "I believe I have had a good time," she wrote to Rachel Moore Warren early on in 1941, "and have felt as free to act on my own initiative as anyone in the U.S.A. I feel no sense of possession and no reluctance to give over. Unlike Miss Hewins I did not marry a library neither that of Pratt Institute nor the N.Y.P.L."

Words well spoken! But how seldom do the turbulent floods of emotion follow the watercourses that reason designs! The actuality of retirement was a shock, and the pain of it was compounded by the fact that she had to surrender the Balcony as a setting and live haphazardly until such time as she should start for California in December. Moreover, she was not clear of Room 105. The files had been systematically cleaned out, but thirty-five years of personal mementoes were everywhere on hand. She could not bring herself to erase them. Consequently, many days in October and November Anne spent in the stacks, where space had been allotted her, sorting books and papers left as unfinished business. She worked in a faded blue voile dress reserved for grime and desolation as she confronted herself and the future in the dusty residue of the past. There she was on the very day of the Children's Room Book Week celebration, having refused all invitations, determined not to appear.

There had been no special retirement party for Anne. The library had staged a collective reception for all staff retiring at that time. Anne had declared she wanted no further fete, ever, after the perfection of the twenty-fifth-anniversary celebration, but the staff gathered informally in the Central Children's Room one evening and presented her with a handsome clutch of baggage in view of her forthcoming trip to California. To the delight of ACM, the collection included a leather jewel case—it resembled a miniature suitcase—and stamped in gold upon it the initials N.K.

The trip to California was charted to touch as many points of the compass of her interest and affection as possible. The strongest and youngest of her friends, hearing account of it, questioned their own abilities to endure the rigor of so widespread an undertaking. But Anne, always an inspired traveler, found her strength renewed by each change of scene, each diverse encounter. First to St. Louis to visit Mary Douglas Carpenter;

to Cincinnati to see Julia Carter; to New Orleans, the ties with library people there strong and lasting; to Abbeville, Louisiana, where she spent Christmas with her cherished great-nephew, Dr. Edgar Warren and his family; to Houston, Texas, and Julia Ideson, librarian of a splendid institution that ACM admired, the Houston Public Library; to San Antonio; to Galveston, Texas, to visit Emma Lee, the noted children's librarian of the Rosenberg Library there; and the family of Anne's blood cousin, Charles Moore, known to his intimates as "Yellow Pine Charlie" because yellow pine had been the chief source of his considerable fortune; and from there she entrained for Los Angeles, for a visit with "Cousin-by-mutual-consent-Oscar" and his daughter, Marie Clarke.

Children had been encountered at each of these points, in library groups and schools as well as in the homes of friends, children spellbound as usual by accounts of Anne Caraway and Nicholas, who exhibited his new treasure chest of miniatures to their delighted eyes.

ACM found the Berkeley campus spacious and welcoming in that year of 1942. She was put up at the Women's Faculty Club, which meant that she walked to classes by a wooded path, the creek running beside for company. With her gift for vivid response to spirit of place she enjoyed the campus, climbed to the top of the Campanile, and became the friend of the young musician who played upon the keyboard to make the bells ring.

As for her lectures, she publicly forswore outline or syllabus, but among her papers there remains an impressive document, including a series of penetrating examination questions, that give the lie to the myth of her completely spontaneous approach to the subject. In all of her life she never spoke for as much as five minutes without knowing exactly what she intended to say and how she intended to say it. The monthly meetings of her library staff were carefully planned and outlined on paper. The Berkeley course was centered on the writers and artists of the twentieth century whom she had known. Some students resented this approach because they had come to the library school to learn how to head up a library for children in the state of California. But others among them were exhilarated, realizing that a quarter of a century of living, vivid experience among major artists and authors was being put into their hands by one who had shaped much of it with her own spirit. They were never to forget it.

Leonore Power Mendelson was living in San Francisco then, and this made possible weekly celebrations of old times in New York, seasoned with the beauty of the Bay cities and the comfort of good food and festivity on every hand. Anne was the great personality on the campus, and there were fitting celebrations in her honor. But a curious note of sorrow runs through her letters of the period, faint but persistent, until at last it emerges, foreign to her but there. She was homesick for New York! She confessed to her niece, Margaret Bedell, that she could not begin her day at Berkeley without first tuning in the radio to hear from Kate Smith what the weather was in New York. "Kate Smith, of all people!" her niece said, astonished at the revelation.

The course at Berkeley ran from the middle of January until May. Anne had no further commitments until late in August, when she had agreed to speak before the Library Association of the Pacific Northwest meeting in Seattle. The time between she determined to spend in writing, and she chose Logan, Utah, with its quiet moun-

tain grandeur, its memories of good encounters and welcoming friends, as a place propitious for fresh beginnings.
She went to stay in the home of one of the Peterson
family, Mrs. Huhne, who made her so comfortable that
Anne reported, in a letter to Ruth Sawyer, that she was
tempted to stay indefinitely. The garden, the hammock
on the porch, the fresh mountain trout, all the hospitality
showered upon her—these she reveled in—but the writing would not come. Mrs. Huhne, remembering that
time, spoke of the muted mood in which Anne seemed
suspended and of her dismay at finding Anne slumped
over her desk, head sunk upon her arms in an unaccustomed show of despair.

But the talk at Seattle was restorative, and ACM set
off for home by as roundabout a route as she had followed on her westward journey: to Minneapolis and St.
Paul, reaffirming friendships with Della MacGregor and
Alice Brown, and to Buffalo on a like quest. When she
came home, the beloved city bore a new guise, dim and
somber in the half-light of the wartime blackout. Anne
found it beautiful and her spirits rose, though she arrived without the slightest idea of where she would go
or what her abode would be. Storer Lunt met her at the
train. He meanwhile had taken quarters at the Grosvenor Hotel, Fifth Avenue and Tenth Street, in which a
few apartments were to be had in the upper reaches of
the building. He invited Anne to be his guest at the hotel
until such time as she could find a place that appealed
to her.

It was a neighborhood she knew and loved of old—
a part of Greenwich Village and therefore heir to its
color and life but not in the middle of the cluttered,
crowded streets, the noise and dirt, all of which one endured for the sake of charm and architectural eccentric-

ity. As a region, it invited walking and poking about. Eighth Street was near, with its small moving-picture theaters, its galleries and shops, chief among them the Washington Square Book Store, boasting an extensive lending library. There were small grocery stores, sausages and cheeses hanging from the ceiling, and stalls of fresh fruit at the entrances; and bakery shops, one of which, on Sixth Avenue, the legendary Ugobono's, Anne had pictured in the pages of *Nicholas*.

In one of the two windows of Ugobono's pastry shop there was a wonderful thin cake watch, with a chocolate stem winder, pink and white dots for the minutes, and vanilla hands. . . . In the other window were the most fascinating tin boxes and glass bottles swinging from basket hangers. They quickly filled a box with almond cakes and macaroons, panitoni and marrons, and Nicholas bought a big tin box with twenty-four little packages of nougat inside, each with a different picture of Italy on the wrapper.

East of Fifth Avenue there stood the high-ceilinged, old-fashioned charm of Wanamaker's department store, and dark shops full of secondhand books, a wig shop with displays of antique jewelry in the window, and at the corner of Tenth Street and University Place a flower shop that by some act of grace transcended the limits of its show windows, which were free of fixed and set pieces, and seemed actually to bloom and blossom into the street. It was run by Louis Chingo, who knew the taste and judgments of each of his customers. A friend of Anne's, stopping there one day, thought Louis psychic. He recognized for whom the flowers were purchased though she said not a word. She had chosen boughs of hawthorn. "Don't break off the branches," she admonished him. "My God, no," he said. "I wouldn't break anything for Miss Moore."

Restaurants were plentiful thereabouts: Schrafft's, Longchamps, Charles on Sixth Avenue, and Asti's at Twelfth Street, where live song and music enhanced the appetite.

The churches of the region, open-doored and consoling, were indigenous to the neighborhood, leading ministers of the time appearing there and liturgical music abounding in practiced perfection: the Church of the Ascension, directly across the street from the Grosvenor; the Presbyterian Church at Twelfth Street; St. George's and St. Mark's close by.

Friends lived near: Maria Cimino and Will Lipkind around the corner; May Massee, Anne Eaton, and numerous others within walking distance. Recounting all these blessings of familiarity and convenience, Anne decided to take a room on the twelfth floor and settle in on her own. Later she moved to the sixteenth floor, where she could more easily avail herself of the hospitality of Storer Lunt's place when he was absent from the city. There she cooked in his small kitchen and entertained her friends for luncheon, with table set against the window that looked out across the rooftops of the Village to the thread of the Hudson River far beyond and the cranes and smokestacks of great ships in the harbor.

There was work to be done. The "Three Owls" articles for *The Horn Book* kept her *en rapport* with current children's books. Bertha Mahony Miller came increasingly to depend on the advice and criticism of Anne as contributing editor as the time approached for her own signing off from Horn Book responsibilities. ACM's involvement was extensive in the publication of the Horn Book's monumental book on illustrators of the period as well as in other independent ventures of its publishing. Editors consulted ACM on any number of problems. Pratt Institute Library School demanded, by tradition, at least one lecture a year, and Anne became vigorously involved in the administrative affairs of the institution by virtue of the honors its officers had bestowed on her and by her own conviction on certain matters for which she waged active and telling campaigns. The affairs of Bradford and its Alumnae Club concerned her. There were lectures before the New England Library Association, especially at the time tribute was paid to Caroline Hewins; to the New York State Library Association meeting at West Point and various other meetings. Compton's Pictured Encyclopedia relied on her for periodic revisions of her famous lists, which continued to be the major feature of their service to libraries. The English-Speaking Union commanded her interest, as did the wartime programs of Books Across the Sea and the Treasure Chest campaign whereby children's books were shipped by the crate to allies everywhere. Well she might say of herself, "Retiring into activity."

But as for the creation of the two books concerning the reading of boys and girls and the biography of Mary Wright Plummer—nothing seemed to rise up within her and overflow the margins of her inspiration. She left evidences of many a brave try, but come it did not.

Anne was one, apparently, who worked best in the heat of the battle. Gone was the urgency of struggle in the midst of daily complications and complexities involving many people. A kind of loneliness possessed her and an anger that time should have robbed her of her greatest arena—the New York Public Library. She could not forswear responsibility for it.

Came the day, after her return to New York, when

she visited Room 105 for the first time. The staff recognized the light dancing shuffle of her feet on the marble floor long before she appeared in the doorway. They had lifted their eyes in a unison of expectancy at the first sound of the clearing of her throat. There she stood, looking on top of the world, wearing a hat so gay, so much in character, that one wanted to laugh aloud at the charm of it. As she greeted everyone she looked about the office. It was much the same as it had been, but a brass candlestick that had stood on a catalogue case had been moved to the top of a bookcase on the east wall. "The candlestick's in the wrong place," she said. "It should be put back where it was. The catalogue case is lower." It was pointed out that as a matter of actual measurement the catalogue case was the taller of the two locations. "But it *looks* lower on the catalogue case," she said. Then she slouched down in a chair as though she were lounging comfortably at home, slung one slim leg across the other, pushed the French hat to the back of her head, its saucy little streamers gone suddenly absurd, and made her pronouncement, "Push Babette Deutsch's *Walt Whitman*. It's the book of the year."

Anne would not recognize the fact that each of her successors claimed the right to make her own decisions in her own time. She professed to them time and again her eagerness to be of help. The difficulty was that by virtue of her genius and experience she could not resist assuming full control. If she were asked for aid she made no distinction between assistance and command. In a letter to Bertha Mahony Miller, Anne complained of one successor, "She never asks for help. I can understand her wanting to stand on her own feet, but I wish she were not so Spartan about it."

At times Anne knew an anguish of longing for the sight of children in the library, and on such days she would set out on branch visits of her own. She was always an expected and hoped-for guest at the celebrations the children's rooms staged with such diligence the length and breadth of the city, and a fete in her honor held every St. Nicholas Eve in the Central Children's Room created afresh the bond between past and present. But her unannounced presence in a library was sometimes an embarrassment, especially to newly appointed members of the staff who were not always able to cope with her praise or criticism.

The staff met this circumstance with generous spirit and professional aplomb, weighing no set of loyalties against another. But the habit of concern Anne never surrendered. In the last years of her life she wrote to Bertha Mahony Miller, describing a certain exhibition in the Central Children's Room. "It is something I brought off by remote control," she said. The ghost of a chuckle is written there in invisible ink.

Little of this was known outside the library. Her letters of the period read like accounts in the life of a busy debutante. Such arrivals and departures of visitors around the world; such quantities of friends coming to see Anne, bringing, like Squirrel Nutkin's kin, small gifts of homage to Old Owl. No stay-at-home was she! Countless were the theaters enjoyed, the art exhibitions explored and evaluated, the pilgrimages to favorite neighborhoods, to museums and cherished spots, the little zoo in Central Park, the Sheep Meadow, the Shakespeare garden, the feasts consumed at proven restaurants, the walks taken in solitary pleasure, the countless rides on the Staten Island ferry, the bridges encompassed on moonlit nights by taxi and in Storer Lunt's "little red car."

Journeys were embarked on: to Ashburnham and Boston for visits with the Millers; to the Edward King family at Biltmore, North Carolina; to Bradford and to Maine, especially to Saco, where family roots ran deep.

The habit of festivals continued with hardly a month of the year that did not hold one day sacred to some private celebration, not to mention the customary holidays of Christmas and Easter, St. Patrick's Day and Halloween.

Patterns of her birthday celebrations ranged all the way from a small gathering in her own place with champagne at hand through theaters and dinners in New York and Boston to the all but legendary revels that Ruth Sawyer Durand arranged one summer in Maine with her daughter and son-in-law, Peggy and Bob McCloskey. The Durands had built a home called Gull Rock on the coast of Maine at Hancock. Anne gives account of that most gracious time in a letter to Edward and Virginia King:

Mrs. Durand had hidden my mail since my arrival on the 7th. It now appeared on the breakfast table in a setting of wild roses and strawberries. She rose betimes to make a birthday cake and soon after breakfast we loaded up the car and took off for the island where the McCloskeys lived—a lovely drive of thirty-odd miles through blue hills and over a high toll bridge across Eggemoggin Reach to Little Deer Isle and along a narrow stony road to the cove where Bob awaited us with the dinghy to transport us to the motorboat in which we crossed to the larger of the two islands where their house is. We were met at the dock by a visitor with a wheelbarrow and made our way through Christmas tree woods, past the boathouse, where Bob has his studio, on by a winding fern-bordered path to the house on the other side of the island. It faces Penobscot Bay with Camden Hills in the distance. . . . The fire was already lighted in the big fireplace on the wide terrace of native stone and a birthday table bearing treasures from all over the island—a tiny Christmas tree, a curious branch of driftwood with seaweed and shells—masses of bayberry, wild strawberries—gave Mrs. Durand a setting for more of the letters and the cards she had held in reserve.

While lobsters writhed in the big copper kettle over the fire we drank numerous healths in the double rounds of old-fashioneds. Luncheon on the terrace with Sally (two in May) waking up in time for the birthday cake and a most wonderful sense of Christmas as well as birthday cheer. The island is perfect. Seven acres of Christmas trees —grassy point—sandspits, on which one can walk at low tide—five beaches—all fascinating to explore.

The Durands went back to Hancock in the late afternoon and next morning the two visitors and David [Durand] left, leaving Nicholas and me alone with Peggy, Bob and Sally for a week. We visited the mainland only once for supplies. That meant a 6 mile crossing to Cape Rosier and a drive of several miles to the store at South Brooksville. We feasted on lobster-clams-mussels with a ham for solid background. Bob rowed us to the smaller island one afternoon to look for wild strawberries. In the evening I read to them from *The Country of the Pointed Firs* which they had not known before but felt its likeness to their own setting. Their house, the only one on the island, was built twenty years ago by an actress and later was sold to some English people. The husband died and his wife sold everything as it stood at a sacrifice. It is spacious and convenient—well heated and they plan to spend the winter there. Bob hopes to pick up his Prix de Rome a year from September and go to Italy taking Peggy and Sally along. . . .

Peggy drove me back to Hancock leaving Sally with Bob overnight. We made a detour from Blue Hill and called on the E. B. Whites at North Brooklin. They have a beautiful place with such delphiniums and other flowers as I haven't seen all summer.

ACM was never one to boast of the number of years she had attained, but when the eighties caught up with her she could not help but acknowledge the fact, and she did so by renewing old pledges to the enjoyment of each day with all the vigor she could summon. She knew a lessening of physical powers—the ears lazy to hear, the eyes to see—and there were recurring bouts of respiratory illnesses, but the spirit sufficed. Moreover, the neighborhood boasted a doctor in whom she had complete confidence, as did hundreds of other Villagers: Dr. Eugenia Ingerman. Anne, with her predilection for the wisdom of the male in such matters, had been skeptical of women in medicine, but when one day she was introduced to Dr. Ingerman in the lobby of the Grosvenor and had seen the strength and compassion in that grave face she knew she had found a rare physician.

Anne professed time and again to an enjoyment of this late decade. "She spoke exultantly of the eighties," Bertha Mahony Miller reported. The degree of her protest had lessened with the years, though she continued to write to authors, editors, artists—anyone whom she considered to have betrayed their own best gifts or the highest goals of excellence in books produced for children.

That she lived among books literally was plain to see, her living quarters chock-a-block with books—books that had been sent to her for review, brought to her for reading by her publisher nephew, or borrowed from the Washington Square Book Store. "The best thing about retirement," Anne wrote to Katherine Carnes in 1954, "is the freedom to read what one really wants to. Only last month I read *Bleak House* for the first time and last summer *War and Peace*, which Maria Cimino says she read in the jungles of Brazil." Accounts of her reading thread the letters she wrote during these years, and the scope of the books mentioned bears witness to the fact that she lived in the thick of things. "I am reading Virginia Woolf's diary with great interest," the letter to

Katherine Carnes continues. "If you haven't, do turn to page 88 and read what she writes of Thomas Hardy. I read it aloud yesterday to someone and we laughed to the point of tears. I've now got to read her books all over again in the light of what she says while writing them."

"My latest reading was Sir Anthony Eden's memoirs," she reported in a letter to Bertha Miller in 1960. "Terribly sad yet containing much of great interest. . . . I was glad I read it before the reviews, thanks to Storer's thoughtfulness." She felt a responsibility for Bertha's selections of books that might appropriately be read aloud to her husband William Miller, and there are wise suggestions all along the line. "I have just begun to read Sholem Asch's *East River* which Siri said seemed to her the best book she read last summer. I found it absorbing and so true to the old East Side I felt I was living with the people of the book. If you haven't read it, let us save it until I come for I am not sure of its appeal to William."

In the last handful of her years—1952 to 1960—four great events crowned Anne's life with such joy that she could do little else but revel in them. The first of these came from England. One day in September 1952 Mr. Arthur Treble, the American representative of the English publishing firm of Frederick Warne, telephoned her and asked if he might come to call, mentioning that he had at hand the manuscript of a proposed book on Beatrix Potter. "It's rather bulky," he said. When he came he set before her a treasure chest—six portfolios containing unpublished drawings by Beatrix Potter, the finished layout for a book tentatively entitled *The Art of Beatrix Potter*, which was in such a state of meticulous perfection as to make one gasp and wonder what extraordinary mind and hand had produced such a piece of work. On the proposed title page, faintly penciled in, were the words, "With an introduction by Anne Carroll Moore."

At this moment Anne must have felt like the Tailor of Gloucester, who, when he beheld the Lord Mayor's wedding coat completed on his work table, could only exclaim, "Oh joy!" A formal letter of invitation to write an appreciation was presented to ACM at the same time from Mr. W. A. Herring of Warne, the very man who had seen all of Beatrix Potter's books through the presses over the long years. ACM knew Mr. Herring of old in London. She had, in fact, put him in a book, for it was he who appears as the make-up man in *Nicholas and the Golden Goose*.

> Here's the make-up man, the make-up man
> Who makes up books as fast as he can.

But who was L. Linder? His was the name of the builder of this celestial dummy of a book. He must have loved Beatrix Potter books all of his life to have produced such a work. ACM made discreet inquiry and in time established with him ties of enduring friendship, held firm by long letters over their years of correspondence.

Mr. Leslie Linder is well known in this day as the man who, among others feats, broke the code in which Beatrix Potter kept her journal and "translated" the minute writing of that document into the fascinating book we know today. He lives in Essex, England, and is by profession an engineer whose specialty is the study of stresses. It was not through a conscious memory of childhood that he came to be obsessed first by the art of Beatrix Potter and then by the character of the artist herself but by an accidental encounter with a battered copy of *Squirrel Nutkin* in a Sunday-school library in which he was involved when he was in his forties. The sight of that one tattered little volume suddenly brought to mind the pleasures he had had in such small red books when he was a child. Not one remained in his possession, the family having cleared away all childish things while he was only seven, and he set out to find all titles, known and unknown. He became positively captivated by the worlds of Beatrix Potter, the worlds in which she lived and the worlds she had engineered. Tales of joyous obsession are always sources of great pleasure. The tale of Leslie Linder is an important one and most endearing. In the appreciation which ACM brought off after a struggle of two years, she told the story of her relationship with Beatrix Potter. But the piece is no mere adventure in nostalgia; it is an incisive criticism of Beatrix Potter's work, a clear statement of the scope of L. Linder's book as it stands and of its future service to the art world. As always happened whenever ACM put pen to paper, something lives and glows there.

In February 1954 she wrote to Katherine Carnes in Atlanta, "You will be glad to know that the Beatrix Potter appreciation got finished at last and I have had two enthusiastic letters from Mr. Linder who says it's even better than he dared hope. The pictures are in proof and I suppose the publication date will be announced in due time by Warne."

It was published in 1955 and immediately went into a second edition. Anne was eighty-four in that year, clear of the book and fully equal to all the year held for her. The second cause for pride originated at Pratt Institute. The trustees voted to confer on her the degree of Doctor of Letters. On June 3, 1955, she walked triumphant in the academic procession, her partner in the march Robert Moses, the famous Parks Commissioner of New York City.

When she was invited to go to Toronto in November to celebrate Young Canada's Book Week, she went off in a new red dress with a black velvet stole and a red hat to match, to such a festival of books, old friends, speeches, theaters and puppet shows, luncheons and banquets, as to intimidate the staunchest soul. After it was over she wrote to Mr. Linder, saying, "I feel as though I could live forever."

Canada had always held a special significance for ACM. It was in Montreal, the year 1900, at a meeting of the American Library Association, that a children's librarians' club was formed with Anne Carroll Moore its president and Mary E. Dousman its secretary. Within months the club had become, at the invitation of the American Library Association, the Children's Librarians' Section and its officers were the first officers of the section. Thirty-four years later, when Siri Andrews was president of the section, the ALA met again in Montreal and at that time Anne delivered a memorable paper, "The Creation and Criticism of Children's Books: a Retrospect and a Forecast." It remains to this day a brilliant summation of the past, but its significance lies in the timeless and ageless truths that were expressed there:

> Having advertised children's books and children themselves to the extent that we have since the war, shall we look upon the mass production and wide distribution of mechanical triumphs of American color reproduction, upon mediocrity, vulgarity, and commonplace unimaginative treatment of theme as acceptable; or shall we continue to search for the intelligence, the wit, the sound basis of creative ideas we associate with the living children's book of any age?

As for Lillian Smith, the genius of the Boys' and Girls' Library in Toronto, she had served apprentice time in the New York Public Library, and she and ACM were bound together by years of friendship and shared admiration for each other. By 1955 Lillian Smith had retired, which meant she could give full strength to the enjoy-

ment of the festivities and, with her successor, Jean
Thompson, oversee the celebration.

This was a working fiesta. ACM was the guest of
S. J. Reginald Saunders, publishers. The executives of
Saunders were careful that there should be periods of rest
for her each day, but there was no diminution of scheduled appearances on account of the years accruing to
the guest of honor. Press, radio, and television each had
a scheduled interview and appearance, with the addition
of a personal appearance at Eaton's big department store.
Anne also spoke before a group of librarians for an hour,
after a buffet luncheon at the Boys' and Girls' House in
the lovely room where the famous Osborne collection
of old children's books is housed, reading letters from
Mr. Linder, talking of Leslie Brooke and Beatrix Potter.
Her letters reveal how great was the release of all her
powers in that setting and tradition with old friends close
at hand. She felt no change of direction in library work
with children as far as Canada was concerned but only
growth and reaffirmation of founding truths. She was
no longer certain of a like turn of affairs in her own
country.

The television interview centered on *The Art of Beatrix Potter*. The interviewer took the book home with
her the night before the screening in order to make a
selection of pictures that would be well served by the
camera. She had confessed to ACM that *The Tailor of
Gloucester* was a favorite of her childhood. All this
meant that ACM felt *en rapport* with the interviewer,
and the affair went off with a blaze of glory, as was
proved by the following day's repercussion from stations coast to coast. She had made her debut on television at the age of eighty-five.

On the way home to New York, as she ate breakfast
in the train diner Sunday morning, a young man paused

as he passed her table. "Did I not see you on television Thursday night?" he said. "I could not resist telling you how delightful it was."

On St. Nicholas Eve of 1959, as if the good saint himself had had a hand in it, Anne Moore received a letter from the Catholic Library Association telling her that she was to be the recipient of the Regina Medal in 1960. This signal honor was created by the Catholic Library Association: "To single out for recognition and emulation those writers, editors, and illustrators who have given unstintingly of their creative genius to children's literature, finding in the field a challenge worthy of their talents and demanding always their very best." It is not limited to any one country or any creed and is to be bestowed not for a single work or series of works but for the entire lifetime work of the individual. The first medal had gone to Eleanor Farjeon. The second was for Anne Carroll Moore, to be presented on April 18, 1960, at a luncheon at the Statler Hilton in New York as part of a Catholic Library Association conference. "It was the most complete surprise I have ever had," she wrote to Bertha Mahony Miller in March of that year. There had been a hiatus in the "Three Owls" pages in *The Horn Book*, due to a period of physical depletion for Anne. As usual, she was invigorated by joy. She describes the thoughtfulness of the committee, Miriam Wessel of the Detroit Public Library and Sister M. Camillus of Mount Mercy College, Pittsburgh, who had first written and then called on her. "Both bore out the spirit of their letter which really touched me deeply and has given me a fresh incentive—the Three Owls will fly again!"

What celebrants of ACM that fair occasion called forth, countrywide—librarians, friends, artists, authors— the whole kit and caboodle of the literary world. The honoree looked frail but beautiful in a blue and green printed silk dress, Margaret Lunt, Dudley's wife, having come up from Wilmington to help in the choice of costume.

Anne did not attempt a speech, since Ruth Sawyer had agreed to accept the honor in her behalf. This she did in splendid fashion, showing in her tribute how boundless was Anne Carroll Moore's world of children's books. ACM contented herself with an airy wave of her hand and a brief "This is the happiest moment of my life."

The exaltation and the vigor continued through the fall, and friends returning from Europe who had not seen her for years found her happy, boasting that her hearing had improved, and able to journey about the city for appropriate festivity. Moreover, during the fall she fulfilled her prophecy that the Owls would fly again and produced a piece for the December *Horn Book*.

But the winter was severe, and Anne fell victim to old bouts of depleting chest colds. The Christmas season found her longing to be astir but unable to battle the blowing corner winds of Tenth Street.

For Anne Carroll Moore, Christmas had always held all the enchantment that a young child finds in it. In addition there was the adult exhilaration of new books pouring from the presses. Every year, as early as in August, Anne drew an anticipatory breath, often choosing to be on hand in that vacation month because the new children's books blossomed then in their bright jackets. She read like a whirlwind and followed the fate of certain titles not only in the reviews but throughout the bookshops of the city, gathering the reactions of buyers and sales people, testing the winds of opinion from every direction.

The twelve days of Christmas she devoted to private

rituals of observance, going from church to church, not as a devout religious person but as a lover of tradition. She found affirmation of her own glee in secular shrines as well as in holy places—the carol service at St. George's Church, where the boys' choir sang the old songs in voices of unearthly beauty; the midnight mass at St. Patrick's; the music at the Church of the Ascension; the golden bells hung at Lord & Taylor; the lighting of the Christmas tree at Rockefeller Plaza and along Park Avenue—even the clang and fury of Woolworth's five-and-dime. Small wonder that she faced Christmas Eve of 1960 with some unhappiness, having been house-bound since the day of the big blizzard, December 12.

She sat surrounded by Christmas roses and boughs of pine from South Carolina, and visitors galore had come to call on the day before Christmas. But nothing could compensate for the deprivation of not seeing with her own eyes the lights that gathered momentum and broke in splendor against the Christmas sky of her beloved city.

When Alexandra Sanford appeared that Christmas Eve, Anne's hopes rose, for here was an old companion skilled in the art of happy prowling, one who, like H. C. Andersen's small hero, was numbered among the staunchest and most steadfast of children's librarians, having first come to the New York Public Library in 1918. She sent account of that Christmas Eve to the "Hunt Breakfast" of *The Horn Book* and it is her story that is told herewith:

> We had a festive dinner in the Grosvenor Bar, then while up in her "Little Book Room" the phone rang to announce callers. They turned out to be Mary Farren Jones and her husband. . . .
> Their visit was brief, as they had to get back to their

children and to trimming their tree. When talk of hat and coat began, I hedged a bit, claimed I could see snowflakes coming down again and the wind coming up. . . . When I suggested the lights would remain all through the holidays and we could go some other evening not so cold, she replied in a tone which put an end to the discussion, "Why, Sandy, it wouldn't be the same." So, well bundled up, off we went in a *big* taxi, after letting several small ones go. It was well heated, so we rolled up Fifth Avenue as far as Fifty-ninth Street to see the fountain illuminated for the first time, in front of the Plaza. Then down the other side of Fifth Avenue to Thirty-fourth Street and over to Eighth Avenue so we could swing around and be on the side near the fascinating scenes like something out of the Arabian Nights, along the second floor windows of Macy's on the Broadway side. Marcia Brown had told her of them, and she wanted to see them. The Venetian one was enchanting. When I said where next? she replied, "Around Gramercy Park." When we passed there last year on Christmas Eve she spoke about where she had lived there with a view of the Park from her high-up window. But she didn't talk much as we rode. . . . Then after bouncing along some dark, bumpy streets we spied that gem of a City Hall she loved, looking superb all illuminated. Then we swung across Brooklyn Bridge, and she leaned forward eagerly not to miss a bit of it. . . .

Then back to Manhattan by way of the Manhattan Bridge, and so to the Grosvenor, but not to bed. Nothing of the sort. If *I* wasn't too tired would I read aloud to her the ballad composed for Helen Masten's party she hadn't been able to attend, but had heard it had been read with gusto? So it was about one-thirty Christmas morning when I reached my diggings!

16

A JOYOUS SUFFICIENCY

> *But that there is a top to a thing and a*
> *bottom to the thing doesn't make it that*
> *there are two things; and that there is a top*
> *called birth and a bottom called death*
> *doesn't make any difference to that which is*
> *free, and sufficient, and joyous, and eternal.*
>
> JAMES STEPHENS

SHADOWS FOLLOWED the Christmas lights. In the dusk of the days Anne reached out from her couch for a slim volume of a book and slipped a handful of letters from past decades between its pages. With these epiphanies she confronted the dark.

The book was Walter de la Mare's *O Lovely England,* which Grace Hogarth brought to her from Walter de la Mare in England, and his was one of the letters harbored there. Another had come from Dr. Billings, the first director of the library. Through the years she had cherished the memory of Dr. Butler, the physician of her Pratt days, and his letter she hoarded as talisman. Another came from Dr. George Putnam, who had been Librarian of Congress. A child had written one letter,

Anne Carroll Peterson, her namesake. A card from Storer Lunt and a note from Eugenia Ingerman completed the portfolio.

There was a fall of snow on January 20, 1961. "Those are the white bees swarming," said the old grandmother in *The Snow Queen*. The entire Eastern seaboard was filled with snow. It fell upon the inaugural ceremonies of John F. Kennedy, and a wind blew the page out of the hand of the bare-headed poet Robert Frost even as he read from it. "The land was ours before we were the land's." Early on that day, Anne Carroll Moore "changed worlds."

No funeral marked her death. The Church of the Ascension opened its doors for a memorial service on the first day of February 1961 at four o'clock in the afternoon. The young clergyman explained that usually the Episcopal Church forswore the speaking of tribute to the dead but that an exception had been made in the case of this good neighbor who had enjoyed the informal fellowship of the church for many a day.

He knew Anne Carroll Moore in her last years and saw her as a frail elderly lady with a sharp blue eye. He spoke of her as he saw her, a somewhat whimsical character who loved children, never sensing that whimsy was the least of it. Some among the group longed for tribute to her strength, her endurance and resolve, her clear-sighted wisdom, generosity of spirit, and emotion. Others hoped for a recapitulation of her accomplishment and its far-reaching power. Each remembered in sorrow, in separate recollection, her significance as a friend.

But the family, in their wisdom, and especially Storer Lunt, realized that all held in common gratitude to Anne her love of life at its joyful peaks and at the simple level of small felicities. Therefore, after the solemn words were spoken the group was invited to cross the street to the Grosvenor Hotel for a festive gathering in the Mark Twain Room, where they ate and drank and spoke together. There was sadness, but there was also laughter and glasses raised high in the toast Ann Caraway herself had spoken "to the living in both worlds."

The ashes were taken to Limerick, Maine, over the Memorial Day weekend, to the cemetery where the Moores are gathered. There, on a typical spring day, with wild flowers all about, intermittent showers, patches of blue sky, and billowing wild clouds, Anne was buried. Sprigs of lilac and apple blossoms were laid on the earth and a cluster of lilies of the valley from the Tenth Street flower shop in New York.

A fitting and appropriate epitaph might be spun from the multiple threads revealed in tributes that swept down upon the family of ACM after she was gone. But it was Bertha Mahony Miller, walking across the lawn's green grass at Ashburnham in the half-light of a summer's evening, who said the significant word: "What life she gave us."

NOTES

CHAPTER ONE

1. Many of Anne Carroll Moore's *Bookman* articles were subsequently published in book form by George H. Doran, their titles being *Roads to Childhood* (1920), *New Roads to Childhood* (1923), and *Cross Roads to Childhood* (1926). The three books were combined and brought up to date in 1939 under the title *My Roads to Childhood*, Doubleday, Doran, publisher. The Horn Book, Inc., acquired publishing rights to the title in 1961, and it is currently available in hard cover and paperback. It is from this edition that much quoted material is given here.

A second major source of quotations has been the three volumes comprising a selection of articles from the New York *Herald Tribune Books*, the "Three Owls" section, edited and written by Anne Carroll Moore. The titles are: *The Three Owls: A Book About Children's Books* (The Macmillan Company, 1925); *The Three Owls, Second Book* (Coward-McCann, 1928); *The Three Owls, Third Book* (Coward-McCann, 1931). These titles are no longer in print, invaluable though they are.

2. The friendship between ACM and Ruth Sawyer Durand, distinguished writer and noted storyteller, was a sustaining force in the lives of both women. Anne was friend and adviser, and Ruth for her part offered practical help as well as intellectual counterpoint. Anne had no thimble sense. Ruth Sawyer, on flying visits to New York, between festivals and feasts, would send her skilled needle flying through Anne's wardrobe, setting aright all small disorders.

3. Two daughters of the colorful Overton family, native New Yorkers, contributed to the distinction of the New York Public Library: Florence Overton as head of the Circulation Department and Jacqueline as Children's Librarian.

CHAPTER THREE

1. The accounts of Bradford's founding are taken from Jean Sarah Pond's book *Bradford, A New England School,* Sesquicentennial Edition, revised and supplemented by Dale Mitchell, Bradford, Massachusetts, 1954.

2. "Cousin Oscar" was O. L. Clarke of Galveston, Texas. He first met Miss Moore in 1919 when he visited his daughter Frances, who was an assistant in the Central Children's Room in New York. Before she introduced her father to ACM she exacted a promise of circumspect behavior. He was a great tease, often an embarrassment to his daughters. Upon catching first sight of Anne standing at the telephone in her office Mr. Clarke waved his arm exuberantly and shouted, "Hello, old girl." This was the basis of their lasting friendship.

Subsequently, after ACM had lectured in Houston, Texas, a woman from the audience approached her and said, "Do you know my cousin Oscar? His daughter is in the New York Public Library." From that time forward she called him "Cousin Oscar."

CHAPTER FIVE

1. Louis Sherry was primarily a caterer when he opened his first candy shop and restaurant on New York's Sixth Avenue in 1881. The world of fashion moved northward, up Fifth Avenue, and Sherry's moved with it. In 1898 he built his own lavish establishment on the corner of Fifth Avenue and Forty-fourth Street: twelve stories of elegance, including several restaurants of various types, a splendid ballroom and smaller rooms for public entertaining, a catering and confectionery department, and, in the upper stories, a few lavish apartments for the convenience of a chosen clientele among the great. It was here that Marie Shedlock made her American debut in 1902.

2. Dr. Earl Barnes (1861–1935) was a professor of education at Stanford University who abandoned teaching to devote himself to lecturing and writing. In 1900 he became staff lecturer, London Society for Extension of University Teaching. It was during that period that he came to know Marie Shedlock.

3. Yvette Guilbert, a famous French *chanteuse* who appeared in the United States in the early 1900s.

4. The quotation from W. H. Auden is from his book *Secondary Worlds,* "Words and the Word," Random House, 1968.

CHAPTER SEVEN

The *History of The New York Public Library* by Harry Miller Lydenberg, published by the library in 1923, is the source for the historical background given in this chapter. Dr. Lydenberg was Chief Reference Librarian at the time of the book's publication. He later became director of the library.

1. Each of these young men became famous. George Bancroft (1800–1891) was statesman, diplomat, and historian, his *History of the United States*, in ten volumes, fixing his place among major historians of the world. George Ticknor (1791–1871), "this grand and chilly old scholar," as Van Wyck Brooks describes him in his *New England: Indian Summer*, wrote a distinguished *History of Spanish Literature*. Edward Everett (1794–1865), statesman and orator, was acclaimed at the time for his speech at the dedication of Gettysburg. It remained for the ages to recognize the grandeur of the words Abraham Lincoln spoke on that same day and occasion.

2. Fitz-Greene Halleck (1790–1867) was an American poet who with Joseph Rodman Drake wrote satirical verse. One of his best-known poems, an elegy on the death of his friend Drake, continues to find a place in certain anthologies of poetry.

CHAPTER EIGHT

1. The phrase "No badge or button . . ." was aimed at the practice of the Cleveland Public Library. Children signed a pledge involving clean hands and the care of books and were awarded a badge or button enabling them to make a display of their virtue.

CHAPTER NINE

1. The quotation is from "The Three Owls," appearing in *The Horn Book*, November–December 1939, pp. 369–72.

The event is told in more detail in a long letter Nicholas wrote on his own stationery to Walter de la Mare, dated December 14, 1927, signed Nicholas and A(nn) C(araway).

. . . We saw Arthur Rackham on board the *Olympic* last Friday night after taking him around Brooklyn and Manhattan bridges. His first visit to America. . . .

I had a good deal of fun with Mr. Rackham and a young artist named Paget-Fredericks who says he has met you. . . . Do you remember the young man himself? He needs simplifying in certain ways. He was horrified when A.[nn] C.[araway] suggested Childs as a typically American restaurant when Mr. Rackham asked for one where he might invite us to dine with him. "Better perhaps for breakfast between midnight and five o'clock," said A. C. reflectively and we went eventually to the Brevoort Grill.

CHAPTER TEN

The text of Justice Holmes's dissent is given in Harry Golden's book, *A Little Girl Is Dead* (World, 1965), p. 315. Leonard Dinnerstein's *The Leo Frank Case* (Columbia University, 1968), richly documented, provides an excellent résumé of the case.

In Boston, on September 1, 1915, a great demonstration denouncing the lynching of Frank was held in Faneuil Hall, Asa P. French, a former U.S. District Attorney, acting as chairman. The New York *Herald* described the meeting thus:

A more impressive cry of indignation was never heard in Boston, and never did Faneuil Hall more fitly perform its function as "the cradle of liberty."

ACM sent to Mr. French a copy of her letter that had appeared in the New York *Times*. He wrote her, on September 3, an account of the Boston meeting:

I read the letter very early in the proceedings in Faneuil Hall, on Tuesday night, and its effect was marked. It gave an atmosphere to the meeting which it would have otherwise hardly had, I think. I am glad it occurred to you to let me see it.
We had a crowded hall and a large overflow outside, and the whole thing was successful beyond our expectations. . . .

Anne Carroll Moore continued to fight for the vindication of Leo Frank, offering articles to several magazines of the time, but editors were unwilling to pursue the subject in the immediate future.
ACM sustained her friendship with Leo's father and mother as long as they lived. Judging from the outlines and observations she preserved, it seems probable that she considered writing a biography of Leo Frank.

CHAPTER TWELVE

1. Eugene Saxton, an editor at George H. Doran, was the initial editor of *The Bookman*. He went subsequently to Harper and Brothers (1925), eventually becoming vice-president and secretary of the firm. He was by all counts a talented and sympathetic editor, who abandoned his profession of the law in favor of journalism and publishing.
2. Stephen Vincent Benét's *Western Star* was published by Farrar and Rinehart in 1943, a few months before Eugene Saxton's death. Anne thought of that event in relation to the friendship between the three men—Stephen Benét, John Farrar, and Eugene Saxton.

CHAPTER THIRTEEN

1. The book under discussion was *Come Hither* by Walter de la Mare, "a collection of rhymes and poems for the young of all ages." The introduction is in truth an allegory, purporting to be "The Story of This Book," full of anagramatic names—the scene "Thrae" which is easily "earth" and the region of "The Laps" which becomes "planets." It is a piece of writing that reveals the poet at his eeriest and mystical best, yet it contains sound advice on the reading of poetry. In Anne's copy the thin marginal line that marks the paragraph she wanted to find at a glance stands at the following:

Having discovered, then, that every poem must have been written as it was written, on purpose, I took a little more pains with those

I cared for least. In some even then I could not piece out the meaning; in others I could not easily catch the beat and rhythm and tune. But I learned to read them very slowly, so as fully and quietly to fill up the time allowed for each line and to listen to its music, and to see and hear all that the words were saying.

2. When "Ann" was used as the name by which Walter de la Mare addressed ACM, it indicated that he was answering a letter from Nicholas, and the Ann was Ann Caraway. When he addressed her in her own person, it was "Anne."

CHAPTER FOURTEEN

1. The summation of ACM's Utah experience and her relation to the Peterson family is movingly told on the fly leaf of her presentation copy of *The Art of Beatrix Potter*, sent to Mrs. Peterson in 1956:

> For Phoebe Nebeker Peterson, with whom I explored new roads to childhood in Utah, leading from her beautiful home on College Hill with President Peterson and their children back to her father's and mother's home on the shores of Bear Lake. Truth and Beauty were the guiding stars of a joyous pilgrimage which began in 1927 under the spell of the Wasatch Mountains. The same stars have continued to shine with increasing radiance wherever we meet—Utah—Concord—Boston—Harvard Yard—Alexandria on Easter Day. With love and gratitude for a beautiful friendship and my share in a living child of the Peterson family.
>
> N.Y.   ACM
> Sept. 1956

CHRONOLOGY

1871   Anne Carroll Moore born on July 12, at Limerick, Maine.

1881   Entered Limerick Academy.

1889   Graduated from Limerick Academy. Entered Bradford Academy at Bradford, Massachusetts.

1891   Graduated from Bradford Academy, June 1891. Read law with her father from June 1891 until January 1892.

1892   Death of Anne's father and mother.

1895   Entered the Library School of Pratt Free Institute, Brooklyn, New York.

1896   Graduated from Pratt in June. Lectured to teachers in the Summer School at Saco, Maine, at the invitation of the State Superintendent of Schools; the topic: "Library Methods of Study." Appointed head of the library for children, the Pratt Free Library of Brooklyn.

1900   Chosen as President of the first Round Table organization of librarians actually in charge of children's work at the American Library Association's annual meeting in Montreal, Canada.

1901   At the invitation of the American Library Association, the Round Table organization became a section of the Association, with Anne Carroll Moore its first chairman.

First trip to England, Scotland, and Ireland.

1902 Taught at the Iowa State Library Commission Summer School. Her *A List of Books Recommended for a Children's Library* published, for the Iowa State Library Commission.

1906 Appointed to organize work with children in the New York Public Library.

1911 The Central Library opened its doors to the public. The Central Children's Room was established as a major department of a reference library.

1918 Joined the staff of *The Bookman* with responsibility for criticism of books for children in its pages.

1920 *Roads to Childhood* first published.

1921 Journey to England, Belgium, and France to report for the American Library Association on children's work in other countries, she being chairman of a subcommittee on library cooperation with other countries. Report published in the ALA Bulletin of July 1921.

1922 To France for the Marie Shedlock festival of storytelling in the devastated regions, and to England for ceremonies at the opening of the David Copperfield Library.

1924 First appearance of "The Three Owls" in the New York *Herald Tribune Books*. Publication of *Nicholas: A Manhattan Christmas Story*.

1927 Delegate to the International Conference of Librarians at Edinburgh, Scotland.
First visit as lecturer to the Utah State Agricultural College at Logan, Utah.

1931 The Anne Carroll Moore Children's Library opened in the new library of the Agricultural College at Logan, Utah.

1932 Pratt Institute bestowed upon Anne Carroll Moore a Diploma of Honor in recognition of her eminence as "a commanding influence and authority in the choice of children's literature within and without the library profession."

1940 The first Constance Lindsay Skinner Gold Medal for outstanding work as a pioneer in the field of better books for children was awarded Anne Carroll Moore by the Women's National Book Association and the Booksellers' League of New York.

The University of Maine honored Anne Carroll Moore by bestowing upon her the honorary degree of Doctor of Letters.

1941 Retirement from the New York Public Library. Accepted teaching appointment at the Graduate School of Librarianship at the University of California, Berkeley.

1954 Publication of *The Art of Beatrix Potter*.

1955 The honorary degree of Doctor of Letters awarded Anne Carroll Moore by Pratt Institute.

1960 The Regina Medal of the Catholic Library Association was given to Anne Carroll Moore.

1961 Died on January 20 in New York City.

INDEX

Frances Clarke Sayers

Frances Clarke Sayers is a Texan who, as she says, "happens to have been born in Topeka, Kansas." Her father, an official of the Santa Fe Railroad, was transferred to Galveston. She was brought up there in an atmosphere that combined the aura of the old South with the varieties of internationalism a seaport affords. Her father was a conservative, her mother "a fighting liberal." For Mrs. Sayers and her sister, the household was a lively one.

An article in the *St. Nicholas* magazine, read by Mrs. Sayers when she was ten or twelve, aroused her interest in a new profession for women: children's librarianship. In time she came to be a student at the Carnegie Library School in Pittsburgh. Anne Carroll Moore, the subject of this biography, came to the school as a visiting lecturer and asked Mrs. Sayers to come and work in New York City. For five years, Mrs. Sayers worked in the Central Children's Room of the New York Public Library. Later, after a span of years in California, Mrs. Sayers returned to the New York Public Library as Superintendent of Work with Children from 1941 to 1952. From 1954 to 1964, she was Senior Lecturer in the School of Library Science and the English Department at the University of California in Los Angeles.

Miss Moore, New York, the children of that city, and Alfred Henry Paul Sayers, librarian and bookman whom Mrs. Sayers met there and later married, have, she says, constituted the major themes of her life.

Mrs. Sayers now lives in Ojai, California. She is the author of six books for children: *Bluebonnets for Lucinda, Mr. Tidy Paws, Tag Along Tooloo, Ginny and Custard, Sally Tait,* and *Oscar Lincoln Busby Stokes.* Her adult books are *Summoned by Books* and *Anthology of Children's Literature* (with Evelyn Sickels).